COOL
BEANS

COOL
BEANS

The Ultimate Guide to Cooking with
the World's Most Versatile Plant-Based
Protein, with 125 Recipes

JOE YONAN

Photographs by Aubrie Pick

TEN SPEED PRESS
California | New York

CONTENTS

INTRODUCTION

"We're just here for the beans."

That's what we told the waiter at Maximo Bistrot in Mexico City, where my husband, Carl, and I were honeymooning.

We had considered a handful of destinations, but CDMX was at the top of our list for several reasons: we had scored cheap nonstop flights from Washington, DC; Carl had never been and I was eager to show him just what he had been missing; and what he had been missing, more than anything else, was the food.

For me, the appeal goes even deeper: Mexico City is not just the capital of our vibrant, fascinating neighbor to the south. It's the seat of a culinary culture ruled by three kings: corn, chiles, and beans. And as a longtime vegetarian who reveres beans as the most important plant-based protein in the world and as someone who grew up in West Texas, immersed in Mexican-American culture, I consider Mexico the bean-all and end-all. Every Mexican chef I've ever met has waxed poetic about them: scoops of frijoles borrachos (drunken beans) nestled in fresh corn tortillas; complex stews made from slowly cooked black beans, fresh and dried chiles and the pungent herb epazote; and smoke-kissed purees slathered on fried masa boats, topped with lime-dressed greens. It's one of the many reasons I've always felt at home there.

This time, I knew that on and among our visits to the floating gardens of Xochimilco, Frida Kahlo's and Diego Rivera's homes and museums, street food tours, art galleries, and markets, I would be on a mission to taste as many bean dishes as I could find. And in my research, one chef emerged as the bean whisperer: Maximo owner Eduardo "Lalo" Garcia. I had heard that he was passionate, with a fascinating background, and that he served a spectacular bean soup at his tasting-menu restaurant.

We got to Maximo an hour before our reservation, just so we could talk to Garcia about beans, which, no surprise, are one of his favorite subjects. In addition to his history lessons about them, Mexican cooking, and the impact of NAFTA on his country's culture, he described his "very, very old-fashioned" soup, made with beans he gets from the state of Hidalgo. They're called cacahuate, because they resemble peanuts when raw, but . . . he was fresh out.

Out? I'm sorry, what? We had come all that way to see the master of beans in the world capital of beans only to be told . . . no dice, no beans. A young Los Angeles chef had visited just a day or two earlier, Garcia explained, and he had sent her home with the rest of his stash. I had a hunch: "Was it Jessica Koslow from Sqirl?" He nodded, laughed that I would, of course, know all the other American bean obsessives, and then, when he saw my face fall and recognized the depth of my disappointment, he turned serious. He started scrolling through his phone, I assumed checking emails, texts, or calendar reminders. Good news: He was scheduled for another bean delivery that weekend. He hadn't planned it, but he'd make the soup for us— that is, as long as we would still be in town and could return.

We would, we could, and we did. A few days later, as we sat down for lunch—the only customers in the place getting just the bean soup rather than the multi-course tasting menu—the anticipation started nagging at me. How good could these beans actually be?

The waiter brought us two big bowls of soup: the beans were super-creamy and golden in color, fatter than pintos, with a broth that was so layered and deep and, well, beany, that it made me swoon. It seemed so simple—just beans and broth and pico de gallo—that I could hardly believe how much flavor I was tasting. My husband, still recovering from a bout of Montezuma's Revenge, seemed to come back to life before my very eyes. We tore into a basket of blue corn tostadas, and I slugged a Minerva beer in between spoonfuls of the soup. We left happy and restored.

Such is the power of the humble bowl of beans.

As a category of food, beans are old, ancient even. Forward-thinking cooks have been talking about ancient grains for years now—my friend Maria Speck helped popularize the idea in her book *Ancient Grains for Modern Meals*—but some beans are just as old as grains. According to Ken Albala's masterful 2007 book *Beans: A History*, among the first plants domesticated, some 10,000 years ago, were einkorn wheat, emmer, barley—and lentils.

Lentils are so old that people who say lentils are shaped like lenses have got it backward; the world's first lenses got their name because they were shaped like lentils. That's old. In fact, there's evidence that thousands of years before they were domesticated, in 11,000 BC, people in Greece were cooking wild lentils.

Pythagoras talked about fava beans, Hippocrates about lupinis, and one particularly famous orator is even more deeply connected to chickpeas: His family took its name (Cicero) from the legume's genus (*Cicer*). Ancient Indian rituals and early Sanskrit literature feature mung beans. In the New World, the remains of beans were found in a Peruvian Andean cave dated to 6000 BC. Mentions of black beans show up in the writings of ancient Mayans. A little younger is the soybean, but it has made up for lost ground by becoming, as Albala writes, "the most widely grown bean on the planet, the darling of the food industries and genetically one of the most extensively modified of all plants."

So why do beans have, well, something of a fusty reputation, especially here in the West?

I think a couple of things are going on: first, there's the unavoidable association with hippies, the memories of three-bean chilis stirred by pot-smoking countercultural types. But perhaps more importantly, beans worldwide have almost always been associated with poverty. (An exception is India, where the prominence of vegetarian eating ensures that beans have been appreciated by the highest castes.) America, as a relatively young country built on grand ambitions and looking for inspiration, perhaps has historically paid more attention to the cooking of the world's elite and less to the cooking of the more resourceful lower classes.

That's been changing, thankfully. As immigrants continue to shape American cuisine and we pay more attention to our own native traditions, we've started to realize just how deep the roots of bean cookery go.

Mexico. India. Nigeria. Israel. China. Italy. Japan. Spain. The United States. Morocco. Peru. It's hard to think of a country where beans aren't part of the culinary fabric.

When Lalo Garcia was growing up in a farming village in Guanajuato, he said, "The one thing we always had in the house was a big clay pot of beans." Indeed, the incredible cuisine—or as the great Mexican-cooking authority Diana Kennedy puts it, *cuisines* plural—of Mexico owe everything to the triumvirate of beans, corn, and chiles.

Ran Nussbacher is co-owner of Shouk, a plant-based, fast-casual Middle Eastern restaurant with two locations in DC. With falafel, a fantastic veggie burger, an "omelet" made of chickpea flour, and more, "We are bean heavy," he says.

In Tel Aviv, where Nussbacher grew up, falafel and hummus were the first, second, and sometimes only, order of business most every day of the week. When he was in the army, stewed chickpeas mixed with rice was a staple. And when he would meet friends for drinks, "The bar always had small bowls of warm chickpeas with a small amount of chickpea water sitting out, heavily seasoned with salt, pepper, sometimes a little cumin, and you'd pick them up with your fingers as you drank beer."

Ozoz Sokoh, who writes the *Kitchen Butterfly* blog from her home in Lagos, says beans are "central to Nigerian food culture." In Lagos, the streets abound with women selling akara, a black-eyed pea fritter. "If you take a poll, almost everyone eats akara on Saturday mornings." There's also ewa riro (page 93), stewed black-eyed peas with spices; moinmoin, a steamed black-eyed pea pudding somewhat akin to a Mexican tamal; ewa aganyin, a slow-cooked bean stew topped with a black chile sauce and often paired with a soft bread; and more.

India is another great bean-loving culture. Lentils, chickpeas, split peas, and mung beans are used not only to make the great dals and South Indian dosas (page 135) but also such bean-and-rice dishes as khichdi (page 179). "You can't argue with legions of Indian cooks," says Priya Ammu, who grew up in India and owns the restaurant DC Dosa. "I loved khichdi growing up. We always had it with cucumber raita and roasted papadums on Sundays."

What made beans so ubiquitous?

As Albala writes, "Though all great agricultural societies have their own staple starch . . . beans are perhaps the one food common and indispensable to all."

For much of the world, they have always been a way to sustain through times of poverty, as the cheapest (by far) source of protein around. And now, with a growing interest in plant-based eating even among people who can afford to eat whatever they want, beans have become more appealing than ever.

They are truly unique, as the only food that can be categorized, according to the U.S. Department of Agriculture (USDA), as both a protein and a vegetable. What's more, according to a 2016 study published in the journal *Food & Nutrition Research*, meals based

on these vegetable proteins are more satisfying than those based on animal proteins. The list of beans' health benefits is long: they're nutrient-dense, rich in cancer-fighting antioxidants and heart-healthy fiber, and they have been shown to help improve our gut health, help stabilize blood sugar, and possibly even lower cholesterol.

If there's one idea that best summarizes their health benefits, it's this: eat beans, live longer.

It's more than just a fun thing to say. The idea has a basis in some of the most intensive research around longevity of the past few decades. I'm talking about the "Blue Zones" project, in which Dan Buettner and his fellow researchers identified and studied the habits of people in five populations around the world who live significantly longer than average. They share many habits in common—daily exercise, strong social connections, family commitment, moderate alcohol intake—but the one that jumped out at me when I first read about the project was this: the cornerstone of all their diets is beans, about 1 cup per person per day. When Buettner was asked on *The Splendid Table* radio show what dietary takeaways the rest of us could gather from his project, his response was, you guessed it, "Eat more beans."

The good news: eating more beans doesn't need to seem like a chore. Far from it. With hundreds of varieties grown all over the world, it's easy to find beans that are incredibly delicious, and they're all so versatile, too.

Bean lovers already know how magical beans are. When cooked from dried, with precious few other ingredients added, they create a rich broth to rival anything that ever came from boiling a chicken. They freeze beautifully in this liquid, making them perfect for make-ahead, finish-quickly meals. They're pretty darn good straight from a can—perhaps the best plant-based ingredient available in such a format, with the possible exception of tomatoes. And they can play into every kind of dish, in every part of the meal, from dips and snacks to salads and soups to main courses, sides, and even desserts. Frankly, anything meat can do, beans can do better—and they're starting to catch up to the work of eggs, too.

Open my refrigerator and you'll find a quart-size Mason jar or two of, say, chickpeas, black turtle beans, or cranberry/borlotti (another name for Lalo's cacahuate) beans, immersed in that glorious liquid gold, awaiting whatever use I have in store for them. In my freezer might be zip-top bags of cooked (or farm-fresh) Jacob's cattle beans and black-eyed peas, along with various stews, soups, and purees I've made with them. On my stovetop might just be the next pot simmering away—heirloom flageolet beans, perhaps, or red kidney beans, or green lentils—and on my counter might be a batch of dried gigante beans, big enough to live up to their name, soaking in water for yet another round.

In my pantry are more than a dozen jars of dried beans and lentils in a multitude of colors and sizes. And I always keep on hand several cans of this bean or that, for those times when I'm caught without home-cooked versions at the ready. Beans are showing up in some of the precious few packaged snack foods I keep around, too, particularly the spiced and roasted chickpeas and pickled lupini beans I like to nibble on between meals.

I've liked beans since my childhood, when chants about "the magical fruit" tickled me and my friends. In my college days, paying my own way and poor as the dickens, I depended on cans and bags of black, pinto, and kidney beans (along with instant ramen noodles) to get by. I spent a few decades also eating meat when I could afford it, but as a vegetarian for the last eight years (and plant-centric for many years before that), I've doubled down on my commitment to beans in as many guises as I can find—or create. And I'm always on the lookout for the newest ways of cooking them.

My own bean journey took a turn about a decade ago, when I first learned of the heirloom beans sold by Steve Sando's Rancho Gordo in Napa, California. We at *The Washington Post* were the first national publication to write about this bean missionary who started to get attention in the food world when famed chef Thomas Keller put Sando's beans on his menu at the French Laundry. I started buying Sando's beans, and I can remember the revelation of those first few pots: the varieties I was familiar with were outstanding representatives, cooking up so much more quickly and evenly, no doubt because they were simply fresher, and presenting me with flavor complexities I had never experienced tasting beans. And then there were the varieties I was encountering for the first time, as most of Sando's customers were. The Rio Zape bean, with its notes of chocolate and coffee, made me a Rancho Gordo customer for life.

In fact, I don't think it's too big of a stretch to say that without Rancho Gordo, I would never have transitioned to a plant-based diet, or if I had, it sure wouldn't have been as much fun. There are many reasons for my transition—it's about my own health, the health of the planet, and compassion for animals—but Rancho

Gordo beans showed me that plant-based cooking can produce unapologetically luscious flavors and textures. As Sando himself told me, one thing that has changed for him over the years of cooking these beans is how much simpler his treatments have gotten. "Even though I'm an omnivore," he says, "I think vegan beans are the way to go. Vegan cooking is so not hard when you have really good ingredients. Just cook it simply—onion, garlic, olive oil. People sometimes say, 'And a ham hock, right?' But you don't need that if it's a really good bean. Even chicken stock is a waste."

Sando isn't the first to try to bring heirloom varieties of beans to a mainstream customer. Zürsun in Idaho, Baer's Best in New England, and Timeless Natural Food in Minnesota are among the other companies with a commitment to the product. But few have been as evangelical about their approach as Sando, who has become the country's largest retailer of heirloom beans, selling more than a half-million pounds of them a year. Along the way, he has rescued old varieties and found farmers to grow them for his company—including small farmers in Mexico.

I've been thrilled to see Sando's company continue to thrive. His bean club—in which subscribers get a shipment every quarter, along with a newsletter and first crack at the rarer varieties—has sold out at 5,000, with a waiting list of 1,500. And a *New Yorker* profile of him in 2018 caused his sales to increase by 30 percent over the previous year. "And that's without a single discounted pound of beans," he tells me. At $6 a pound, three times the price (or more) of supermarket beans, Sando's remain a bargain.

These days, I draw inspiration from traditional bean recipes from all over the world, including the ones I've already mentioned, along with the giant-bean stews with lemon, honey, and dill of Greece; the bean-stuffed breads (khachapuri) of Georgia; the chickpea-and-bread soup of Tunisia; and so many more.

As the longtime food editor at *The Washington Post*, I have the perfect perch to see all the trends and recipes bubbling up in the food world, from bloggers and authors and chefs and home cooks, and I love that the way people are treating beans today in some cases has very little to do with tradition. There are riffs on the soccas and farinatas of France and Italy that combine them with mushrooms and whole chickpeas for gorgeous flavor, color, and texture. There are lovely, light, gluten-free cakes made with pureed cooked beans in place of flour and some of the fat, recipes that remind me of the old diet standby of black beans and chocolate cake mix to make brownies—but are so much better. There are the veggie burgers—plural!—that have taken New York by storm. There are even cooks using aquafaba, the liquid from canned or cooked beans, to make dishes for which you formerly needed eggs: meringues, mousses, and mayos, not to mention the leavening power this aquafaba provides cakes, muffins, and more. (See page 18 for more information.)

Now that the Instant Pot has become such a sensation, millions of people are discovering that pressure cooking can make bean cooking a weeknight affair. When I posted a pot-of-beans photo recently on Facebook, one commenter—southern food writer extraordinaire Kathleen Purvis—replied, "Instant Pots: the second best thing that ever happened to beans. The first best thing? Rancho Gordo."

Even Sando, who loves old-school ways of cooking beans, especially in his traditional clay pot, has to admit that the IP is a game-changer. "It's not the way I cook, but I've never seen anything that encourages more noncooks to cook, so I'm all for it." In the Rancho Gordo Bean Club? Lots of IP users.

So for all of you excited about cooking beans, either for the first time or the 1,000th, here's something I've learned while researching this book: you can take many a favorite or even classic recipe that doesn't have anything to do with beans and find a way to easily—even beautifully—fit beans into it. I sometimes think it would be fun to find a way to make a chickpea version of every chicken dish in the world. (The next book, perhaps?) But I don't just use beans as a meat substitute. In tabbouleh, for instance, the Lebanese salad of (mostly) parsley and (a little bit of) bulgur, navy or cannellini beans sub in perfectly for the grain. (See White Bean Tabbouleh, page 65.)

Beans have something more serious going for them, too: in these days of justifiable worry about climate change—about whether we're taxing our planet to the point of destruction—beans may represent the key to feeding the Earth's rapidly growing population. Compared to animal proteins, these crops require far less water and other resources. Rather than taking a toll on the land, they improve the soil by helping to fix nitrogen. Along with grains, they're also one of the world's first (and best) storage crops, making them easily portable and eminently usable. Those are some of the reasons the United Nations declared 2016 the International Year of Pulses, using a word for the edible seeds of the legume family that's more common in other parts of the world than in America.

Whatever you call them, beans are a little mysterious and perhaps even intimidating, which might be why they're not as wildly popular in the United States as I think they deserve to be. The fact is, questions abound about the best ways to buy and cook them. How do you know how old a bean in that supermarket bulk bin really is? Should you soak them or not? Salt at the beginning, middle, or end—or, as some new tests have suggested, salt them in the soaking water? Avoid acidic ingredients until later, or does it really matter? Stovetop, oven, pressure cooker, slow cooker, Instant Pot? And how, really, do you mitigate the gaseous side effects of eating them?

This is why I've written this book: to explore new ways and pay tribute to the still-relevant old ways that people love to cook beans and to proselytize to the unconverted. That means, I hope, inspiring you to get into the kitchen and answering any questions you might have once you've opened a can, poured water over dried beans in a pot, or are standing at the stove wondering how long you might be there.

If beans don't have your affection yet, I think they soon will.

The world of beans is large, and in this book, I'm concerning myself primarily with pulses, the dried seeds of the legume family. That means you won't see recipes for green beans or other dishes in which we consume the legume fresh, with the exception of a few standouts, just because I think they're so unusual and fun, including charred green chickpeas, popped out of the pod like edamame. I'm also giving short shrift to soybeans, because when cooked from dried like other beans, they take an exceedingly long time to start to get tender, and they don't have much flavor at all. Instead, they've been used to make other, more flavorful products that are probably very familiar to you: soy milk, tofu, and my fermented favorites: soy sauce, miso, and tempeh. Those are used throughout the book.

There are hundreds and hundreds of bean varieties, but I will confess to a few favorites, and you'll pick up some tendencies in this collection. From hummus to aquafaba to all the dishes made with their flour, chickpeas possess an unparalleled versatility. Given my longstanding affection for Mexican food, black beans will always have my heart. And I don't know if it's my Middle Eastern blood or just an appreciation for particularly large, meaty beans, but I adore favas, limas, and gigante beans.

Other than those, I've never met a bean I didn't like, and in the moment, when they're cooked right, I always love the one I'm eating.

ROYAL CORONA

BLACK-EYED PEAS

LUPINI

CHRISTMAS LIMA

JACOB'S CATTLE

LENTILS DU PUY

BLACK TURTLE

LADY
CREAM
PEAS

RED LENTILS

FLAGEOLET

ADZUKI

BLACK CHICKPEAS

HOW TO USE THIS BOOK

Most, but not all, of these recipes call for already cooked beans. I suggest that you get in the habit, then, of cooking a pot of beans every week, storing them in their liquid, and using my recipes for creative ways of cooking them that you might not have considered. If you're left with extra liquid, freeze it for later: it makes a fantastic base for soup or a delicious broth all on its own.

Or feel free to use canned beans, of course. As acclaimed chef Rich Landau of Philly's Vedge and other restaurants told me, "Canned beans are your best friends. There's no shame in it."

For any of the recipes that call for cooking the beans from dried with other ingredients, you'll want to make the dish from start to finish, and in many instances, you can speed things up with a pressure cooker or Instant Pot. In a few cases, I instruct you to cook the beans very low and very slow, which of course means you could use a slow cooker instead.

Plenty of the recipes are my own creation from the get-go, while others have at least a basis in tradition. For the latter, I call for ingredients here and there that you might not be able to find in your average supermarket. While I offer substitution tips where I can, I also encourage you to seek out global markets if possible, even if it means taking a longer drive than you're used to on any given weekend, or order them online. (See my preferred list of sources on page 222.) These ingredients, including spices, blends, and condiments, can open up new paths to excitement in your kitchen. Here's a reason to try to buy in person rather than through the interwebs: you can more easily ask the proprietors of these markets—trust me, they're cooks, every one—for their own favorite ways to cook beans and other dishes from their culture. Devour the inspiration.

TECHNIQUES

I used to follow the conventional wisdom when it came to cooking beans: Always soak, to help the beans cook more quickly. Never salt until the end, or near the end, of cooking, to avoid making them tough. Ditto for acidic ingredients of any kind. Only use a pot on the stovetop, so you can peek from time to time and add water as needed. But over the last several years, much of that has gone out the window. Now, here's how I make the most flavorful pot of simple beans ever. These are all based on 1 pound of beans, and you can use the results to make many of the recipes in this book that call for precooked beans.

Preparation

PICKING OVER/RINSING. I often quickly sift through a batch of beans, looking for any foreign matter or dust, and rinse if they're not going to be soaked and it seems necessary. Most beans I get, though, are very clean, so this step has become more and more moot.

SOAKING. For the most part, I don't bother. That's partly because I am usually buying beans from sources like Rancho Gordo, Camellia, and other high-end purveyors, and their beans tend to be pretty fresh. See more on this on page 17, but the upshot: it usually doesn't speed things up enough to make it worth it, and I get more flavor and color in the beans when I skip it. This is especially true of such thin-skinned varieties as black beans and black-eyed peas. The exception: when I suspect a batch of beans might be very old or I'm unsure of the age, and I want to give them a fighting chance to cook in my usual hour or two on the stovetop or in the oven. (When I use a pressure cooker, which I do often, there's no need for soaking at all.) When I do soak, I follow the advice I first read from food scientist/writer Harold McGee and later from America's Test Kitchen, and I add 1 tablespoon of kosher salt to enough water to cover the beans in a bowl by 3 inches, creating a brine that adds flavor to the beans and helps them soften faster. I soak them overnight (or for at least 4 hours), covered, at room temperature, then drain before proceeding.

ADDING SALT. If I have brined the beans, I add 1 teaspoon of kosher salt to the cooking water at the outset. If I haven't brined them, I add 1 tablespoon.

USING OTHER SEASONING. For every pound of beans, I usually throw in half an onion, a few garlic cloves, a bay leaf or two, and a strip of kombu, a dried seaweed that's been known to have as positive an effect on softening the beans as soaking does. Enzymes in kombu can also help the digestibility of beans, including reducing the gaseous effects. (For more on how to combat beans' "musical fruit" qualities, see page 20.) Sometimes I add a dried chile pepper or two.

TOMATOES/CITRUS/ACIDS. If it's no more than a few tablespoons as part of the seasoning, I go ahead and put it in at the beginning if desired. The hardening effect of acidic ingredients kicks in only when they're included in higher proportions.

WATER. I don't typically measure the amount of water, instead filling the pot with as much water as needed to cover the beans by 2 inches if they've been soaked, 3 inches if they haven't. Less than this, and I almost always need to add more water before the beans are ready, especially when cooking in a stovetop pot. Much more, and the bean liquid—liquid gold, as far as I'm concerned—isn't as concentrated as I like. (The exception is when pressure cooking, when I use 3 cups of water for every 1 cup of beans.) I use tap water, even though DC's municipal water is considered "moderately hard," meaning it has moderate amounts of such minerals as calcium and magnesium, and hard water can cause beans to take longer to soften than distilled water. If you have particularly hard water or want to shorten your bean-cooking time, feel free to consider using distilled water, or add ¼ teaspoon baking soda to the water for each pound of beans. (Some say the baking soda can make the beans taste a little soapy; if you find this, feel free to rinse them before using.)

QUANTITY GUIDELINES

1 pound of dry beans = 5 to 6 cups cooked beans plus 2 to 3 cups liquid

1 can of beans = 1½ to 1¾ cups cooked beans plus ½ to ¾ cup liquid

1 pound of dry beans = 3 to 4 cans of beans

A Note About Cans

When buying beans in cans, look for those marked "BPA-free," especially (but not only) for recipes in which you plan to use the liquid in the can. Traditionally, cans have been lined with plastic containing bisphenol A, which some research has linked to fertility problems, heart disease, male impotence, and other conditions. Thankfully, more and more brands—including Eden, Westbrae Naturals, and Whole Foods' house brand—have switched to a lining that doesn't contain BPA. Another option is beans that come in glass jars or asceptic pouches.

I also prefer beans with no salt added so that I can control the amount of salt (and therefore sodium) more easily myself. If you can't find unsalted canned beans, be sure to rinse them well before using.

Bean Substitutes

There are hundreds and hundreds of varieties of beans, many with very distinctive qualities, and I encourage you to explore beyond the basic supermarket varieties and look at heirloom beans such as those sold by Rancho Gordo and other high-end purveyors and in international markets to find the beans beloved by particular cultures that you might not be familiar with.

Some beans stand alone, and there's really no comparable substitute for them, although that shouldn't keep you from experimenting. A pasta dish with chickpeas will be very different if you sub cannellini beans, which are much more buttery and less starchy; and enchiladas made with black beans

CONTINUED ON PAGE 18

It's got to be at the top of any list of FAQs about bean cookery: Do you have to soak them before cooking? Or can you skip it?

The answers to those exact questions are easy: no and yes, respectively. Soaking is certainly not a requirement: Just ask millions of cooks in Mexico (a bean-loving country if there ever was one) who never have, never would.

But just because you don't have to soak beans before cooking doesn't mean you shouldn't. Soaking shaves a little off the cooking time, although for the most part it's probably not enough of a savings to make it worth the planning just for that advantage alone.

So why soak?

Well, soaking can help reduce some of the so-called anti-nutrients, such as lectins and phytates, that keep you from absorbing all of the beans' nutrition when you eat them. (For more on this, see page 19.) And soaking and changing the water can help reduce what food scientist Harold McGee calls "the gassy potential" of beans (see "Let the Music Play," page 20), but there's a catch: you also lose nutrients, along with color and flavor. Both J. Kenji López-Alt of Serious Eats and *The Food Lab* and former *Los Angeles Times* food editor Russ Parsons have campaigned against soaking, especially when it comes to thin-skinned black beans, and I would agree: I've never made a pot of black beans more flavorful and with more inky black color than when I've skipped the soaking.

Now, brining—soaking the beans in a saltwater solution—is another story. It helps soften the beans' skins and makes them cook up creamier, as the obsessives over at America's Test Kitchen (ATK) have proven. But it turns out that using kombu, a form of dried seaweed—an old macrobiotic technique that my ex-hippie sister Rebekah taught me long ago—actually accomplishes the same thing. The ATK cooks found that the kombu works the same way as the brine, with the seaweed's "sodium and potassium ions trading places with minerals in the beans to create a smoother, creamier consistency," with no need for soaking.

Why soak, again?

There is actually one good reason, IMHO. Soaking, to me, is the great bean equalizer.

One of the mysteries of cooking beans is that, particularly with mass-market and bulk-bin products, you never are truly sure just how old the beans are. And the older they are, the longer they can take to cook. That means cooking time can vary widely between batches—even among different beans in the same batch, if you're buying from a bulk bin that's not managed well. But soaking seems to reset everything: once the beans take that overnight bath, they seem to all behave more like a batch that's no more than a year or two old, and they cook up more evenly.

If you buy from a consistent source or a dependable brand (see page 222) and get to know how long they typically take, it doesn't matter. But if you're not sure, I say soaking is your insurance.

Since it's even harder for me to know how old your beans are than it is for you, I include soaking instructions in most of these recipes. But you should feel free to skip it; just realize that the recipe might take a little longer—or a lot longer if the beans are particularly old.

CONTINUED FROM PAGE 15

will be distinct from those made with pinto beans, although each is delicious in its own way.

With that in mind, I tend to group many varieties of beans not by their botanical family—especially since so many of the most popular beans in the United States are all part of *Phaseolus vulgaris*—but by taste, texture, and color. In the recipes in this book I make frequent substitution suggestions, but feel free to play with the following switches to shake up your bean cookery. Be aware that cooking times vary, as will the size of the beans and, in some cases, the texture.

Round, starchy, nutty, firm:
chickpeas = black chickpeas = cicerchie

Very large, creamy, slightly sweet:
large lima = fava = gigante = corona = scarlet runner

Medium, creamy, nutty:
pinto = cranberry/borlotti = pinquito = Jacob's Cattle

Medium, starchy, almost a tad crunchy:
black-eyed peas = lady cream peas = cowpeas

White/light green, creamy, smooth, firm:
navy = cannellini = great Northern = flageolet = tarpais = coco

Red, meaty, full-flavored:
red kidney = small red bean

Quick-cooking lentils/etc. that get soft but hold their shape: brown/green lentils = mung beans

Small lentils/etc. that collapse completely into creaminess: red/orange lentils = split mung beans (moong dal) = split black urad (urad dal)

Small lentils that stay firm and intact:
French green lentils = black Beluga lentils = Umbrian lentils = pardina lentils

Aquafaba

Before you open the can of chickpeas, shake it. Then open and drain the chickpeas through a sieve over a measuring cup or bowl. A 15-ounce can of chickpeas contains about ½ cup of aquafaba, the liquid in a can of chickpeas. Keep any left over in an airtight container in the refrigerator for up to 1 week or freeze in ice cube trays, then transfer to zip-top bags and freeze for up to 6 months. Defrost before using.

It's possible to use the cooking liquid from chickpeas that you cook from dried beans, but the concentration is more variable, so it's less consistent than working with canned. Besides, I prefer adding seasonings to all my beans when cooking them from dried, and you don't want those flavors in aquafaba for most purposes. When using aquafaba as a substitute for eggs in baked goods or as a thickener, 2 tablespoons of aquafaba equals one egg white, and 3 tablespoons of aquafaba equals one whole egg.

Cooking Methods

I vary my cooking methods depending on the amount of time I have, how much attention I feel like paying, and whether I want the intoxicating aroma of beans to fill the house or to be sealed up inside a pressure cooker. Note that when it comes to cooking beans, all times are approximate, because there is so much variation depending on the age of the beans. Here are your options:

Lectins: A Nonissue

If you've read the bestselling work of a certain supplement-selling doctor, Steven Gundry, you might think beans are the enemy, or close to it.

The idea goes like this: Just about everything that ails us can be traced to lectins, a type of plant protein classified as an "anti-nutrient" because they can disrupt absorption. Gundry says they can bind to sugar molecules and penetrate the intestinal lining, leading to immune disorders.

Sounds awful, right? Well, plenty of nutrition professionals have questioned whether lectins are indeed the bogeyman Gundry says they are. But here's the thing: We don't have to worry about lectins in beans, because guess what? They're virtually eliminated by something that happens to virtually every bean recipe ever written: cooking. (In a follow-up book, Gundry allows his followers to eat beans if they pressure-cook them first; while pressure-cooking is a fine way to cook beans, my analysis of the research indicates that it's not necessary to significantly reduce the lectin content.)

The concerns about lectins seem to be rooted in the small number of cases of people who ate raw or undercooked red kidney beans, which are particularly high in lectins, and ended up in the hospital. And there's evidence that slow cookers, particularly if they're set on the lowest setting, might not get hot enough to destroy the lectins. Boiling the beans for 10 minutes first seems to do the trick, according to some research.

That's an easy solution to a paradox that might not be so paradoxical after all.

PRESSURE COOKER. This has become my most common method, by a hair, because it means I can cook most varieties of beans on any given weeknight in only 15 to 30 minutes (not including the time it takes to come to pressure or to naturally release), with no soaking required. You can use a stovetop model, an Instant Pot, or another multicooker. Prepare the beans as described on pages 14–15, cook at high pressure according to the chart on page 224, and let the pressure naturally release. If the beans are undercooked, either bring the machine back to pressure and cook for another 5 minutes, then manually release the pressure to check again, or cook the beans uncovered. Even once the beans are ready, I like to cook them uncovered for 10 to 20 minutes to reduce and concentrate the broth. As Rancho Gordo's Steve Sando puts it, this step "breathes life" back into what can be a lackluster broth.

STOVETOP POT. The old standby. I usually use a Dutch oven, follow the method described on pages 14–15, and bring the beans to a boil for 10 minutes; this helps make sure to get rid of some of the so-called anti-nutrients such as lectins (see more on this above). Then lower the heat as low as it will go, cover the pot, and cook until the beans are very tender (usually 1 to 1½ hours, but see the chart on page 225); you can continue to cook them uncovered for a bit, if you'd like, to reduce and concentrate the broth.

Storage

Unless using them immediately, I remove the kombu, bay leaf, and onion (the garlic disintegrates), and pour the beans into glass Mason jars with all their liquid, which should cover them for the best storage. (Add water if needed to cover.) One pound of dried beans results in enough cooked beans plus liquid to barely fit in two quart-size jars. I refrigerate them for up to 1 week. If I need to keep them longer than that, I'll store them in gallon-size zip-top freezer bags, in their liquid (or water if needed to cover), freezing them flat for easy defrosting later. They also freeze well in tempered glass.

Let the Music Play

"The more you eat, the more you toot," goes the childhood rhyme about the "magical" (or "musical," depending I guess on where you grew up) fruit. But this was no anti-legume screed; the next line, again with regional variations, goes something like, "The more you toot, the better you feel, so let's have beans at every meal."

Let's!

First, let's acknowledge that it's impossible to talk about beans without talking about farting. Beans earned their magical/musical reputation the hard way: through repetition. Noisy, sometimes smelly repetition.

Why do beans cause flatulence? Blame it on the oligosaccharides, certain carbohydrates in beans for which we don't have the enzymes to process, so they accumulate in the lower intestine, where our gut bacteria feed on them, fermenting them and releasing gas in the process. But it's not just beans: any high-fiber diet, especially when it's first adopted, can result in increased gas.

But what if you are particularly sensitive—or prone to embarrassment? Can you cut down on beans' musicality? Yes, you can. Here are some tips:

1 If you're just starting to add beans to your diet with any regularity, stick with it. One 2011 study in *Nutrition Journal* showed that while half the participants reported experiencing more flatulence in the first week of adding ½ cup of beans a day to their diet, almost three-quarters of those said the symptoms dissipated by the second or third week.

2 Try a variety of beans to see which you tolerate best. The *Nutrition Journal* study showed remarkable variance in individual responses to different types of beans. Canned beans typically have the lowest levels of oligosaccharides because of the processing, so that's a good place to start.

3 Soak your beans overnight in water, discard the water, and use a pressure cooker. A 2009 study in *LWT–Food Science and Technology* found that this combination reduced the oligosaccharides by 75 to 80 percent. The reduction was even higher when baking soda was added to the soaking water, according to a 1985 study in the *Journal of Agricultural and Food Chemistry*, but that also results in some loss of B vitamins. In fact, all soaking results in the loss of some nutrients, so be aware of that trade-off. (See "To Soak or Not to Soak," page 17.)

4 Cook beans with kombu, which has long been purported to help with the digestion of beans. There is a scientific basis for this: kombu (*Saccharina japonica*) is indeed among the marine algae that contain alpha-galactosidase, the same enzyme we lack that's required for breaking down the oligosaccharides. Other traditional additions that purportedly help with digestion include the Mexican herb epazote and the Indian powder asafoetida (also known as hing or heeng). Cumin and ginger, too.

5 Try a commercial product such as Beano, which also uses the enzyme alpha-galactosidase to help digest the oligosaccharides in beans. Research has proven its effectiveness.

I happen to believe that beans are so healthful we shouldn't let fear of farting get in the way of our enjoying them. Some researchers, such as Harold McGee, say that since the oligosaccharides are feeding our bacteria, they themselves are part of what makes beans good for us.

Just make a joke of it—or a song.

DIPS & SNACKS

With their creamy texture, all it takes is a little mashing or blending to turn beans into a luxurious spread or dip. Hummus is arguably the most beloved bean spread in the world, acting not just as a dip but as the base for countless bowls. But chickpeas aren't the only bean that can become dippable or spreadable. If you get into the habit of regularly cooking a pot of beans and then looking for various ways to eat them, their last iteration can happen when you whir them in a food processor or blender with seasonings and a little oil. On the other end of the spectrum, far from creamy, when you roast or fry beans, they become as addictive as popcorn.

HARISSA-ROASTED CARROT AND WHITE BEAN DIP

The combination of harissa and mint—one spicy, one cooling—takes this dip into can't-stop-eating territory. Use cannellini, navy, great Northern, or another white bean.

Preheat the oven to 450°F.

On a small rimmed baking sheet, toss the carrots with the harissa, 1 tablespoon of the olive oil, and the salt. Place the garlic on one side of the sheet. Roast until the carrots are fork-tender, 20 to 25 minutes. Let cool slightly.

Squeeze the soft garlic cloves out of their skins into the bowl of a food processor or blender. Add the carrots and use a spatula to scrape in as much of the browned roasted harissa bits from the pan as possible. Reserving a few whole beans for garnish if desired, add the rest to the food processor or blender, plus the remaining 2 tablespoons of olive oil, mint, and lemon juice and puree until smooth, scraping down the sides of the bowl as needed. Add a little water or some of the reserved bean liquid, a few tablespoons at a time, to loosen the mixture if it is too pasty in texture. Taste and add more salt if needed.

To serve, spoon the dip onto a shallow plate and use the back of a spoon to swirl it. Add the whole beans and a little dollop or two of harissa, if desired, drizzle with olive oil, and sprinkle with the chopped mint. Serve with pitas, crackers, or raw vegetables.

Refrigerate in an airtight container for up to 1 week.

Makes about 2 cups

½ pound carrots, cut into 1-inch pieces

1 tablespoon harissa, plus more (optional) for finishing the dish

3 tablespoons extra-virgin olive oil, plus more for finishing the dish

½ teaspoon kosher salt, plus more to taste

5 garlic cloves, unpeeled

1¾ cups cooked or canned no-salt added white beans (from one 15-ounce can), drained but not rinsed (reserve the liquid)

¼ cup lightly packed mint leaves, plus more chopped mint for finishing the dish

1 tablespoon fresh lemon juice

PERFECTLY SIMPLE AND LIGHT HUMMUS

(PICTURED ON PAGE 24, LEFT)

Makes about 3½ cups

3½ cups cooked or canned no-salt added chickpeas (from one 29-ounce can or two 15-ounce cans), drained but not rinsed (reserve the liquid; see page 18)

⅓ cup tahini

2 garlic cloves, chopped

2 tablespoons fresh lemon juice

½ teaspoon kosher salt, plus more to taste

Extra-virgin olive oil, for serving

Smoked paprika, za'atar, or sumac, for serving (optional)

There are two schools of thought about making hummus: One is that you can just throw everything in a food processor and hope for the best. The other is that you must pay attention to every detail, cooking the chickpeas from scratch (with baking soda to loosen their skins), peeling them (a laborious task, trust me) and being careful how you blend them, and exalting in the creamy smooth perfection that results. I propose a third school, one that calls for no peeling or even home cooking of the beans, but one that can still give you something luscious and light—a far cry from the leaden, grainy sludge that too many of us have come to expect. The key is in the order of your blending and in the liberal use of aquafaba, the liquid from a can of chickpeas—of course.

Measure out 1 cup of the chickpea cooking liquid (aquafaba) into a liquid measuring cup and add a few ice cubes to it.

In a blender (preferably a high-powered one such as a Vitamix) or food processor, combine the chickpeas, tahini, garlic, lemon juice, salt, and ¼ cup of the aquafaba. Puree until very smooth, scraping down the sides of the bowl as needed and continuing to process for several minutes.

With the motor running, slowly pour another ½ cup of the aquafaba into the chickpea mixture, stopping the machine every now and then to scrape down the sides of the bowl. The mixture should be light and about the texture of thick pancake batter. If it's thicker than that, resume processing and slowly pour in a little more aquafaba, until you reach the right texture. Taste and add more salt if needed.

To serve, spread the hummus on a shallow bowl or platter, swirling it if you'd like. Drizzle with a little olive oil and sprinkle with the smoked paprika, if using. Serve with pitas or raw vegetables or use as the base for roasted vegetables.

SPICY ETHIOPIAN RED LENTIL DIP

This is basically a thicker version of misir wot, the traditional lentil stew spiced with berbere, Ethiopia's intoxicating mix of chiles, ginger, garlic, fenugreek, coriander, and other warming spices. (You may have to go to a good spice store for berbere or look for it online, but it's worth the effort.) Since red lentils fall apart during cooking, this becomes dippable without the need for pureeing. Misir wot is often cooked with hefty quantities of clarified butter, but vegetable oil works wonderfully, too. I like to punch things up with more fresh garlic and ginger.

Pour the oil into a medium saucepan over medium-high heat. When it shimmers, stir in the onion and garlic and sauté until tender and starting to brown, 6 to 8 minutes. Stir in 1 tablespoon of the berbere, the tomato paste, ginger, and salt and cook until fragrant, about 30 seconds. Stir in the lentils and 2 cups water, bring to a boil, then reduce the heat to low, cover, and cook, stirring occasionally, until the lentils are tender and the mixture is very thick, about 25 minutes.

Stir in the remaining 1 teaspoon berbere, taste, and add more salt, if needed. Serve warm or at room temperature, with pitas or other chips or crudités.

Refrigerate in an airtight container for up to 1 week.

Makes about 2 cups

¼ cup sunflower, grapeseed, or other neutral vegetable oil

1 cup chopped onion

4 garlic cloves, chopped

1 tablespoon plus 1 teaspoon berbere

2 tablespoons tomato paste

1 tablespoon freshly grated ginger

1 teaspoon kosher salt, plus more to taste

1 cup red lentils, rinsed and drained

Water

ROASTED BEET HUMMUS BOWL

WITH TURMERIC TAHINI AND PEANUT DUKKAH

4 servings

BEETS

About 1 cup kosher salt

2 pounds small to medium beets, scrubbed but not peeled

**TURMERIC TAHINI
(MAKES ABOUT 1 CUP)**

Water

1 tablespoon fresh lemon juice

1 garlic clove, smashed and peeled

1 teaspoon kosher salt

2½ teaspoons ground turmeric

1 teaspoon maple syrup

½ cup tahini

**PEANUT DUKKAH
(MAKES ABOUT ¾ CUP)**

Heaping ⅓ cup roasted peanuts

2 tablespoons toasted sesame seeds

2 tablespoons coriander seeds

1 teaspoon cumin seeds

½ teaspoon kosher salt

½ teaspoon sweet paprika

2 cups Little Sesame's Creamy, Fluffy Hummus (page 30), at room temperature

Extra-virgin olive oil, for drizzling

This is one of the fantastic hummus bowls served at DC's Little Sesame. You'll end up with more turmeric tahini and peanut dukkah (an Egyptian spice blend) than you need for this recipe, but you'll find plenty of other uses for them—primarily to drizzle and sprinkle on any roasted vegetable or grain dish that you like.

To roast the beets: Preheat the oven to 425°F.

Spread enough salt to come to a depth of ¼ inch in a baking dish just big enough to comfortably hold the beets. Nestle the beets in the salt, cover the whole dish and the beets tightly with aluminum foil, and roast until a metal skewer or fork can easily pierce the beets with little to no resistance, about 1 hour, depending on the size of the beets. Remove and, when the beets are cool enough to handle, slip off the peels, if desired. Cut the beets into ½-inch-thick wedges.

While the beets are roasting, make the turmeric tahini: Combine ½ cup plus 2 tablespoons water, the lemon juice, garlic, salt, turmeric, and maple syrup in a blender and blend until combined. Pour in the tahini and blend until smooth.

To make the peanut dukkah: Combine the peanuts, sesame, coriander, cumin, salt, and paprika in a mini food processor or large dedicated spice grinder and process until combined but still chunky.

To assemble, spread the hummus in a large shallow bowl, pile the beets in the center, drizzle with some of the tahini, and sprinkle with some of the peanut dukkah. Drizzle with olive oil and serve.

The turmeric tahini can be refrigerated in an airtight container for up to 2 weeks, and the dukkah can be stored in an airtight container at room temperature for up to 2 months.

LITTLE SESAME'S CREAMY, FLUFFY HUMMUS

Makes about 3 cups

1 cup dried chickpeas, soaked overnight and drained

1 tablespoon baking soda

Water

1 cup extra-virgin olive oil, plus more if needed

4 garlic cloves

1 teaspoon kosher salt, plus more to taste

2 tablespoons fresh lemon juice

Scant ⅔ cup tahini

This is the hummus I make when I have time to cook the chickpeas from scratch. I learned it from chefs Ronen Tenne and Nick Wiseman, two of the founders (along with Nick's cousin David Wiseman) of DC's Little Sesame, where hummus is the main attraction. Their top tips: Cook the chickpeas until they're so tender as to practically be falling apart (using baking soda to speed things up). Use a little raw garlic and a little garlic confit (cooked in olive oil for more sweetness and a little less bite). Don't be afraid of salt. Use good tahini—but not so much that it weighs down the hummus. And never, ever put olive oil in the blend. What you'll get is something super-creamy and light, perfect for topping with roasted vegetables, along with their Turmeric Tahini and Peanut Dukkah (page 28), or just swiping up with pita, of course.

Combine the chickpeas with the baking soda and enough water to cover by 2 inches in a large pot over medium-high heat. Bring to a boil; foam will rise to the top within the first few minutes. While continuing to boil, skim off the foam repeatedly until very little remains. Reduce the heat to medium-low, cover, and cook until the chickpeas are so tender you can very easily smash them against the side of the pot with a wooden spoon, and the water is dark brown, about 40 minutes. Drain.

(I don't recommend using a pressure cooker for this one because the baking soda foam can clog it up—and because it's quick enough that you won't save much time, especially when you count the bringing-up-to-pressure time.)

NOTE

This will leave you with extra garlic-scented olive oil; refrigerate it and use it within 2 weeks, anywhere you would use regular olive oil.

While the chickpeas are cooking, pour the olive oil into a very small saucepan over low heat. Add 2 of the garlic cloves, adding more oil if needed to cover them, and cook until they are very tender, about 30 minutes. Drain, reserving the olive oil.

Combine the drained chickpeas in a high-speed blender or food processor with the remaining 2 raw garlic cloves, the 2 garlic confit cloves, salt, and lemon juice and puree for 3 minutes, until very smooth. With the motor running, pour in the tahini and ¾ cup water and keep pureeing until very smooth. Add more water, if needed; you want the consistency to be like thick, pourable pancake batter. Taste and add more salt if needed.

Swoosh the hummus onto a shallow platter or serving bowl, drizzle with a little of the garlic-scented oil, and serve. (To store, before drizzling with the oil, refrigerate in an airtight container for up to 1 week. Bring to room temperature before serving and whisk in more water if needed to loosen, since the hummus will thicken as it sits, and drizzle with the garlic-scented oil before serving.)

CUMIN-ROASTED CARROTS, ONIONS, AND LEMONS
WITH BEAN SPREAD

This is a gorgeous pileup, indeed, with flavors to match. I like to serve it right on large flatbreads for a fun, interactive dinner-party dish.

Preheat the oven to 450°F. Set a rack in the upper position. Put a large rimmed baking sheet in the oven while it heats.

Cut the carrots in half lengthwise. If they are particularly fat, cut the halves again in half lengthwise.

Seed the lemon halves as best you can, then thinly slice them (removing more seeds as you go).

Toss the carrots and lemon slices in a bowl with the olive oil, onion, cumin, and salt. Spread them evenly on the baking sheet.

Roast until the carrots are lightly browned and tender, the lemon has started to char in spots, and the onion is bright red, about 30 minutes. (Toss with tongs and respread on the sheet halfway through.) Remove the pan with the carrot mixture, turn off the oven, and put the lavash directly on the oven racks for a few minutes to warm.

Drizzle the carrot mixture with the honey and toss while warm.

To serve, lay the warm lavash on large platters. Spread half the bean spread on each lavash, top with half the carrot mixture, garnish with the whole beans, if using, and scatter with the dill.

NOTE

If you don't have the bean spread on hand, make a quick version by mashing 1 cup canned lima beans (drained and rinsed) with 6 pressed garlic cloves, ¼ cup vegan or dairy yogurt, ⅔ cup roasted chopped almonds, a drizzle of olive oil, and kosher salt to taste.

4 servings

6 carrots, trimmed and scrubbed

1 lemon, halved

¼ cup extra-virgin olive oil

1 red onion, thinly sliced or cut into thin wedges

2 teaspoons ground cumin

2 teaspoons kosher salt

2 large pieces lavash or another flatbread

2 tablespoons honey or agave nectar

2 cups Garlicky Gigante Bean Spread (page 34 or see Note below)

A few whole cooked gigante or lima beans, for garnish (optional)

1 cup lightly packed fresh dill, chopped

GARLICKY GIGANTE BEAN SPREAD
(SKORDALIA)

Makes about 2¾ cups

1¼ cups roasted unsalted almonds

1½ cups cooked gigante beans, drained but not rinsed

10 garlic cloves, inner sprouts removed (see Note below)

⅓ cup extra-virgin olive oil

2 tablespoons fresh lemon juice

1½ teaspoons kosher salt, plus more to taste

½ cup Coconut–Cashew Yogurt (page 215), or your favorite coconut or almond milk or dairy yogurt

1 teaspoon finely grated lemon zest

This Greek spread is most commonly made with potatoes and bread, but I've seen versions that use my beloved gigante beans instead, so now this is what I make when I have some gigantes left over. My friend Aglaia Kremezi's version calls for blanched almonds that you soak in water to help get the skordalia as smooth as possible, but I prefer the lazy approach of using roasted chopped nuts—I like the extra texture they give.

Put the almonds in the bowl of a food processor and pulse a few times to break up. Add the beans, garlic, oil, lemon juice, salt, yogurt, and lemon zest and puree until incorporated but still a little chunky from the nuts. Taste and add more salt if needed.

Serve this as a dip with pitas or raw vegetables or use it as a base for roasted vegetables (such as the cumin-roasted carrots, onion, and lemons on page 33) or as a sandwich condiment.

> **NOTE**
>
> Unless you are using the freshest garlic, it is probably sprouting inside, and when you're using this much raw garlic, those sprouts can create an unpleasantly sharp and acrid taste. Use a paring knife to cut open each clove lengthwise and remove and discard the center sprout.

SALSA MADRE
(BLACK BEAN MOTHER SAUCE PUREE)

DC chef Christian Irabién was in my kitchen cooking beans when it struck him: "These," he said, pointing at the blender full of pureed black beans, "are like the Mexican mother sauce." At the same time, we both said, "Salsa madre!" What he meant, of course, was that you could use them for so many other dishes: spreading them on fried masa boats known as sopes (page 36), as the base for chilaquiles (page 174), thinned out into a soup with masa dumplings (page 108), or as a smear on the bottom of a tostada, in a taco, or on bread. There are two secrets to Irabién's beans I had never seen before. One is that he blends them with all the aromatics that went into the pot to cook them, the things that usually get left behind: an onion and half a head of garlic, both with their skins and roots left intact; dried avocado leaf, which lends a slight anise-flavored note; and even the bay leaves, which are usually plucked out before serving. The other is his brine: after the beans cook but before he purees them, he drains them (saving that precious liquid, of course) and lets them sit in a very salty brine, which seasons them from the inside out. A third secret, which is not much of a secret to cooks all over Mexico: skip the soaking and you'll have a much more flavorful, inky broth—which is key for this dish.

Combine the black beans with 3 quarts water in a Dutch oven or heavy stockpot over high heat. Add the bay leaves, avocado leaves, onion, and garlic. Bring to a boil, then lower to a simmer and cook, uncovered, until the beans are very tender, 2 to 3 hours.

While the beans are cooking, make the salt brine: combine 1 quart water with the salt and whisk until the salt is completely dissolved.

When the beans are tender, remove from the heat. Pour them through a fine-mesh strainer, reserving all the cooking liquid and aromatics. Add the beans to the brine and let them sit for at least 1 hour.

Drain the beans thoroughly, discarding the brine, and combine them in a blender (preferably a high-powered one such as a Vitamix) with 1 cup of the cooking liquid and the bay leaves, avocado leaves, onion, and garlic from the pot and puree until smooth. Add a little more cooking liquid if needed but only enough to help the blades turn.

The puree can be refrigerated in an airtight container for up to 1 week or frozen for up to 6 months.

Makes about 5 cups

1 pound dried black beans, rinsed

Water

3 bay leaves

3 dried avocado leaves (may substitute 1 teaspoon anise or fennel seeds)

½ white onion, with peels and roots

½ head garlic, with peels and roots

¼ cup plus 1 tablespoon kosher salt

BLACK BEAN SOPES

Makes 8 sopes

1 cup instant masa harina, plus more as needed

½ teaspoon kosher salt

Hot water

3 tablespoons unsalted vegan or dairy butter, at room temperature

Safflower, grapeseed, or other neutral vegetable oil, for frying

1 cup Salsa Madre black bean purée (page 35) or see note below), warmed

½ cup Herb-Marinated Tofu Feta (page 217) or store-bought vegan or dairy feta, crumbled

½ cup Quick and Simple Charred Salsa Verde (page 217) or your favorite store-bought salsa

1 cup lightly packed mixed lettuce greens, tossed with 2 tablespoons fresh lime juice

These hearty little snacks that DC chef Christian Irabién taught me how to make feature crispy fried masa that's still a little creamy inside—heaven. The forming takes a little practice, especially since you need to cook them briefly first before finishing the shaping and frying. Top them with black bean puree, feta, salsa, and crunchy lettuces. These make a great passed appetizer.

Combine the masa harina and salt in the bowl of a stand mixer fitted with the beater attachment. (Alternatively, you can use a large bowl and a hand mixer.) With the mixer on low speed, slowly pour in ¾ cup hot water until the mixture forms a dough. It should be moist and tacky but not sticky or dry. If it's sticky, sprinkle in a little more masa harina and mix to combine; if it's dry, pour in a tablespoon or so more hot water and mix to combine. When the dough feels right, turn the mixer to medium-high speed, pinch off a small piece of butter, and drop it into the dough, beating until it disappears before dropping in another piece. When all the butter is in the dough, turn the mixer to high and beat for another minute, until the masa dough is very fluffy. Check to see if it has remained slightly tacky but not sticky or dry; beat in more masa harina or water if needed to correct it.

Using a small cookie scoop or large tablespoon, form the masa into eight equal pieces. Pat each one into a 3-inch disk.

Pour 1 tablespoon of the oil into a large skillet over medium-high heat. When it shimmers, add as many of the masa disks as will fit without overcrowding. Cook until very lightly browned, 1 minute per side, then remove to a plate and let cool slightly. While they're still pretty hot but you can (barely) handle them, pinch the edges of the masa disks all around, turning them up to form a rimmed basket shape.

Pour enough oil into the skillet over medium-high heat to come up ½ inch. When the oil shimmers, add enough of the masa boats (sopes) to fit without overcrowding and fry until crisp, 2 minutes per side. Transfer to a paper-towel-lined plate.

Scoop 2 tablespoons of the black bean puree into each of the sopes, then top with feta, salsa verde, and dressed lettuce. Serve while hot.

NOTE

If you don't have any Salsa Madre on hand, puree 1½ cups cooked or no-salt-added canned black beans, drained and rinsed, with ¼ teaspoon kosher salt, ½ teaspoon ground cumin, and just enough water or bean cooking liquid to help the blender blades turn, then blend until smooth.

CORN HUMMUS
WITH SPICY CORN RELISH

8 to 12 servings

HUMMUS (MAKES ABOUT 5 CUPS)

3 large ears corn, husks intact

1 cup dried chickpeas, soaked overnight and drained

2 (3 by 5-inch) strips kombu (dried seaweed)

1 bay leaf

1 yellow onion, halved

1 garlic clove

1½ teaspoons kosher salt, plus more to taste

Water

½ cup tahini

¼ cup extra-virgin olive oil

¼ cup fresh lemon juice, plus more to taste

1 teaspoon ground turmeric

When I saw this corn hummus on the menu at Oleana, one of my favorite restaurants in the Boston area—actually, make that the world—I had to try making it myself. After all, chef-owner Ana Sortun had years earlier stunned me with her warm, buttered Turkish hummus. Oleana's talented chef de cuisine, Paige Lombardi, has clearly caught the hummus bug, because she loves to use the dish (and variations on it) to showcase seasonal produce, adding the warm spark of Mediterranean and Middle Eastern spices. She makes this beautiful dish by throwing corn cobs into the pot to flavor the chickpeas, adding turmeric for an earthy backdrop (and beautiful golden color), and topping it with a relish of corn, tomatoes, and spices—including fruity-hot Marash chiles. Besides scaling it down from restaurant yields, I made just one tweak: I like to throw some of the fresh corn kernels into the hummus, too—just to amp up that summer flavor.

To make the hummus: Run water over the corn cobs in their husks and microwave on high for 5 to 7 minutes, until steaming hot. Let cool slightly, then use your fingers to feel where the row of kernels ends on the wide end of the cob (opposite the silk end) and use a sharp knife to cut through those last kernels and through the cob. Holding the silk end, squeeze each cob out of the husk from that end; it should pop out clean and slightly cooked. Rinse if needed to get more of the silks off. Cut each cob in half crosswise, then stand one half at a time on a cutting board, cut side down, and slice off the kernels. Reserve 1 cup of the kernels for the hummus and the remainder for the relish.

Add the cobs to a large pot, along with the chickpeas, kombu, bay leaf, onion, garlic, 1 teaspoon of the salt, and enough water to cover everything by 1 inch. Set over high heat, bring to a boil, boil for 5 minutes, then reduce the heat to medium-low. Cover and cook until the chickpeas are very soft, 60 to 90 minutes. (Check the water periodically and add more as needed to keep everything covered.)

(You can also make this in a stovetop or electric pressure cooker: bring to high pressure and cook for 25 minutes if using a stovetop model or 30 minutes if using an electric model, then turn off and let the pressure naturally release.)

When the chickpeas are soft, remove the bay leaf, cobs, onion, and kombu. Drain the chickpeas, reserving the cooking liquid.

Transfer the chickpeas to a high-speed blender or food processor. Add 1 cup of the reserved corn kernels, plus the tahini, olive oil, lemon juice, turmeric, the remaining ½ teaspoon salt, and 1 cup of the reserved cooking liquid and process until very smooth. You want the consistency to be like thick, pourable pancake batter. Add more cooking liquid ¼ cup at a time if needed to loosen. Taste and add more salt and lemon juice, if needed.

To make the corn relish: Pour the olive oil into a medium skillet over medium-high heat. When it shimmers, stir in the pickled peppers, coriander, cumin, chile flakes, oregano, salt, and pepper and cook until fragrant, about 30 seconds. Stir in the corn and cook until the corn loses any raw taste, 1 to 2 minutes. Stir in the lemon juice and use the spoon to scrape up any browned bits on the bottom of the pan. Stir in the tomatoes and parsley and remove from the heat. Taste and add more salt if needed.

To serve, scoop the hummus onto a large serving platter (or platters) and use the back of a spoon to swoosh it around the edges of the platter, creating a well in the center. Scoop the corn mixture into the center, sprinkle with the sunflower seeds and parsley, and drizzle with olive oil.

CORN RELISH (MAKES ABOUT 2½ CUPS)

1 tablespoon extra-virgin olive oil, plus more for drizzling

2 Turkish pickled hot peppers (or Greek or Italian pepperoncini), chopped

2 teaspoons ground coriander

1 teaspoon ground cumin

1 teaspoon Marash chile flakes (may substitute ½ teaspoon crushed red pepper flakes)

1 teaspoon dried oregano

½ teaspoon kosher salt, plus more to taste

½ teaspoon freshly ground black pepper

1½ to 2 cups reserved corn kernels

2 tablespoons fresh lemon juice, plus more to taste

1 cup cherry tomatoes, halved

3 tablespoons roasted unsalted sunflower seeds

¼ cup flat-leaf parsley or cilantro leaves, chopped, plus more for garnish

CHARRED GREEN CHICKPEAS

WITH CHILE AND LIME

If you're ever lucky enough to come across fresh green chickpeas sold in the pod, snap them up and make this great party appetizer, the type of thing that will keep guests occupied in the kitchen while they watch you cook. I love this treatment because it feels like the best cross possible between charred shishito peppers and steamed edamame. Season the chickpeas heavily with Mexican Tajin seasoning (a combination of chile powder, salt, and dried lime powder) as soon as they come out of the skillet, then when you pop the chickpeas out of the pod and into your mouth, you can taste the spices right off the pod and off your fingers, too.

Pour the olive oil into a large cast-iron or other heavy-duty skillet over medium-high heat. When it shimmers, add the chickpeas in one layer, working in batches, if necessary, to avoid overcrowding. (Pour in more oil between batches if needed.) Cook until the pods blacken in spots, 5 to 6 minutes, stirring occasionally.

Transfer the pods to a serving bowl as they become ready and sprinkle immediately with the salt and Tajin seasoning. Repeat with the remaining chickpeas.

VARIATIONS

Instead of the Tajin seasoning, try chaat masala, Madras curry, Chinese five-spice powder, ras el hanout, za'atar, berbere, or any of your other favorite spice blends.

4 to 6 servings

2 tablespoons extra-virgin olive oil, plus more if needed

1 pound fresh chickpeas in the pod (may substitute fresh or frozen and thawed edamame in the pod)

1 teaspoon kosher salt, plus more to taste

1 tablespoon Tajin seasoning or Rancho Gordo's Star Dust dipping powder (or see other variations below)

BLACK CHICKPEA HUMMUS
WITH BLACK GARLIC AND PRESERVED LEMON

Makes about 4 cups

14 ounces dried black chickpeas, soaked overnight and drained

Water

2 (3 by 5-inch) strips kombu (dried seaweed)

1½ teaspoons kosher salt, plus more to taste

½ cup tahini

½ cup chopped preserved lemon, plus more for garnish

4 black garlic cloves

¼ cup smoked olive oil (may substitute regular olive oil)

Flat-leaf parsley leaves, for garnish

I first made this when my favorite DC grocery chain, Mom's Organic Market, which has a stellar collection of dried beans, started carrying Timeless Natural Foods' black kabuli chickpeas, which are a striking deep black color. Most of the color is in the skins, so the hummus turns out brown and not inky black, but the flavor is super-nutty. Black garlic adds even more of that note, plus a little sweetness, while preserved lemon gives a pop of salty tartness. You can also find black chickpeas sold as ceci neri in Italian specialty stores and lighter-colored, smaller ones sold as kala chana in Indian stores.

Combine the chickpeas, 6 cups water, kombu, and 1 teaspoon salt in a large pot over medium-high heat. Bring to a boil, reduce the heat to medium-low, and cook, covered, until the chickpeas are tender, 60 to 90 minutes. Let the chickpeas cool slightly (or refrigerate for up to 5 days), then drain the chickpeas, reserving the cooking liquid.

(You can also make this in a stovetop or electric pressure cooker. Bring to high pressure and cook for 25 minutes if using a stovetop model or 30 minutes if using an electric model, then turn off and let the pressure naturally release.)

Scoop out ¼ cup or so of the chickpeas to save for garnish.

Combine the remaining chickpeas with 1 cup of the reserved cooking liquid, the remaining ½ teaspoon salt, tahini, preserved lemon, and garlic in a blender, preferably a high-powered one such as a Vitamix. Blend until smooth, adding more cooking liquid, ½ cup at a time, if needed to keep the mixture from stalling the blender. Continue adding liquid and blending until the mixture is creamy and light textured but not runny. (It should be the texture of thick cake batter.) You might need to use all of the cooking liquid. Taste and add more salt if needed.

To serve, dollop the hummus onto a large serving platter, use the back of a large spoon to swirl it around the plate, and drizzle with the olive oil. Garnish with the reserved chickpeas, preserved lemon, and parsley. Serve with bread, pickles, and/or raw vegetables.

HUMMA-NOUSH

That's right: it's a cross between hummus and baba ghanouj, with each lending some of its texture to the other for something wholly unique yet familiar. I got the idea from Ron Pickarski, executive chef at Eco-Cuisine in Boulder, Colorado, who offered it to the Food and Agriculture Organization of the United Nations for its work on the 2016 International Year of Pulses. My version is a little simpler than his, and I add sumac for a burst of earthy tartness and a touch of smoked paprika to play up the smokiness of the eggplant. This is even better if you cook the eggplant on a charcoal grill, to really get the smoke that baba ghanouj traditionally requires (and in that case, you can skip the smoked paprika if you'd like).

Prepare a grill for direct heat with a medium-hot fire. If using charcoal, you should be able to hold your hand about 6 inches above the grate for 4 to 6 seconds. For a gas grill, preheat for 10 minutes to 450°F (medium-high). For cooking indoors, turn the oven to broil (high if your oven has different broiler settings) and set the rack position so the eggplant on a baking sheet will be just a few inches from the flame or element. (It will get smoky, so consider yourself warned!)

Pierce the eggplants all over with a sharp paring knife. Rub the eggplants with the grapeseed oil and place them directly on the grill or on a large rimmed baking sheet under the broiler. Cook the eggplants, turning as needed, until they have thoroughly blackened and burned to an ashen crisp on each side and completely collapsed, 40 to 60 minutes. Remove from the grill or oven and let cool.

When the eggplants are cool enough to handle, slash each one open and scrape the flesh into the bowl of a food processor or blender. (You should have about 1½ cups eggplant flesh.) Add the chickpeas, garlic, tahini, lemon juice, sumac, salt, and smoked paprika, if using, and puree until smooth. Taste and add more salt if needed.

To serve, scoop into a shallow bowl and use a large spoon to make a swoosh. Drizzle with the olive oil and sprinkle with a little sumac.

Serve with pita, carrot chips, or any other raw vegetable of your choice.

Makes about 2 cups

3 medium to large Italian eggplants

2 tablespoons grapeseed oil

1¾ cups cooked or canned no-salt-added chickpeas (from one 15-ounce can), drained and rinsed

2 garlic cloves, chopped

3 tablespoons tahini

1 tablespoon fresh lemon juice

1 teaspoon sumac, plus more for sprinkling

½ teaspoon kosher salt, plus more to taste

¼ teaspoon Spanish smoked paprika (pimenton; optional)

Smoked olive oil (may substitute regular olive oil), for drizzling

ECUADORIAN LUPINI BEAN CEVICHE

(CEVICHOCHOS)

8 servings

2½ cups jarred lupini beans in brine (chochos), drained and rinsed

1 small red onion, or 2 large shallots, thinly sliced

Water

1 tomato, thinly sliced

⅓ cup fresh orange juice

⅔ cup fresh lime juice

¼ cup lightly packed cilantro leaves, chopped

1 tablespoon safflower, grapeseed, or other neutral vegetable oil

1 tablespoon tomato paste

1 teaspoon kosher salt, plus more to taste

½ cup corn nuts, for garnish

Flesh of 1 ripe avocado, cubed, for garnish

Your favorite hot sauce (optional)

Plantain chips or tortilla chips

All ceviche isn't made with fish: this traditional one from the mountains of Ecuador that my friend and scholar Sandra Gutierrez told me about uses lupini beans (chochos). They have to be boiled repeatedly to make them safe for consumption, which might be why they're typically cooked, brined, and packed into jars. They are sold in Latin and Italian markets (pickled lupinis are a popular snack in Rome). That makes this ceviche a much easier prospect to make than if you were preparing them from the dried beans, but there is still a laborious task that awaits: I much prefer eating these peeled, which requires a little knife work—much like peeling and deveining the world's smallest shrimp. It's all downhill after that, with no cooking required, and you're left with a delicious snack that's particularly refreshing during the dog days of summer. If you happen to have some cooked gigante or large lima beans on hand, this is a good use for them, too.

Peel the lupini beans by holding a bean between the thumb and forefinger of your non-dominant hand so the tiny opening is exposed. Use a paring knife in your dominant hand to carefully slash the little opening larger, then squeeze the bean to pop it out into a large bowl. Repeat until all the beans are peeled.

Add the onion to the bowl with the peeled beans, cover with water, and let them both soak for about 10 minutes. Drain and rinse thoroughly with water and return to the bowl. (This takes the bite out of the red onion and removes some of the extra brine from the lupini beans.)

Add the tomato, orange juice, lime juice, cilantro, oil, tomato paste, and salt. Taste and add more salt if needed. Refrigerate in an airtight container for at least 2 hours or up to 24 hours.

To serve, transfer to a serving bowl, garnish with the corn nuts and avocado, drizzle with the hot sauce, if desired, and serve with the chips.

RED BEAN, WALNUT, AND POMEGRANATE PÂTÉ

Makes about 1¾ cups

1¾ cups cooked or canned no-salt-added red kidney beans (from one 15-ounce can), drained and rinsed

½ cup chopped walnuts

2 garlic cloves, chopped

3 tablespoons unsalted vegan or dairy butter or refined coconut oil

3 tablespoons pomegranate molasses, plus more for drizzling

½ teaspoon kosher salt, plus more to taste

½ teaspoon freshly ground black pepper, plus more to taste

¼ cup pomegranate seeds, for garnish (optional)

This twist on a traditional Armenian snack is garlicky and creamy with a little fruity tartness that comes from the pomegranate molasses (a decidedly non-traditional addition I couldn't resist). This recipe is based on ones by two of my favorite women in the food world: Boston chef Ana Sortun and cookbook author Naomi Duguid. I hope they'll forgive my liberties.

Combine the beans, walnuts, garlic, butter, pomegranate molasses, salt, and pepper in the bowl of a food processor or blender and blend until very smooth, scraping down the sides of the bowl as needed. Taste and add more salt and pepper if needed.

Scrape the mixture into four ½-cup ramekins, cover with plastic wrap, and refrigerate until firm, at least 2 hours. Or if you'd prefer, form it into a log and roll in plastic wrap before refrigerating, then cut it into thick slices. Before serving, unwrap, drizzle with the molasses, and sprinkle with pomegranate seeds, if using.

Serve it with crackers and pickles.

Refrigerate in an airtight container for up to 5 days or freeze for up to 3 months.

ROASTED FAVA BEAN CRISPS

I modeled these after a store-bought snack that I find particularly difficult to resist. The secret, I found through trial and error, is to soak—but not cook—the dried fava beans before roasting. (When you cook them in water, split and dried favas can turn into a delicious mush without warning, which meant my "errors" were put to good use.) If you can't find beans that are split before being dried, feel free to soak dried whole ones, which split easily after soaking, but avoid those that still have the skin around the inner bean—they are very difficult to peel without cooking. These crisps are primarily meant for snacking, but they also make a nice crunchy garnish for soups and salads. Note that you can shake up the spices here: instead of one or both garlic and onion powders, try za'atar, sumac, garam masala, smoked paprika, Old Bay, or another favorite.

Preheat the oven to 350°F.

Spread the beans out on paper towels in a single layer and use more paper towels to pat them dry. Remove the paper towels and let them air-dry for a few minutes.

In a large bowl, whisk together the rice flour, salt, garlic powder, and onion powder, then whisk in the olive oil. Add the beans and stir to thoroughly coat. Spread them out on a large rimmed baking sheet, being careful not to overlap them.

Bake for 25 minutes, then turn off the oven (resist the urge to open it!) and let them sit while they cool, about 20 minutes. Take them out and transfer them to a large plate to continue cooling.

Serve when cool or store in an airtight container at room temperature for up to 2 weeks.

Makes about 2 cups

1 cup large dried split fava beans, soaked overnight and drained

¼ cup rice flour

1 tablespoon kosher salt

1 tablespoon garlic powder

1 tablespoon onion powder

¼ cup extra-virgin olive oil

CRUNCHY SPICED ROASTED CHICKPEAS

It took food-science geek Alton Brown of the Food Network's *Good Eats* to figure out that the way to make roasted chickpeas as crispy as the fried ones was to let them dry in an oven as they cool. I take the method further than he does: to guarantee that they'll be even crispier, I like to roast them slowly and let them sit in the oven for even longer. Now, finally, the homemade thing can approach the store-bought snack. I like to experiment with various spices and spice mixes as seasoning for these: use your favorite or keep experimenting.

Preheat the oven to 300°F. Put a large rimmed baking sheet in the oven as it heats.

Put the chickpeas in a salad spinner and spin to dry. Transfer them to a line of paper towels and put another section of paper towels on top, rubbing gently to further dry. Let air-dry for at least 30 minutes. In a bowl, toss them with 1 teaspoon of the olive oil, ½ teaspoon of the salt, and the spice(s).

Transfer the chickpeas to the preheated baking sheet and roast for 1 hour, until the chickpeas have slightly darkened and begin to get crisp on the edges. Leave them in the oven but turn off the heat and let the chickpeas cool in the oven (resist the urge to open the door!) as the temperature drops, about 2 hours.

Remove and let finish cooling at room temperature. When completely cool, drizzle with the remaining 1 teaspoon olive oil and sprinkle with the remaining ½ teaspoon salt. Taste and add more salt and/or spices if needed.

Serve immediately or transfer to an airtight container and store at room temperature for up to 1 week.

Makes 1¾ cups

1¾ cups cooked or canned no-salt-added chickpeas (from one 15-ounce can), drained and rinsed

2 teaspoons extra-virgin olive oil

1 teaspoon kosher salt, plus more to taste

1 teaspoon za'atar, sumac, Chinese five-spice powder, Madras curry, Tajin seasoning, smoked paprika, chaat masala, or other favorite spice or blend, plus more to taste

GIGANTE BEAN AND PORTOBELLO SATE

4 to 6 servings

MARINADE

4 scallions, chopped

2 tablespoons freshly grated ginger

¼ cup fresh lemon juice

2 teaspoons finely grated lemon zest

2 tablespoons safflower or grapeseed oil, plus a little more for the pan

4 garlic cloves, chopped

2 tablespoons low-sodium tamari

2 teaspoons light brown sugar

Water

3 large portobello mushroom caps, each sliced into 4 strips

1½ cups cooked gigante beans, drained and rinsed (may substitute the largest lima beans you can find)

SAUCE

Reserved marinade (from above)

½ teaspoon cayenne pepper

½ cup smooth peanut butter

Water

1 cup unsweetened small-flake dried coconut

Why not turn beans into sate (aka satay), one of the great culinary gifts of Indonesia to the world? Over there, it's not just chicken that gets grilled, of course. You can find sate made from fish, shrimp, and even tempeh, one of their other great culinary gifts. Gigante beans are big enough to skewer and meaty enough in texture to stand up to an aggressive marinade and spicy peanut sauce. Note that you'll have sauce left over; it can be refrigerated in an airtight container for up to 1 week—toss it with pasta and a little sesame oil to make cold sesame noodles!

To make the marinade: Combine the scallions, ginger, lemon juice, lemon zest, oil, garlic, tamari, brown sugar, and ¼ cup water in the bowl of a food processor or blender and puree until smooth, scraping down the sides of the bowl as needed.

Toss the mushrooms with half the marinade in a small glass bowl and toss the beans with the remaining half of the marinade in another small glass bowl. Cover and refrigerate for at least 2 hours or overnight.

Soak 12 wooden skewers in hot water for 10 to 15 minutes, then drain.

Drain the mushrooms and beans and reserve the marinade.

To make the sauce: Heat the reserved marinade in a small saucepan over medium heat until lightly bubbling, then stir in the cayenne pepper and whisk in the peanut butter and ½ cup water. Cook until hot and thick but still pourable, adding a little more water if needed. Remove from the heat and cover to keep warm.

Thread three slices of mushrooms lengthwise onto a skewer and repeat with the remaining mushrooms. Thread the gigante beans on separate skewers.

Heat a griddle, grill pan, or large cast-iron skillet over medium-high heat. Brush with a little oil. Cook as many mushroom skewers as will fit until softened and browned, about 4 minutes per side (pressing with a spatula if needed to help the mushrooms stay in contact with the pan). Repeat with the remaining mushroom skewers. Cook the bean skewers until heated through and lightly browned, about 2 minutes per side. Transfer to a platter as you work and lightly tent the skewers with foil to keep them warm.

To serve, pass the skewers and set out bowls of the sauce and coconut and let your guests dip and sprinkle as they see fit.

WHITE BEAN BRANDADE

Traditional brandade is made with salt cod, but vegetable whisperer Rich Landau of Vedge and V Street in Philly and Fancy Radish in DC came to me with this fabulous version using cannellini beans. It's a perfect party appetizer, especially in the cold-weather months when something warm and bubbly—not to mention delicious—will be a particular hit.

Preheat the oven to 425°F.

Pierce the potatoes all over with a fork. Microwave on high for 4 minutes, then transfer to a large rimmed baking sheet and bake until soft inside, about 45 minutes.

While the potatoes are baking, combine the beans, aioli, garlic, shallot, olive oil, chives, lemon juice, mustard, salt, pepper, and vinegar in the bowl of a food processor or blender and puree until very smooth, scraping down the sides of the bowl as needed. Transfer to a large bowl.

When the potatoes are ready, let them cool for a few minutes until they're easy to handle and increase the oven temperature to 450°F.

Slash open the potatoes and use a fork to flake the flesh into the bowl with the bean mixture. Gently mix in the potatoes until incorporated. Let the mixture stand for 20 minutes so the potatoes can absorb the moisture. At this point, the mixture can be refrigerated in an airtight container for up to 1 week before being baked.

Transfer the mixture to a 3- to 4-cup gratin dish or small casserole. Bake until the top is bubbly and lightly browned, 15 to 20 minutes.

Serve with crusty bread.

6 to 8 servings

1 pound russet potatoes

1½ cups cooked or no-salt-added canned cannellini beans (from one 15-ounce can), drained and rinsed

1 cup Chickpea Aioli (page 214) or store-bought vegan or traditional mayonnaise

1 garlic clove, chopped

1 small shallot, chopped

3 tablespoons extra-virgin olive oil

2 tablespoons chopped chives

1 tablespoon fresh lemon juice

2 teaspoons Dijon mustard

1 teaspoon kosher salt

½ teaspoon white pepper

½ teaspoon sherry vinegar

BLACK LENTIL CRACKERS

Makes about 24 crackers

1 cup rice flour

¼ cup chickpea flour

½ cup black lentils, soaked overnight and drained

½ cup sunflower seeds

¼ cup chia seeds

¼ cup sesame seeds

2 teaspoons kosher salt

1 teaspoon chopped fresh rosemary

2 tablespoons extra-virgin olive oil

Boiling water

These gluten-free crackers, which I adapted from a recipe by Swedish bean-loving baker Lina Wallentinson, are super-crisp and full of texture, thanks to all the lentils and seeds. Wallentinson's version uses no flour, and the chia seeds (and their gel-producing quality) create the "dough," which is pretty miraculous. But I wanted something sturdier for scooping up any of the dips in this chapter, so I added rice flour and a little chickpea flour. Note that this base recipe tastes great simply seasoned as is, but you could stir in such warm spices as za'atar, cumin, oregano, and/or smoked paprika.

Preheat the oven to 350°F. Set a rack in the lower third of the oven.

In a medium bowl, mix the rice flour, chickpea flour, lentils, sunflower seeds, chia seeds, sesame seeds, salt, rosemary, and olive oil. Pour 1 cup boiling water over the mixture and stir to thoroughly combine. Let the dough sit for 10 minutes, then cover and refrigerate for at least 1 hour.

Scoop the dough onto a standard sheet of parchment paper (about 12 by 17 inches). Place another sheet of parchment on top and roll out the dough so it comes all the way to the edges of the paper. (If it comes out from between the sheets, you may need to pinch it off in some places and press it back in where needed.)

Peel off the top sheet of parchment and transfer the dough still on the bottom sheet of paper onto a large cookie sheet or rimmed baking sheet. Bake on the lower oven rack until it feels dry to the touch and lightly browns, about 1 hour. Remove it, turn it over, and peel off the parchment, then return it to the oven to lightly brown the other side, about 15 minutes. Remove to a cooling rack and let cool; it should crisp up as it cools.

Break it up into big pieces and serve immediately or store in an airtight container at room temperature for up to 1 week.

HOT AND CREAMY WHITE BEAN, SPINACH, AND ARTICHOKE DIP

Makes about 6 cups

1 cup raw cashews

Water

2 tablespoons extra-virgin olive oil

1 large yellow onion, chopped

4 garlic cloves, chopped

1 teaspoon kosher salt, plus more to taste

½ teaspoon crushed red pepper flakes

1 pound baby spinach, finely chopped (may substitute mustard greens, Swiss chard, kale, or collard greens)

1¾ cups cooked or canned no-salt-added cannellini or navy beans (from one 15-ounce can), drained and rinsed

1 cup plain vegan or dairy cream cheese, whisked to loosen

One 14-ounce can quartered artichoke hearts, drained and chopped

2 tablespoons sumac

12 mild pickled jalapeño slices, chopped, plus 2 tablespoons of the pickling liquid

½ cup panko-style or other dried bread crumbs

This is my take on that gooey, irresistible spinach–artichoke dip, bulked up with creamy white beans and given a (little) punch with two forms of chiles. BTW: The amount of sumac may seem excessive on paper, but trust me, it works.

Preheat the oven to 400°F.

Combine the cashews with 1 cup water in a small saucepan over medium-high heat and bring to a simmer. Turn off the heat, cover, and let sit for at least 15 minutes. Transfer to a high-powered blender, such as a Vitamix, and blend until very smooth. Set aside.

Pour the olive oil into a large cast-iron skillet over medium-high heat. Once it shimmers, add the onion and garlic and sauté until they start to lightly brown, 7 to 8 minutes. Stir in the salt and red pepper flakes and cook until fragrant, about 30 seconds.

Reduce the heat to medium and stir in the spinach. Cook until the leaves wilt, 3 to 4 minutes. (If you use sturdier greens, this will take longer.) Turn off the heat and stir in the reserved cashew puree plus the beans, cream cheese, artichoke hearts, sumac, jalapeño slices, and pickling liquid. Taste and add more salt if needed.

Sprinkle with the bread crumbs and bake until the top and edges are browned and the inside is piping hot, about 45 minutes. (You can also cover and refrigerate the dip, before baking, for up to 1 week.)

Serve hot with crackers, chips, or toasted bread.

CANNELLINI BEAN PUREE
WITH GIARDENIERA AND TOGARASHI

Mike Friedman, chef-owner of the Red Hen and All-Purpose restaurants in Washington, DC, serves this killer spread, which I refuse to call hummus, even with quote marks around it, because of the lack of chickpeas, which is what the word means. Mike takes an Italian-American approach, using cannellini beans and topping it with giardeniera (jarred pickled vegetables), but adds a Japanese touch, too, with a sprinkle of togarashi (chile peppers plus other spices) at the end. This is a truly global spread, obviously.

Combine the cannellini beans, lemon juice, tahini, salt, and garlic in the bowl of a food processor or blender and process until very smooth, about 1 minute, scraping down the sides of the bowl as needed.

With the food processor running, slowly drizzle in the olive oil and continue blending until the puree is incredibly smooth, 2 to 3 minutes.

Refrigerate in an airtight container for at least 2 hours before serving.

To serve, smear onto a plate or shallow bowl, pile the giardeniera in the center, and sprinkle with the togarashi.

Makes about 1¾ cups

1¾ cups cooked or canned no-salt-added cannellini beans (from one 15-ounce can), drained and rinsed

¼ cup fresh lemon juice

¼ cup tahini

2 teaspoons kosher salt

2 garlic cloves, minced

¼ cup extra-virgin olive oil

½ cup giardeniera, drained and chopped

1 teaspoon togarashi (may substitute red chile flakes)

SALADS

Beans that hold their shape are a fabulous way to add heft and nutrition to a salad. And with few exceptions, this is where canned beans can come in handy: just open, drain, and toss with the rest of your ingredients. What other source of protein is so convenient? Most of these salads play well as either side dishes or main courses, depending on what you serve them with—and how much, of course.

RED GEM SALAD
WITH GREEN CURRY GODDESS AND CRISPY LENTILS

When I had this salad at Ellē in Washington, DC, it was the sexiest dish using beans I had ever seen: stunning green leaves with red-tinged edges, a pale green dressing, and shiny black lentils. The taste was even better: the spicy, tart, and herbaceous dressing, crisp lettuce, and earthy and crunchy lentils (plus seeds). It was simple and complex at the same time, almost elemental in its appeal. I streamlined Chef Brad Deboy's recipe for my own home cooking: instead of making a curry paste from scratch for the dressing, I started with a store-bought version and amped it up with lime and fresh basil. You'll have more dressing than you need for this recipe, but you can refrigerate it in an airtight container for up to 1 week and use it for potato salads, other greens, and as a dip.

To make the dressing: In the large bowl of a food processor, combine the tofu, basil, olive oil, curry paste, garlic, lime zest, lime juice, agave, and salt. Process until smooth, scraping down the sides of the bowl as needed. Taste and add more salt if needed.

To make the salad: Combine the lentils with 1 cup water in a small saucepan over medium-high heat. Bring to a boil, reduce the heat to low, cover, and simmer until the lentils are tender, 20 to 30 minutes. Drain in a fine-mesh strainer and rinse with cold water, then scatter on paper towels and gently pat dry.

Pour the oil to a depth of 1 inch into a small saucepan over medium-high heat. Line a bowl with paper towels. When the oil shimmers, sprinkle in the lentils, being careful to avoid splatters. Cook until the lentils stop bubbling, about 5 minutes, then use a slotted spoon to scoop them into the paper-towel-lined bowl. When the lentils are cool, remove the paper towels, and stir in the sesame seeds, flaxseeds, salt, and garlic powder.

To assemble the salad, scrape ½ cup of the dressing into a large bowl. Add the lemon juice, drizzle in a little olive oil, and whisk to combine. Drop in the lettuce leaves and gently toss until they are well coated. Sprinkle with half the lentil mixture and gently toss to coat. Add another ¼ cup of the dressing, if you'd like, and toss to coat.

To serve, divide the salad among serving plates, sprinkle each serving with the remaining lentil mixture, and garnish with the chopped basil and mint.

6 servings

GREEN CURRY GODDESS DRESSING

12 ounces silken tofu, drained (preferably in a shelf-stable aseptic package, not packed in water and refrigerated)

½ cup lightly packed basil leaves

¼ cup extra-virgin olive oil, plus more for assembling the salad

2 tablespoons Thai green curry paste

1 garlic clove, minced

1 teaspoon finely grated lime zest

2 tablespoons fresh lime juice

1 tablespoon agave nectar or honey

½ teaspoon kosher salt, plus more to taste

SALAD

¼ cup black lentils, picked over and rinsed

Water

Sunflower or safflower oil, for frying

2 tablespoons toasted white sesame seeds

2 tablespoons flaxseeds, toasted

¼ teaspoon kosher salt, plus more to taste

¼ teaspoon garlic powder

1 tablespoon fresh lemon juice

6 cups lightly packed red gem lettuce leaves (may substitute romaine hearts), chilled

½ cup packed basil leaves, chopped, for garnish

½ cup packed mint leaves, chopped, for garnish

THREE-BEAN SALAD

WITH FETA AND PARSLEY

6 servings

1 pound yellow wax beans (may substitute green beans)

1 yellow onion, thinly sliced

4 garlic cloves, peels left on

5 tablespoons extra-virgin olive oil

½ teaspoon kosher salt, plus more to taste

⅓ cup apple cider vinegar

2 tablespoons sugar

¼ teaspoon freshly ground black pepper

1½ cups cooked or canned no-salt-added great Northern, navy, or cannellini beans (from one 15-ounce can), drained and rinsed

1½ cups cooked or canned no-salt-added red kidney beans (from one 15-ounce can), drained and rinsed

2 celery stalks, thinly sliced

1 cup lightly packed flat-leaf parsley leaves, chopped

¼ cup Herb-Marinated Tofu Feta (page 217) or store-bought vegan or dairy feta, crumbled

When I was growing up, I loved the traditional American three-bean salad, but my palate has changed, and now I can't stand the requisite canned green beans. So instead, I roast yellow wax beans with onions and garlic, combine them with cooked great Northern and red kidney beans in a sweet-and-sour (although not as sweet as my mother's!) dressing, and top them with a little feta. This salad tastes even better the next day, so don't fear the leftovers.

Preheat the oven to 450°F. Place a large rimmed baking sheet in the oven while it heats.

In a large bowl, toss the wax beans, onion, and garlic with 2 tablespoons of the olive oil and the salt. Transfer to the baking sheet and spread out evenly. Roast until the beans are lightly browned and tender, 20 to 30 minutes, then scoop the bean mixture onto a cutting board and let cool slightly.

Pick out the garlic and squeeze the soft cloves into the bowl you used for tossing the vegetables before roasting. Use a fork to lightly mash the garlic. Whisk in the remaining 3 tablespoons olive oil, the vinegar, sugar, and pepper.

Cut the roasted beans and onion into 1-inch pieces and add them to the bowl with the dressing. Stir in the white beans, kidney beans, celery, and parsley and gently toss to combine. Taste and add more salt if needed. Sprinkle the feta on top and serve.

FRENCH GREEN LENTILS
WITH A TRIO OF MUSTARDS

This warm salad was inspired by the classic pairing of French green lentils—the famous du Puy variety, which hold their shape so beautifully—and a Dijon-heavy vinaigrette, like the beautiful one my friend David Lebovitz writes about in *My Paris Kitchen*. I added mustard in two more forms: black mustard seeds for a pop of texture and flavor and peppery mustard greens. A little feta and some toasted pistachios take the dish over the top, in the best possible way.

Combine the lentils, 5 cups broth, bay leaf, and 1 teaspoon of the salt in a saucepan. Bring to a boil, reduce the heat to medium-low, and cook until the lentils are just tender, about 20 minutes.

While the lentils are cooking, pour the olive oil into a large deep skillet over medium-high heat. When it shimmers, add the onion, garlic, and carrot and sauté until the vegetables are tender, about 5 minutes. Stir in the remaining 1 teaspoon of the salt and the mustard seeds, then stir in the mustard greens and cook until they fully wilt, about 5 minutes.

When the lentils are tender, drain them, discard the bay leaf, and add them to the mustard greens mixture in the skillet, stirring to combine. Turn off the heat and stir in the shallot, vinegar, and Dijon mustard. Taste and add more salt if needed.

To serve, divide the salad among six serving plates and top with the pistachios and feta.

6 servings

1½ cups dried French green lentils, picked over and rinsed

Vegetable Broth (page 216), store-bought no-salt-added vegetable broth, or water

1 bay leaf

2 teaspoons kosher salt, plus more to taste

¼ cup extra-virgin olive oil, plus more for drizzling

1 small yellow onion, finely chopped

2 garlic cloves, chopped

1 carrot, finely chopped

1 tablespoon yellow or black mustard seeds

1 large bunch mustard greens, chopped

1 shallot, finely chopped

1 tablespoon red wine vinegar

1 teaspoon Dijon mustard

1 cup toasted pistachios

1 cup Herb-Marinated Tofu Feta (page 217) or store-bought vegan or dairy feta, crumbled

FALAFEL FATTOUSH

6 to 8 servings

3½ cups cooked or canned no-salt-added chickpeas (from two 15-ounce cans), drained and rinsed

1 yellow onion, cut into large chunks

5 garlic cloves, peeled but left whole

2 tablespoons extra-virgin olive oil

¾ teaspoon kosher salt

2 teaspoons ground cumin

1 teaspoon ground coriander

¼ teaspoon cayenne pepper

2 large pitas, split and torn into large pieces

1 tablespoon sumac

DRESSING

Roasted garlic (from above)

¼ cup fresh lemon juice

¼ cup tahini

Water

½ teaspoon kosher salt, plus more to taste

6 cups torn romaine lettuce leaves

1 cup lightly packed flat-leaf parsley leaves

1 pint cherry tomatoes, halved

4 large sour pickle spears, coarsely chopped

This bread salad reminiscent of Middle Eastern fattoush packs all the elements of a falafel sandwich—spiced chickpeas, of course, plus pita, lettuce, parsley, pickles, and tahini sauce—into a bowl. It's best when freshly made, because the pita chips retain some crunch, so if you want to reserve some for leftovers, separate out the pita chips after roasting and save them in an airtight container at room temperature while you refrigerate the rest, until you're ready to serve the salad.

Preheat the oven to 425°F.

On a large rimmed baking sheet, toss together the chickpeas, onion, garlic, olive oil, salt, cumin, coriander, and cayenne. Roast until the onion and garlic have started to soften, 15 to 20 minutes.

Scatter the pita pieces on top, sprinkle them with sumac, and continue roasting until the pitas are crisp and the onion and garlic are very soft, 8 to 10 minutes.

Remove from the oven, fish out the garlic to use in the dressing, and let everything cool to room temperature.

While the chickpea mixture is cooling, make the dressing: In a small bowl, mash the reserved roasted garlic with a fork, then whisk in the lemon juice, tahini, ¼ cup water, and salt. Taste and add more salt if needed.

To assemble the salad, toss the chickpea mixture with the romaine, parsley, tomatoes, and pickles. Drizzle with the dressing and serve immediately.

BLACK BEAN, CORN, AND COCONUT SALAD

6 to 8 servings

2 ears corn, husks intact

2 small or 1 medium poblano chile

1¾ cups cooked or canned no-salt-added black beans (from one 15-ounce can), drained and rinsed

½ cup grated fresh coconut (see Note below) or frozen grated coconut

¼ cup lightly packed mint leaves, chopped

2 tablespoons fresh lime juice

1 cup cherry tomatoes, halved (if small) or quartered (if large)

1 tablespoon extra-virgin olive oil

½ teaspoon kosher salt, plus more to taste

This is a cross between a salad and a salsa; if you want to push it in the latter direction, add 1 seeded and chopped jalapeño or serrano chile. It's great as a crunchy, fresh side dish, as a dip with tortilla chips, or as a topping on tacos, sandwiches, grain bowls, or salads.

Run water over the corn cobs in their husks and microwave on high for 5 minutes, until steaming hot. Let cool slightly, then use your fingers to feel where the row of kernels ends on the wide end of the cob (opposite the silk end) and use a sharp knife to cut through those last kernels and through the cob. Holding the silk end, squeeze each cob out out of the husk from that end; it should pop out clean and cooked. Cut each cob in half crosswise, then stand one half at a time on a cutting board, cut side down, and slice off the kernels. Transfer them to a large bowl.

Roast the poblanos by setting them on the grates over a gas burner turned to high and use tongs to turn them until they are blackened in spots all over. (Alternatively, you can do this under a broiler.) Transfer to a small bowl, top with a plate, and let steam for 10 minutes, then uncover. When cool enough to handle, use your fingers to slip off the blackened skins, then remove and discard the stems and seeds. Chop into ½-inch pieces and add them to the bowl with the corn.

Add the beans, coconut, mint, lime juice, tomatoes, olive oil, and salt and toss to combine. Taste and add more salt if needed. Serve immediately.

NOTE

For grated fresh coconut, wrap a whole coconut in a towel, put it in a stainless-steel bowl, and whack it with a hammer or a rolling pin several times until it cracks open. Use a butter knife to pry the flesh from the shell and grate it on the coarse side of a box grater or using the grating disk of a food processor.

WHITE BEAN TABBOULEH

Tabbouleh is misunderstood in America. How many times have you had a soggy salad of couscous or bulgur with a few flecks of parsley, and perhaps some tomato thrown in? Not in the spirit of tabbouleh, my friends. The real deal is a parsley salad, and the bulgur is practically a garnish, in terms of proportion. That's why I didn't feel too bad about subbing the white beans here for the bulgur, since the grain is a secondary element of this classic Lebanese salad anyhow. Besides, it works so well I think it might even be better this way. Caution: This is best made with white beans that have held their shape and are not overcooked. Note, too, that you will want to use curly rather than flat-leaf parsley, since it helps the salad stay fluffy and not mushy. For the same reason, resist the urge to use a food processor.

Pick the parsley leaves off the stems. (You should have about 6 cups lightly packed.) Wash and spin-dry in a salad spinner, then lay out on paper towels and pat dry. Leave to air-dry for at least 30 minutes, if possible, then finely chop.

Spread the cannellini beans on new paper towels, cover with more paper towels, and gently pat dry.

Combine the parsley, beans, tomatoes, scallions, mint, lemon juice, olive oil, garlic, salt, and pepper in a medium bowl and gently toss to combine. Taste and add more salt if needed. Serve immediately.

4 to 6 servings

2 bunches of curly parsley

1¾ cups cooked or canned no-salt-added cannellini beans (from one 15-ounce can), drained and rinsed

1 cup cherry or grape tomatoes, quartered

2 scallions, thinly sliced

10 large mint leaves, finely chopped

3 tablespoons fresh lemon juice

2 tablespoons olive oil

2 garlic cloves, minced or pressed

½ teaspoon kosher salt, plus more to taste

¼ teaspoon freshly ground black pepper, plus more to taste

ITALIAN RICE SALAD
WITH CANNELLINI BEANS

4 to 6 servings

1 cup Carnaroli rice (may substitute Arborio)

Water

1 teaspoon kosher salt, plus more to taste

1 zucchini, cut into 1-inch pieces

1 celery stalk, cut into 1-inch pieces

1 yellow or red bell pepper, cut into 1-inch pieces

½ cup oil-packed black olives, pitted

½ cup lightly packed flat-leaf parsley leaves

½ cup cherry or grape tomatoes, halved

5 teaspoons fresh lemon or lime juice

1 tablespoon Chickpea Aioli (page 214) or store-bought vegan or traditional mayonnaise (see Note opposite)

1 tablespoon Dijon mustard

2 tablespoons extra-virgin olive oil

½ teaspoon freshly ground black pepper, plus more to taste

1¾ cups cooked or canned no-salt-added cannellini beans (from one 15-ounce can), drained and rinsed

This is the Italian equivalent of potato salad—perfect for picnics, cookouts, or just a hot summer's evening at home. I was inspired by a recipe in *Autentico* by Rolando Beramendi for something he called the Contessa's Rice Salad, after a woman who was careful to perfectly dice vegetables fine enough to be the same size as the grains of rice. I don't usually have the patience for that, so I use a food processor instead, first cutting the vegetables into bigger (but even) pieces so they all come out the same size after pulsing. But I do make sure to use Carnaroli rice—a high-starch Italian variety often used in risotto—for the creamiest result.

In a medium pot over medium-high heat, combine the rice with enough water to cover by 2 inches. Stir in ½ teaspoon of the salt. Bring to a boil, then reduce the heat to medium-low so the liquid is at a simmer and cook, uncovered, until the rice is al dente, 7 to 9 minutes. If the rice hasn't absorbed all the water, drain it in a fine-mesh strainer, transfer it to a large bowl, and let it cool completely. (To speed up the cooling, spread the rice on a large rimmed baking sheet and refrigerate until cool, then return to the bowl.)

While the rice is cooling, combine the zucchini, celery, bell pepper, olives, parsley, and tomatoes in the bowl of a food processor and pulse several times until everything is about the size of grains of rice, scraping the sides of the bowl as needed and being careful not to overprocess it to mush.

Add the vegetables to the bowl of rice and toss just to combine—and to break up the rice if it has gotten clumpy when cooling.

In a small bowl, whisk together the lemon juice, aioli, mustard, olive oil, the remaining ½ teaspoon salt, and the ground pepper. (If you'd like, you can do this in the food processor instead, especially if it's a small one—just combine the ingredients in the same bowl you used for the vegetables; no need to clean it.) Pour this over the rice mixture and toss just to combine. Gently fold in the cannellini beans, being careful not to break them up. Taste and add more salt and pepper if needed.

Serve at room temperature or chill and serve cold.

NOTE

If you use a store-bought mayonnaise instead of the Chickpea Aioli, add 1 minced garlic clove to the dressing.

WINTER SALAD
WITH CRANBERRY BEANS, SQUASH, AND POMEGRANATE

This salad has the chewy texture and nutty flavors I particularly crave when the nights (and probably the days) are cold, brightened with one of the glories of winter: pomegranate. For something even heartier, replace the arugula with kale; just be sure to remove the stems and to thinly slice and massage the leaves for a few minutes to make them silkier. My favorite here is cranberry beans (aka borlotti), but you can substitute navy, cannellini, pinto, kidney, or chickpeas—really, anything that you love.

Combine the wild rice with 2 cups water in a small saucepan over medium-high heat. Bring to a boil, then lower the heat to low, cover, and simmer until the wild rice is tender and split, 60 to 90 minutes. Drain.

While the wild rice is cooking, set a large rimmed baking sheet in the oven and preheat the oven to 425°F.

Use a serrated knife to slice off the stem end of the squash, then scoop out the seeds. Reserve the seeds for roasting, if you'd like. Cut the squash in half lengthwise and then crosswise into ½-inch slices. When the oven is hot, scatter the squash slices on the preheated baking sheet, making sure not to overlap any, drizzle with 2 tablespoons of the olive oil, and sprinkle with ½ teaspoon of the salt. Roast until tender, about 15 minutes. Let cool.

In a large bowl, toss the roasted squash with the cooked rice, arugula, beans, pomegranate seeds, and the remaining ½ teaspoon salt. Drizzle the pomegranate molasses, lemon juice, and the remaining 1 tablespoon olive oil over the salad and toss to combine. Taste and add more salt if needed. Sprinkle the pumpkin seeds on top, garnish with the flowers or microgreens, if desired, and serve immediately.

4 servings

½ cup wild rice

Water

1 pound delicata or acorn squash

3 tablespoons extra-virgin olive oil

1 teaspoon kosher salt, plus more to taste

3 cups arugula

1¾ cups cooked cranberry beans, drained and rinsed

1 cup pomegranate seeds

1 tablespoon pomegranate molasses

1 tablespoon fresh lemon juice

½ cup toasted pumpkin seeds (pepitas)

Arugula flowers, microgreens, or other edible blossoms (optional)

INDIAN FRUIT AND CHICKPEA SALAD

4 servings

1½ cups cooked or canned no-salt-added chickpeas (from one 15-ounce can), drained and rinsed

Peanut, sunflower, or other neutral vegetable oil

1 tablespoon Madras curry powder

½ teaspoon kosher salt

1 small ripe papaya, cut into ½-inch cubes

1 large ripe mango, cut into ½-inch cubes

½ cup tamarind-date chutney

1 teaspoon fresh lemon juice

2 tablespoons chopped cilantro leaves

½ teaspoon finely chopped Thai green chile

¼ teaspoon ground cumin

This is my adaptation of the signature salad at Bindaas, one of my favorite Indian restaurants in Washington, DC. Owned by Ashok Bajaj and with cooking by the award-winning Vikram Sunderam of Rasika and Bombay Club fame, it specializes in chaat and other street food. This salad hits all my favorite notes: creamy, crunchy, sweet, sour, deep, spicy. My only change to Vikram's recipe was to skip the fresh jackfruit he includes, because I hate the mess involved with cutting open the behemoth specimens that are most often available, and I don't like substituting the canned stuff. Even without it, there are so many wonderfully powerful flavors going on, you'll want to make this salad regularly.

Pat the chickpeas dry between layers of paper towels.

In a large deep skillet over medium-high heat, pour the oil to a depth of ½ inch. When it shimmers, add the chickpeas and fry until crispy, 3 to 4 minutes. Use a slotted spoon to scoop them onto a paper-towel-lined plate and toss with the curry powder and salt.

In a large bowl, combine the papaya, mango, chutney, lemon juice, cilantro, green chile, and cumin. Stir to combine thoroughly. Transfer to a serving bowl, top with the chickpeas, and serve.

NOTE

You can find tamarind-date chutney in any good Indian market or Asian superstore.

CHARRED ZUCCHINI, CORN, AND AYOCOTE BEAN SALAD

Here's my take on succotash, one of the great summer dishes of the South. I usually just throw it together from whatever combination of corn, butter beans, and tomatoes I might have on hand, but after making tacos with one of my favorite filling ingredients—charred zucchini—I knew I would find a place for it in this treatment. I add mayo and avocado, turning it into a salad to serve cold or at room temperature. The bean of choice is something big and meaty: I prefer ayocote beans after falling for them in Mexico City, but gigantes, favas, limas, or other butter beans work beautifully, too.

Run water over the corn cobs in their husks and microwave on high for 5 to 7 minutes, until steaming hot. Let cool slightly, then use your fingers to feel where the row of kernels ends on the wide end of the cob (opposite the silk end) and use a sharp knife to cut through those last kernels and through the cob. Holding the silk end, squeeze each cob out of the husk from that end; it should pop out clean and slightly cooked.

Heat a large cast-iron skillet over high heat until smoking. Add the zucchini to the skillet in a single layer, with no oil in the pan, and cook, without moving them, for 4 minutes, until deeply charred on one side. Use tongs or a spatula to turn them and cook the other side until charred, about 3 minutes. Remove and let cool.

Add the corn, still on the cob, to the dry skillet, and cook—rolling the cobs every minute or two—until they are charred in spots all over. (Some kernels will pop!) Remove and let cool.

When the zucchini and corn are cool, dice the zucchini slabs into ½-inch pieces. Cut each cob in half crosswise, then stand one half at a time on a cutting board, cut end down, and slice off the kernels.

In a large bowl, whisk together the aioli, lime juice, salt, and pepper. Add the zucchini, corn, beans, onion, tomatoes, basil, chile, and avocado and gently fold to combine. Taste and add more salt if needed.

Serve at room temperature or refrigerate and serve cold.

Serves 6

3 ears corn, husks intact

1 small to medium zucchini, cut lengthwise into 1-inch slabs

⅓ cup Chickpea Aioli (page 214) or store-bought vegan or traditional mayonnaise

2 tablespoons fresh lime juice

1 teaspoon fine sea salt, plus more to taste

¼ teaspoon freshly ground black pepper

2 cups cooked ayocote beans, drained and rinsed

½ sweet yellow onion (preferably Vidalia or Walla-Walla), thinly sliced

½ pint cherry or grape tomatoes, halved

½ cup packed basil leaves, chopped

1 jalapeño or serrano chile, stemmed, seeded, and finely chopped

Flesh of 1 ripe avocado, cubed

CHRISTMAS LIMA, KALE, AND CHERRY TOMATO SALAD

WITH HONEY-DILL DRESSING

4 to 6 servings

1½ cups dried Christmas lima beans (may substitute the largest lima beans or gigante beans you can find), soaked overnight and drained

Water

1 (3 by 5-inch) strip kombu (dried seaweed)

2 bay leaves

1½ teaspoons kosher salt, plus more to taste

1 pint cherry tomatoes, halved

¼ cup plus 1 tablespoon extra-virgin olive oil

8 ounces lacinato or curly kale

DRESSING

¼ cup fresh lemon juice

2 tablespoons honey or agave nectar

½ cup lightly packed fresh dill, chopped

½ cup toasted and chopped walnuts

Freshly ground black pepper

This salad is based on a Greek stew called piyaz, a recipe I learned from Michael Costa, chef at DC's Zaytinya restaurant. For a weeknight, I turned the stew into this salad, which involves very little cooking—especially if you already have a couple cups of beans already cooked. If not, it still works, thanks to our good friend the pressure cooker (or Instant Pot). Christmas limas maintain their gorgeous pattern even when cooked, but other large beans are just as delicious. This salad keeps well because of the sturdy kale, so it's a great dish to bring to a picnic or cookout.

Combine the beans in a large pot over medium-high heat with enough fresh water to cover by 2 inches. Add the kombu, bay leaves, and 1 teaspoon of the salt; cover, bring to a boil, and boil for 10 minutes. Reduce the heat to medium-low and cook until the beans are tender, 60 to 90 minutes.

You can also cook the beans in a stovetop or electric pressure cooker: bring to high pressure, then reduce the heat (if using a stovetop cooker) to medium to maintain pressure and cook for 20 minutes. Let the pressure release naturally, then open.

Set the oven to broil and arrange the rack so that it's as close as possible to the element or flame. Drizzle the tomatoes with 1 tablespoon of the olive oil and sprinkle with ¼ teaspoon of the salt. Broil until charred and collapsed, 4 to 6 minutes.

Wash and dry the kale thoroughly, then thinly slice it. Transfer to a large bowl, then use your hands to pick it up by the handful and gently squeeze, repeating for a few minutes until the kale is "massaged" and has turned darker and silkier.

Drain the beans, but don't rinse them, and toss them with the kale.

To make the dressing: In a small bowl, whisk together the remaining ¼ cup olive oil, the lemon juice, honey, dill, and the remaining ¼ teaspoon salt until combined. Stir in the tomatoes and their juices and the walnuts.

Pour half of the dressing over the kale-bean mixture and toss to combine. Grind some pepper over the top. Add more of the dressing if you'd like and save the rest to pass at the table or for another use. (You can refrigerate it in an airtight container for up to 1 week.)

Serve immediately or refrigerate for up to 5 days.

SMOKED TOFU AND NAVY BEAN SALAD

4 to 6 servings

8 ounces smoked tofu, torn into bite-size pieces and crumbled

1¾ cups cooked or canned no-salt-added navy or great Northern beans (from one 15-ounce can), drained and rinsed

2 scallions, thinly sliced

1 carrot, finely chopped

½ cup dried cherries, chopped

½ cup chopped sour pickles

2 tablespoons toasted sesame seeds

½ teaspoon Spanish smoked paprika (pimentón; optional)

½ teaspoon cayenne pepper

1 teaspoon kosher salt, plus more to taste

Flesh of 1 large ripe avocado, mashed

1 tablespoon Chickpea Aioli (page 214) or store-bought vegan or traditional mayonnaise

2 tablespoons apple cider vinegar

I started making this salad when I first tasted the stellar smoked tofu sold at Neopol Savory Smokery in DC's Union Market. When I can't get my hands on it, I use grocery-store smoked (or simply baked and marinated) tofu and add one of my favorite spices, smoked paprika. This is good on soft white bread or buns, in lettuce wraps or flour tortillas, or over greens.

In a large bowl, combine the tofu, beans, scallions, carrot, cherries, pickles, sesame seeds, paprika, if desired, cayenne, and salt. Stir to combine thoroughly. Add the avocado, aioli, and vinegar and stir to combine. Taste and add more salt if needed.

Serve immediately.

LADY CREAM PEA, SWEET POTATO, AND CHARRED OKRA SALAD

This simple salad showcases the creamy, slightly sweet flavor of lady cream peas, part of the family of legumes called cowpeas that were brought by enslaved people from Africa to the South, where they became crucial to the culinary landscape. They're related to the black-eyed pea and the crowder pea, either of which can be substituted here. I like to keep their southern-ness front and center by combining them with sweet potatoes and okra, the latter of which I char in the oven to highlight its nutty flavor and cut down a little on its gelatinous quality. Serve as a side dish or as a main course with a salad and bread.

Preheat the oven to 450°F. Put a large rimmed baking sheet in the oven while it heats.

When the oven is ready, drizzle 1 tablespoon of the olive oil on the baking sheet and set the okra on the sheet, cut side down. Drizzle with the remaining 1 tablespoon oil and roast until the okra is dark brown and a little charred on the cut side, 15 to 20 minutes. Let cool, then cut into bite-size pieces.

While the okra is roasting, bring a medium saucepan of water to a boil, add 1 tablespoon of the salt and the sweet potatoes, and cook until tender, 5 to 10 minutes. Drain and let cool.

In a large bowl, whisk together the aioli, parsley, lime zest, lime juice, harissa, paprika, and the remaining ¼ teaspoon salt. Fold in the cream peas, sweet potatoes, and okra. Taste and add more salt and harissa if needed. Serve cold or at room temperature.

6 to 8 servings

2 tablespoons extra-virgin olive oil

1 pound okra, halved lengthwise

Water

1 tablespoon plus ¼ teaspoon kosher salt, plus more to taste

1 pound red sweet potatoes, into ½-inch cubes

2 tablespoons Chickpea Aioli (page 214) or store-bought vegan or traditional mayonnaise

¼ cup lightly packed flat-leaf parsley leaves, chopped

1 teaspoon finely grated lime zest

2 tablespoons fresh lime juice

1 tablespoon harissa, plus more to taste

½ teaspoon sweet or hot Spanish smoked paprika (pimenton)

2 cups cooked and cooled lady cream peas (may substitute black-eyed peas, crowder peas, or another southern cowpea), drained

PINTO BEAN TORTILLA SALAD

This is my updated version of my mother's "Texas Salad," which she made for special occasions when I was growing up in West Texas. The vinaigrette can be refrigerated in an airtight container for up to 1 week. To save time, feel free to use your favorite store-bought tortilla chips instead of frying your own. After they are fried, the tortillas can be stored in an airtight container at room temperature for up to 3 days.

To make the vinaigrette: Combine the cilantro, olive and canola oils, vinegar, garlic, sugar, and salt in a blender; puree until smooth. Taste and add more salt as needed.

To make the salad: Line a plate with paper towels.

Pour the peanut oil into a large skillet over medium heat. Once the oil starts to shimmer, add 2 or 3 tortillas (or as many as will comfortably fit); fry them on each side until crisp and golden brown, 1 to 2 minutes. Lift each tortilla with tongs and let the excess oil drip off, then transfer it to the paper-towel-lined plate. Working in batches, repeat with the remaining tortillas. Let the tortillas cool, then break them into bite-size pieces.

Toss the tortilla pieces with the lettuce, beans, scallions, feta, tomatoes, and ½ cup of the vinaigrette in a large serving bowl. Add the remaining ¼ cup of the vinaigrette, if desired, or reserve for another use. Serve immediately.

6 servings

CILANTRO VINAIGRETTE (MAKES ABOUT ¾ CUP)

¼ cup lightly packed cilantro leaves, coarsely chopped

¼ cup extra-virgin olive oil

¼ cup canola oil

¼ cup red wine vinegar

1 garlic clove, coarsely chopped

1 teaspoon sugar

½ teaspoon fine sea salt, plus more as needed

SALAD

½ cup peanut oil, for frying

6 (6-inch) corn tortillas

12 cups lightly packed, torn romaine lettuce leaves

3 cups cooked or canned no-salt-added pinto beans (from two 15-ounce cans), drained and rinsed

6 scallions, thinly sliced on the diagonal

1 cup Herb-Marinated Tofu Feta (page 217) or your favorite vegan or dairy feta cheese, crumbled

¾ cup oil-packed sun-dried tomatoes, sliced

SOUPS, STEWS & SOUPY SIDES

Beans make perfect soups and stews, particularly when you cook them from dried, because the liquid gold that results is honestly good enough for a soup all by itself. This chapter is the largest in the book, for good reason: beans love broth and broth loves beans.

3

GEORGIAN KIDNEY BEAN STEW
(LOBIO) WITH CORN FLATBREADS AND PICKLED CABBAGE

Georgians love beans, and their treatment is distinguished by the use of blue fenugreek (aka utskho suneli), the slightly bitter herb crucial to much of the country's cooking; fresh herbs, such as cilantro, dill, and mint; and the accompaniment of a corn flatbread called mchadi. This recipe is something of a mash-up of techniques I learned from Ani Kandelaki, sous chef at DC's Supra restaurant, and Gerald Addison, co-chef at another DC restaurant, Maydan. Even though I love the stew with both the flatbread and the pickled cabbage that Supra serves alongside, I can also attest that it's just as delicious served over rice or any other grain and/or with a crisp salad of arugula or other bitter greens.

To make the pickled cabbage: Combine the vinegar, 1 cup hot water, coriander, salt, and sugar and bring to a boil in a large saucepan. Add the cabbage and garlic and cook for 2 minutes, then remove from the heat. Transfer to a large glass jar, packing down the cabbage so it is covered by the liquid. Let cool while you make the lobio and cornbread. Use immediately or refrigerate in an airtight container for up to 2 weeks.

To make the lobio: Pour the oil into a large saucepan over medium heat. When it shimmers, add the onion and garlic and cook until very soft and lightly brown, about 8 minutes. Stir in the fenugreek, Aleppo pepper, coriander, and salt and cook until fragrant, about 30 seconds. Stir in the beans and the cooking liquid, and cook until the beans are warmed through, about 2 minutes. Use a large fork or masher to mash about half the beans, adding more cooking liquid if needed to make the mixture very creamy but not soupy. Turn off the heat and stir in the cilantro, dill, and mint. Taste and add more salt if needed. Cover to keep warm.

To make the flatbread: Whisk together the masa harina and salt in a small bowl. Stir in ¾ cup hot water until the mixture forms a dough. It should be moist and tacky but not sticky or wet, so add a little more water if it feels too dry and a little more masa harina if it feels too wet. Form into a disk, cut into quarters, and then use your hands to pat each portion into a 4- to 5-inch round, about ¼ inch thick or a little thicker.

Heat a large dry skillet over medium-high heat until very hot. Add as many of the flatbread rounds as will fit without overcrowding and cook on each side until firm and dark brown in spots, 3 to 4 minutes per side.

To serve, divide the lobio into bowls, top with the pickled cabbage, cilantro, dill, and mint, and serve the flatbread on the side for dipping into the beans.

6 servings

PICKLED CABBAGE

1 cup apple cider vinegar or red wine vinegar, or a combination

Water

2 teaspoons coriander seeds

1 teaspoon kosher salt

1 teaspoon sugar

½ head red cabbage, cut into ½-inch pieces

3 garlic cloves

LOBIO

2 tablespoons sunflower or other neutral vegetable oil

½ large onion, finely chopped

3 garlic cloves, thinly sliced

1 tablespoon ground blue fenugreek (may substitute 1 teaspoon ground fenugreek)

1 teaspoon Aleppo pepper (may substitute ground ancho chile)

1 teaspoon ground coriander

1 teaspoon kosher salt, plus more to taste

3 cups cooked or canned no-salt-added red kidney beans (from two 15-ounce cans), drained (reserve the cooking liquid) and rinsed

1½ cups bean cooking liquid or water

½ cup chopped cilantro leaves and tender stems, plus more for garnish

¼ cup chopped dill leaves, plus more for garnish

¼ cup chopped mint leaves, plus more for garnish

CORN FLATBREAD

1 cup instant masa harina, plus more as needed

1 teaspoon kosher salt

Hot water

KIDNEY BEAN AND MUSHROOM BOURGUIGNON

6 servings

2 tablespoons vegan butter or dairy butter

1 pound cremini mushrooms, cut into ½-inch pieces

6 large shallots, halved lengthwise

2 carrots, cut into ½-inch coins

3 garlic cloves, minced

2 teaspoons minced fresh rosemary

½ teaspoon kosher salt, plus more to taste

¼ teaspoon freshly ground black pepper, plus more to taste

1 tablespoon flour

1½ to 1¾ cups dark red wine, preferably Zinfandel or Cabernet Sauvignon

1 tablespoon tomato paste

3½ cups cooked or canned no-salt-added red kidney beans (from two 15-ounce cans), drained and rinsed

One year, seemingly every week for months, I made a comforting take on French boeuf bourguignon from Katy Beskow that doubled down on meaty mushrooms and left out the beef. Then I tried an obvious addition and never looked back: beans return the dish to its original protein-heavy status and add a wonderfully creamy texture that goes beautifully with the red wine sauce. I like to use red kidney beans because their color is already winelike, but flageolets are nice when you want to keep things French, and black beans and cranberry/borlotti beans work well here, too. Serve over mashed potatoes, cauliflower, or polenta or with crusty bread.

Heat 1 tablespoon of the butter in a large skillet over medium-high heat. Add the mushrooms and cook, stirring occasionally, until they soften and exude their liquid and all but about ½ cup of their liquid evaporates, about 10 minutes. Transfer the mushrooms and their juices to a small bowl.

Add the remaining 1 tablespoon butter to the pan. Stir in the shallots and carrots. Cook until the carrots begin to soften and the shallots start to brown, 4 to 5 minutes. Stir in the garlic, rosemary, salt, and pepper. Cook until fragrant, about 1 minute, then sprinkle in the flour and stir to coat.

Pour in 1½ cups of the wine, add the tomato paste, and stir to incorporate. Cook until thick, 2 to 3 minutes.

Stir in the beans and the cooked mushrooms and their juices and cook until warmed through, about 2 minutes. If the sauce has thickened too much, stir in up to another ¼ cup of the wine to keep it loose. Taste and add more salt and/or pepper if needed.

Serve warm.

SMOKY BLACK BEAN AND PLANTAIN CHILI

Ripe plantains—a classic pairing with black beans in Caribbean cooking—add a touch of sweetness to this chili, which I loosely based on a black bean and sweet potato chili by one of my favorite sources of vegan recipes, Gena Hamshaw's *Food52 Vegan*. You can refrigerate this chili in an airtight container for up to 1 week or freeze for up to 3 months.

Peel the plantains and cut them into ½-inch slices, then stack a few at a time and cut them in half again to form half-moons.

Pour the olive oil into a Dutch oven or heavy stockpot over medium-high heat. Once it shimmers, add the onion and garlic and sauté until lightly browned, about 8 minutes. Stir in the chipotles, cumin, paprika, and salt and sauté until fragrant, about 30 seconds.

Stir in the plantains until well coated. Add the tomatoes, beans, and 1 cup water and bring the mixture to a boil. Reduce the heat to low, cover, and cook until the flavors meld and the plantains are very soft, about 15 minutes. Stir in the lime juice and cilantro. Taste and add more salt and/or lime juice if needed.

Divide among serving bowls and top with the avocados and scallions.

4 to 6 servings

3 ripe plantains (yellow with plenty of black spots)

2 tablespoons extra-virgin olive oil

1 large yellow onion, chopped

4 garlic cloves, chopped

2 to 3 chipotles in adobo (depending on how spicy you want it), finely chopped

2 teaspoons ground cumin

½ teaspoon Spanish smoked paprika (pimentón)

1 teaspoon kosher salt, plus more to taste

1 (15-ounce) can diced tomatoes, preferably fire-roasted

3½ cups cooked or canned no-salt-added black beans (from two 15-ounce cans), drained and rinsed

Water

2 tablespoons fresh lime juice, plus more to taste

½ cup lightly packed cilantro leaves (or parsley for the cilantro haters), chopped

Flesh of 2 large ripe avocados, sliced

3 scallions, thinly sliced

ROASTED TOMATO AND PEPPER SOUP

WITH LADY CREAM PEAS

4 to 6 servings

2 pounds tomatoes, cut into large chunks

2 red bell peppers, cut into large chunks

6 garlic cloves

1 large white or yellow onion, cut into large chunks

¼ cup extra-virgin olive oil

1½ teaspoons kosher salt, plus more to taste

½ teaspoon freshly ground black pepper, plus more to taste

½ teaspoon crushed red pepper flakes

1½ cups dried lady cream peas (may substitute black-eyed peas or canned no-salt-added navy or cannellini beans)

Water

2 cups bean cooking liquid

1 cup water or Vegetable Broth (page 216)

½ cup lightly packed basil leaves, chopped

Sherry vinegar (optional)

Sugar (optional)

Roasting concentrates the flavor of tomatoes, meaning you can make this soup with less-than-stellar, out-of-season tomatoes, and it's still fantastic. (But make it when local tomatoes are at their best, and you'll knock your own socks off.) The addition of lady cream peas makes this taste like the best possible version of childhood alphabet soup, with the little white beans playing the part of those pasta letters and numbers—although I'm afraid all you'll be able to spell is "********." The bean cooking liquid helps add a silkiness, so if you are substituting canned beans, you'll lose some of that.

Preheat the oven to 450°F.

Toss the tomatoes, bell peppers, garlic, and onion on a large rimmed baking sheet. Drizzle with the olive oil and sprinkle with 1 teaspoon of the salt, the pepper, and red pepper flakes. Roast until the tomatoes have collapsed and are starting to brown on the edges and the bell peppers are tender, about 45 minutes.

While the vegetables are roasting, cook the lady cream peas (if using canned beans, no need to cook the beans): In a large pot, combine them with enough water to cover by 3 inches. Bring to a boil over medium-high heat, then reduce the heat to medium-low, add the remaining ½ teaspoon salt, and simmer, covered, until tender, 30 to 45 minutes. Drain, reserving the bean liquid. Measure out 2 cups of the bean cooking liquid and save any remaining for another use.

When the vegetables have finished roasting, transfer the contents of the baking sheet to the empty soup pot and set it over medium-high heat. Stir in the bean cooking liquid and the 1 cup water or broth and bring to a boil. Reduce to medium-low and simmer until the flavors meld, about 10 minutes.

Add the basil and use an immersion (handheld) blender to puree the soup until smooth. Stir in the lady cream peas and continue cooking over medium-low until the peas are warmed through, about 5 minutes. Taste and add more salt and pepper if needed, along with a splash of vinegar and/or a pinch of sugar, if desired.

Serve hot.

ROASTED CARROTS AND CANNELLINI BEANS IN ALMOND BROTH

4 to 6 servings

1½ pounds carrots, scrubbed but not peeled

1 tablespoon tomato paste

2 tablespoons extra-virgin olive oil

½ teaspoon ground cloves

½ teaspoon ground ancho chile

1 teaspoon kosher salt, plus more to taste

1¼ cups Vegetable Broth (page 216) or store-bought no-salt-added vegetable broth

¼ cup almond milk

⅓ cup coarsely chopped almonds, plus ¼ cup more for serving

1¾ cups cooked or canned no-salt-added cannellini beans (from one 15-ounce can), drained and rinsed

2 teaspoons fresh lemon juice

½ cup lightly packed mint leaves, chopped

I got this idea from Kismet in Los Angeles: sweet carrots, tinged with a little chile and the warming spice of clove, roasted with beans (they used chickpeas, but cannellinis bring a buttery note that I adore) in a dark, nutty broth. Serve with rice or with crusty bread for sopping up the juices.

Preheat the oven to 400°F.

Cut the carrots into 1½-inch chunks. (If desired, use a "roll cut": make a diagonal cut across the carrot, then roll it a half-turn and, holding your knife at the same angle, cut crosswise again to create a wedge shape, and repeat.)

In a large heavy-duty skillet or deep baking dish big enough to hold the carrots in one layer, whisk together the tomato paste, olive oil, cloves, chile, and salt. Add the carrots and toss to thoroughly coat. Roast until the carrots are barely fork-tender and browned, 35 to 45 minutes.

Combine the broth, almond milk, and ⅓ cup chopped almonds in a measuring cup with a spout.

When the carrots are ready, scatter in the beans and pour in the broth mixture. Return to the oven and continue roasting until the broth has reduced slightly, about 15 minutes.

Stir in the lemon juice. Taste and add more salt if needed.

Sprinkle the remaining ¼ cup chopped almonds and the mint leaves on top and serve hot from the skillet or dish.

WHITE GAZPACHO
WITH CHICKPEAS AND CASHEWS

This is a riff on the classic Spanish soup ajo blanco, sometimes called white gazpacho: a from-the-pantry puree of bread, almonds, garlic, water, olive oil, and vinegar. Chickpeas, my favorite legume, sub in for the bread (adding more nutrition) and creamy cashews for the almonds. Serve in shot glasses or demitasse cups as an elegant starter or passed appetizer, or in larger bowls for a first dinner course.

Combine 2½ cups ice water, the cashews, olive oil, chickpeas, aquafaba, garlic, vinegar, and salt in a high-powered blender, such as a Vitamix. Puree until smooth. If the soup seems too thick, add more ice water, a few tablespoons at a time, until you have reached your desired consistency. Taste and add more salt if needed.

Chill the soup until very cold, 1 to 2 hours (or as long as overnight).

To serve, divide among serving bowls, drizzle with olive oil, and garnish with cashews or roasted chickpeas, if desired, and chive blossoms and/or mint leaves.

4 to 6 servings

Ice water

1¾ cups raw cashews, plus more for garnish

½ cup extra-virgin olive oil, plus more for drizzling

⅔ cup cooked or canned no-salt-added chickpeas (from one 15-ounce can), drained and rinsed (reserve the liquid; see page 18)

½ cup aquafaba (chickpea cooking liquid or liquid from the canned chickpeas)

2 garlic cloves

2 tablespoons apple cider vinegar

½ teaspoon kosher salt, plus more to taste

Crunchy Spiced Roasted Chickpeas (page 49), for garnish (optional)

Chive blossoms and/or mint leaves, for garnish

HOMESTEADER'S NEW ENGLAND BAKED BEANS

8 servings

1 pound Jacob's cattle or other plump creamy beans, such as cranberry/borlotti or pinto

Water

2 (3 by 5-inch) strips kombu (dried seaweed)

1 small yellow or white onion, sliced

¼ cup molasses

⅓ cup maple syrup

2 teaspoons kosher salt, plus more to taste

2 teaspoons dry mustard

1 teaspoon Spanish smoked paprika (pimenton)

½ teaspoon ground ginger

¼ teaspoon freshly ground black pepper

2 tablespoons apple cider vinegar, plus more to taste

On my sister Rebekah and brother-in-law Peter's Maine homestead, the copy of *Woodstove Cookery: At Home on the Range* by Jane Cooper isn't just dog-eared, it's cleaved in two, broken apart at page 144 because of Pete's regular use of the baked beans recipe, which he prepares in the wood-fired brick bread oven he built outside. Cooper credits this recipe to Leila MacGregor of Tunbridge, Vermont, who in turn calls it "an old Vermont family recipe." Besides preferring to use home-grown beans (Jacob's cattle variety beans are particularly good for this treatment), Peter's only deviation is in the sweetener: he uses slightly less molasses than the original recipe calls for and maple syrup (of course) instead of sugar. I take the sweetener down a touch more and add a little vinegar for brightening—plus smoked paprika to approximate the work of the traditional salt pork. Oh, and in keeping with the bean-cooking techniques taught to me by Rebekah (and later proven true by America's Test Kitchen), I put in a little kombu to help soften the beans during their first cooking. Yes, these are twice-baked—first until tender with little other seasoning and then veeeeeerrrrrry slowly with the spices and sweeteners. If you want to shortcut it, use a pressure cooker for the first go and a slow cooker for the second—or an Instant Pot, in two rounds, for the whole shebang. To be even more authentic, fire up the wood oven and/or use a stoneware bean pot.

Preheat the oven to 350°F.

Combine the beans with enough water to cover by 2 inches in a Dutch oven or other large pot over medium-high heat. Add the kombu. Bring to a boil, turn off the heat, cover, and transfer to the oven. Bake until the beans are very tender, 60 to 90 minutes, checking a time or two to add water if they are no longer covered by it.

Remove the kombu and reduce the temperature to 200°F. To the pot add the onion, molasses, maple syrup, salt, mustard, paprika, ginger, and pepper and bake for 8 hours, until the beans are falling-apart tender and infused with flavor. Stir in the vinegar, taste, and add more vinegar and salt if needed.

Serve hot, either as a side dish or over roasted potatoes and with a garden-fresh salad for a true Maine homesteader's meal. Cover and refrigerate for up to 1 week, or freeze for up to 3 months.

SLOW-COOKED MARINATED FAVA BEANS

6 servings

1 pound dried whole (not peeled or split) small fava beans, soaked overnight and drained

Water

4 garlic cloves

1 teaspoon red lentils, picked over and rinsed (optional)

1 tomato, quartered

1 tablespoon kosher salt

5 tablespoons fresh lime juice

⅓ cup extra-virgin olive oil, plus more for finishing

3 tablespoons ground cumin

1 cup lightly packed flat-leaf parsley leaves, chopped

1 small red onion, finely chopped

1 tablespoon sumac

Tahini, for finishing

This incredibly creamy, deeply flavorful dish depends on very slow, gentle cooking—and on your ability to procure small whole dried fava beans, usually imported from Egypt. (I get mine from Kalustyan's in New York City; see Sources, page 222.) Large whole fava beans will split and turn to mush long before the skins become tender, while peeled and split ones will become a soup! Dina Daniel and her cook, Elmer Ramos, at Fava Pot in Falls Church, Virginia, let these go all day, then finish them to order. Eat them as a side dish as is, over rice, or in pitas with hummus and pickles.

Combine the fava beans with enough water to cover by 2 inches in a large pot over medium-high heat. Add the garlic, lentils (if desired), and tomato. Bring to a boil, then reduce the heat as low as possible and cook, uncovered, for 12 hours, until the beans are very creamy and soft. Check periodically and add water to keep the beans covered. (You can also make these in a slow cooker: Boil for 10 minutes in a pot, then transfer to the slow cooker and cook on low for 12 hours. Remove the lid and cook on high for another 1 to 2 hours to reduce the liquid until it's barely covering the beans or transfer to a pot on the stovetop for faster reducing.)

Stir in the salt, 3 tablespoons of the lime juice, the olive oil, and cumin and let the beans sit for at least 1 hour to absorb the seasonings. (You can refrigerate them in an airtight container at this point for up to 1 week.)

When you're ready to finish the beans, return them to the large pot over medium heat and use a potato masher to mash about half of them. (Or you can transfer half of them to the bowl of a food processor or blender and blend very briefly, then return them to the pot.)

While the beans are reheating, combine the parsley, onion, sumac, and the remaining 2 tablespoons lime juice in a bowl and toss to combine.

When the beans are hot, divide them among serving dishes or scoop them into a large serving bowl and top with the parsley-onion mixture. Drizzle with a little olive oil and tahini and serve immediately.

ISRAELI-STYLE MUNG BEAN STEW

This India-meets-Israel dish—stewed mung beans with tahini, onions, spinach, and tomatoes—was shared with me by Ran Nussbacher, owner of DC's Shouk restaurants, whose mother gave it to him. She lives in Tel Aviv and was inspired to recreate the dish after loving it at the popular Café Puaa. "Mung bean is certainly more Indian than it is Middle Eastern, so I think this is a fusion story, as India is a prime destination for Israeli travelers," Nussbacher says. I love Indian spices and their use in dal, but this is proof that mung beans can indeed speak more than one language. The original recipe called for the onions to be briefly cooked, but I like to add even more depth and sweetness by spending the time to caramelize them first.

Pour the olive oil into a large skillet over medium-high heat. When it shimmers, add the onions. Sauté, using tongs to toss frequently, until they wilt, 2 to 3 minutes. Reduce the heat to low and cook, stirring occasionally, until the onions are soft, sweet, and lightly browned, 60 to 75 minutes.

While the onions are cooking, transfer the beans to a large pot over medium-high heat. Add enough water to cover by 1 inch. Bring to a boil, then reduce the heat to medium-low, cover, and cook until they are tender, about 15 minutes. Turn off the heat and let the beans sit until the onions are ready.

When the onions are ready, drain the beans, reserving the cooking water, and return them to the pot. Transfer the onions to the pot, along with the tomatoes and garlic. Add just enough of the cooking liquid to barely reach the top of the mixture. (You want the final dish to be moist but not soupy.) Bring to a boil, then reduce to medium-low, cover, and cook, stirring occasionally, until the tomatoes are soft enough to mash with the back of a wooden spoon, 10 to 15 minutes. Stir in the spinach and cook just until it wilts, about 2 minutes.

Stir in the salt, pepper, and lemon juice. Taste and add more salt if needed.

To serve, divide among serving bowls and drizzle with the tahini. Serve with rustic bread.

4 to 6 servings

3 tablespoons extra-virgin olive oil

2 large onions, thinly sliced

1½ cups dried whole mung beans, soaked overnight, drained, and rinsed

Water

2 large tomatoes, cut into large chunks

4 garlic cloves, chopped

5 cups packed baby spinach, chopped

1 teaspoon kosher salt, plus more to taste

½ teaspoon freshly ground black pepper

2 tablespoons fresh lemon juice

½ cup tahini

NIGERIAN STEWED BLACK-EYED PEAS AND PLANTAINS

(EWA RIRO AND DODO)

This is my favorite order at African restaurants, where my husband (who doesn't like black-eyed peas) always gets chicken. More for me! The first time I made this dish of stewed beans (ewa riro), after scouring the internet and cookbooks for recipes, my version tasted plain compared to what I had eaten, so I turned to Ozoz Sokoh, who writes The *Kitchen Butterfly* blog from her home in Lagos. She turned me on to grains of selim, also known as African pepper, Negro pepper, and Guinea pepper, which add a mysterious muskiness and more of the depth some traditional recipes accomplish with smoked turkey or dried crawfish. I got an in-person lesson from Oyin Akinkugbe, owner of DC's ZK Lounge and West African Grill. Her most emphatic points: make sure the beans are cooked until they are very tender and be generous with the palm oil, which lends the dish an earthy flavor and reddish color. Serve with fried ripe plantains (dodo) and rice.

Combine ½ cup of the onion with the black-eyed peas, kombu, and bay leaf in a stovetop or electric pressure cooker and add enough water to cover by 1 inch. Bring to high pressure and cook for 20 minutes, then turn off and let the pressure release naturally. The black-eyed peas should be very soft. Open the pressure cooker and cook on medium-high heat, stirring frequently to prevent scorching, to reduce the liquid until it is thick and creamy, about 20 minutes.

While the black-eyed peas are cooking, combine 1 cup of the remaining onion with the bell pepper, tomato, and Scotch bonnet (using more or less depending on your appetite for heat) in a blender and puree until smooth.

Scoop the palm oil into a large skillet over medium-high heat. When it melts and starts to shimmer, add the remaining ½ cup onion and sauté until tender, about 6 minutes. Stir in the cayenne, grains of selim, if desired, and ½ teaspoon of the salt and cook until fragrant, about 30 seconds. Pour in the pureed bell pepper mixture, reduce the heat to low, and cook, stirring occasionally, until the sauce reduces, darkens, and loses its raw edge, about 20 minutes.

CONTINUED

4 servings

1 large yellow or red onion, chopped (about 2 cups)

1½ cups dried black-eyed peas, soaked overnight and drained

1 (3 by 5-inch) strip kombu (dried seaweed; optional)

1 bay leaf

Water

½ red bell pepper, chopped

1 small tomato, chopped, or ½ cup canned pureed tomatoes

½ to 1 Scotch bonnet chile pepper, stemmed, seeded, and chopped

¼ cup palm oil

¼ teaspoon cayenne pepper

1½ teaspoons ground grains of selim (see Note on page 94; optional)

1 teaspoon kosher salt, plus more to taste

2 ripe plantains (yellow with plenty of black spots)

Safflower, grapeseed, or other neutral vegetable oil, for frying

NIGERIAN STEWED BLACK-EYED PEAS AND PLANTAINS (EWA RIRO AND DODO)

CONTINUED

When the black-eyed peas are ready, add them to the sauce in the skillet with a little water if needed to loosen the mixture. Stir to combine and cook until the flavors meld, 3 to 4 minutes. Taste and add more salt if needed. Remove from the heat and cover to keep warm.

To make the plantains, line a plate with paper towels. Peel the plantains by using a paring knife to slash a shallow cut down the length of each plantain, then remove the peel. Cut them in half lengthwise, then into ¾-inch half-moons or cut on the bias into ¾-inch slices. Sprinkle the plantains with the remaining ½ teaspoon salt.

Pour the oil to a depth of ½ inch into a large skillet set over medium-high heat. When it shimmers, add the plantains (working in batches, if necessary, to avoid overcrowding) and fry until browned on the bottom, 2 to 3 minutes, then use tongs to turn them over and cook until browned on the second side, 1 to 2 minutes. Transfer them to a paper-towel-lined plate.

To serve, divide the beans among shallow bowls and tuck the plantains on one side. Serve hot, with rice.

NOTE

To prepare the grains of selim, toast 8 pods in a dry skillet over medium-high heat until fragrant and smoking, about 1 minute per side. Let cool briefly, then break apart by hand, discard the shiny seeds (which are bitter), and grind the pods in a dedicated spice grinder.

SOUTHERN BAKED BEANS

I developed this adaptation of Edna Lewis's baked beans recipe from her classic *The Taste of Country Cooking* to go along with an essay included in the 2018 anthology *Edna Lewis: At the Table with an American Original*, edited by my friend and colleague Sara Franklin. I was drawn to it because it proves that our exclusive association of baked beans with New England is flat-out wrong, and that every bean-growing culture seems to have at least one treatment for cooking them slowly, because the results are always so wonderful. Edna's recipe eschews the Yankee inclusion of maple syrup, of course, depending on onion and tomato for a touch of sweetness. I omit her "streaky lean salt pork" and instead use a combination of coconut aminos, which give a dash of almost meaty umami, and one of my go-to spices: Spanish smoked paprika. Serve with a green salad and crusty bread.

Preheat the oven to 250°F.

Combine the beans with 4 cups water in a heavy pot over medium-high heat, bring to a boil, then lower the heat and simmer the beans gently for 15 minutes. Stir in the onion, aminos, tomato paste, paprika, pepper, and mustard, cover, and bake until the beans are very tender and fragrant, about 3 hours. (Check the beans from time to time, and if the liquid has reduced so it is no longer covering the beans, add hot water to barely cover and continue cooking.)

Remove the beans from the oven, taste, and stir in salt if needed. Cover and let them sit until ready to serve.

Store the beans, covered, in the refrigerator for up to 1 week or in the freezer for up to 3 months.

6 servings

1 pound dried navy beans (may substitute cannellini or cranberry/borlotti beans), soaked overnight and drained

Water

1 onion, finely chopped

⅓ cup liquid aminos or coconut aminos (may substitute tamari), plus more to taste

2 tablespoons tomato paste

1 teaspoon Spanish smoked paprika (pimentón)

1 teaspoon freshly ground black pepper

1 teaspoon dry mustard

Kosher salt, to taste (if needed)

CUBAN-STYLE ORANGE-SCENTED BLACK BEANS

8 to 12 servings

BEANS

1 pound dried black beans

1 orange, halved

1 onion, halved

8 garlic cloves

1 green bell pepper, quartered

1 (3 by 5-inch) strip kombu (dried seaweed)

1 bay leaf

2 teaspoons kosher salt

1 teaspoon ground cumin

8 cups Vegetable Broth (page 216), store-bought no-salt-added vegetable broth, or water

SOFRITO

¼ cup extra-virgin olive oil, plus more (optional) for serving

1 yellow onion, finely chopped

3 bell peppers (preferably a mix of red, green, and orange or yellow), finely chopped

3 garlic cloves, chopped

1 jalapeño chile, stemmed and chopped (seeded if you don't want it too spicy)

1 teaspoon ground cumin

½ teaspoon kosher salt, plus more to taste

¼ teaspoon freshly ground black pepper

2 tablespoons tomato paste

1 tablespoon grated orange zest

¼ cup fresh orange juice

1 tablespoon apple cider vinegar, plus more to taste

Quick-Pickled Onions (see page 140; optional), for serving

Hot sauce (optional), for serving

I first started putting an orange in my pressure-cooked black beans for the same reason I imagine a lot of other American cooks have: I read the great and powerful J. Kenji López-Alt's take on the same at Serious Eats. Kenji's techniques never disappoint, although I'll confess to taking shameless liberties with his recipes. In this case, I combined his techniques with other recipes for Cuban-style beans, which always include my beloved orange, and added some flavor-packed touches of my own.

To make the beans: In a stovetop or electric pressure cooker, combine the beans, orange, onion, garlic, green bell pepper, kombu, bay leaf, salt, cumin, and broth. Cover, bring to high pressure, and cook for 40 minutes if using a stovetop pressure cooker or 45 minutes for an electric one. Then turn off and let the pressure naturally release. (If you prefer, you can also make these on the stovetop, simmering the beans over medium-low heat for up to 90 minutes, or baking at 250°F, until the beans are tender.)

While the beans are cooking, make the sofrito: Pour the oil into a large deep skillet over medium heat. When it shimmers, add the onion, bell peppers, garlic, and chile and sauté until tender, about 8 minutes. Stir in the cumin, salt, pepper, and tomato paste and cook just until fragrant, about 30 seconds. Stir in the orange zest, orange juice, and vinegar and cook until the flavors meld, about 5 minutes. Turn off the heat until the beans are ready.

When the beans are ready, fish out and discard the orange, onion, bell pepper, kombu, and bay leaf.

Turn the heat under the skillet with the sofrito to medium and use a slotted spoon to transfer the beans to the sofrito, along with 2 cups of the cooking liquid. Taste and add more vinegar and salt if needed.

Serve hot, with rice, and top with pickled onions, a few dashes of hot sauce, and a drizzle of olive oil, if desired.

QUICK SUNGOLD TOMATO, CHICKPEA, AND GREENS CURRY

2 servings

2 tablespoons extra-virgin olive oil

2 pints Sungold or other yellow or red cherry or grape tomatoes

½ teaspoon kosher salt, plus more to taste

¼ teaspoon freshly ground black pepper

1 teaspoon Madras curry powder

1¾ cups cooked or canned no-salt-added chickpeas (from one 15-ounce can), drained and rinsed

4 cups lightly packed peppery baby greens, such as mizuna, mustard greens, arugula, or a mix

Vegetable Broth (page 216), store-bought no-salt-added vegetable broth, or water (if needed)

This is what can happen when you have a fridge stocked with seasonal vegetables and precooked beans just waiting to be turned into dinner. Serve over rice or another grain of your choice.

Pour the olive oil into a large skillet over medium-high heat. When it shimmers, add the tomatoes and cook until they start to brown and pop, about 5 minutes. Use a fork or potato masher to smash the tomatoes, then reduce the heat to medium and stir in the salt, pepper, and curry powder and cook for an additional 30 seconds.

Stir in the chickpeas and greens and cook, stirring, just until the greens wilt, about 1 minute. Taste and add more salt if needed. If the mixture seems dry, splash in a little broth. Serve hot.

CREAMY INDIAN BLACK LENTIL STEW

(DAL MAKHANI)

Whenever my husband and I order Indian food from one of our go-to spots in DC, he gets butter chicken and I always get this dish, whose savory depth of flavor and indulgent creaminess make it absolutely irresistible. My friend Udai Soni, whose mother, Neha, offered me her own recipe, says it was always his favorite, too. Traditionally—and in Neha's version—this dish includes a good amount of cream; coconut cream makes it just as delicious. I add coconut flakes as a non-traditional garnish. You can find dal makhani masala, along with the beans, at any good Indian market.

Soak the combination of urad dal, rajma, and chana dal in plenty of water overnight, then drain.

Add the beans to a stovetop or electric pressure cooker, along with enough water to cover by 2 inches. Bring to high pressure and cook for 25 minutes if using a stovetop pressure cooker or 30 minutes if using an electric one, then turn off and let the pressure naturally release. The beans should be tender. (If you prefer, you can also make this on the stovetop, simmering the beans over medium-low heat for up to 90 minutes, until the beans are tender.)

While the beans cook, puree the onion in a food processor until smooth.

Pour the oil into a large skillet over medium-high heat. When it shimmers, stir in the pureed onion. Cook, stirring occasionally, until the onion starts to dry out and brown on the bottom, 5 to 8 minutes. Stir in the ginger, garlic, masala, coriander, salt, chile powder, and turmeric and cook until fragrant, about 30 seconds. Stir in the tomato puree and cook, stirring occasionally, until the mixture starts to brown on the bottom, about 10 minutes.

When the beans are ready, transfer the tomato mixture to the pressure cooker and add the butter and coconut cream. With the pressure cooker open and over medium-high heat, bring to a boil and cook, stirring and scraping the bottom of the pot every few minutes to avoid scorching, until the mixture is reduced and thick, about 20 minutes. (You may need a splatter guard!)

While the dal is reducing, toast the coconut in a large dry skillet over medium heat, tossing occasionally, until lightly browned, about 5 minutes.

To serve, garnish the dal with the coconut and cilantro and serve hot, with naan or rice.

6 servings

1 cup whole black urad (lentils), picked over and rinsed

¼ cup rajma (red kidney beans)

¼ cup chana dal (split yellow chickpeas)

Water

1 small red onion, cut into chunks

3 tablespoons sesame oil (not toasted) or other neutral vegetable oil

1 teaspoon freshly grated ginger

1 garlic clove, finely chopped

2 teaspoons dal makhani masala (may substitute garam masala)

1½ teaspoons ground coriander

1 teaspoon kosher salt, plus more to taste

¼ to ½ teaspoon red chile powder (preferably Kashmiri), depending on your tolerance for heat

¼ teaspoon ground turmeric

½ cup (4 ounces) tomato puree

¼ cup unsalted vegan butter or dairy butter

1 (5.4-ounce) can (⅔ cup) coconut cream

1 cup unsweetened large-flake dried coconut, for garnish

½ cup lightly packed cilantro leaves, chopped, for garnish

LALO'S CACAHUATE BEANS
WITH PICO DE GALLO

**4 main-course or
8 side-dish servings**

1 white onion

1 pound dried cranberry/
borlotti (aka cacahuate)
beans, soaked overnight

2 garlic cloves

Water

2 tablespoons extra-virgin
olive oil

2 large tomatoes, chopped

2 dried ancho or guajillo chiles,
stemmed, seeded, and cut into
strips

1 teaspoon kosher salt, plus
more to taste

PICO DE GALLO
(MAKES ABOUT 2 CUPS)

2 Roma (plum) tomatoes,
chopped

⅓ cup finely diced red onion

½ serrano chile, stemmed,
seeded, and diced

1 tablespoon extra-virgin
olive oil

¼ cup fresh lime juice

½ cup lightly packed cilantro
leaves

½ teaspoon kosher salt, plus
more to taste

Mexico City chef Eduardo "Lalo" Garcia's secret is to cook these beans very simply, for a very long time, until they're super-soft, then to add his seasoning—a sofrito of onion, garlic, tomatoes, and dried chiles—and boil them for another half hour, simultaneously infusing them with flavor and concentrating their cooking liquid. These are some of the simplest and yet most complex beans I've ever tasted, let alone cooked. A straightforward pico de gallo adds a little freshness and crunch. Serve with tortillas.

Cut the onion in half. Keep one half intact and throw it into a large pot. Chop the other half and reserve.

Add the beans and 1 of the garlic cloves to the pot, along with enough water to cover the beans by 3 inches, and turn the heat to high. Bring to a boil, then reduce the heat as low as it will go, cover, and cook until the beans are tender, 60 to 90 minutes.

Chop the remaining garlic clove.

While the beans are cooking, make the sofrito: Pour the oil into a medium sauté pan over medium heat. Add the reserved chopped onion and the chopped garlic and cook until the onion softens, about 5 minutes. Add the tomatoes and chiles and cook until the tomatoes break down, release their liquid, and become very soft, and most of the liquid has evaporated, about 10 minutes. Remove from the heat.

When the beans are tender, sir in the sofrito, increase the heat to high, and cook, uncovered, until the beans are very soft and starting to break apart and the liquid has reduced by about one-third but the beans are still brothy, about 30 minutes. Stir in the salt, taste, and add more if needed.

While the beans are cooking, make the pico de gallo: In a mixing bowl, combine the tomatoes, onion, chile, olive oil, lime juice, cilantro, and salt. Taste and add more salt if needed.

When the beans are ready, divide them among shallow bowls and top each portion with some pico de gallo. Serve hot, with tortillas.

Cover and store in the refrigerator for up to 1 week or in the freezer for up to 3 months.

CRANBERRY BEANS
WITH DANDELION GREENS, MISO, AND FENNEL

**4 main-course or
6 side-dish servings**

1 bunch of dandelion greens

¼ cup extra-virgin olive oil

1 yellow onion, finely chopped

4 garlic cloves, finely chopped

¼ teaspoon kosher salt, plus
more as needed

¼ teaspoon crushed red
pepper flakes

3 cups cooked cranberry/
borlotti beans, plus 1½ cups
cooking liquid

2 tablespoons white miso

1 fennel bulb, chopped, plus
chopped fronds for garnish

This recipe was inspired by a side dish at Kismet in Los Angeles that employs fermented turnip tops. I knew I could get the same effect with fresh greens—I like dandelion greens for their earthy bitterness, but peppery arugula or mustard greens would be good, too—plus miso, my favorite all-purpose blast-of-umami ingredient. Eat with rice or another grain as a main course or without as a side. These beans are also excellent on toast. Note that many other beans would work well here, but my top picks for substitution would be cannellinis, flageolets, and gigantes. If you want to use canned beans, rinse and drain them and use vegetable broth instead of the cooking liquid.

Cut the stems off the dandelion greens and thinly slice both the stems and leaves, keeping them separate.

In a large saucepan, heat the olive oil over medium heat. When it shimmers, add the dandelion stems, onion, garlic, and salt and cook, stirring occasionally, until very soft, about 10 minutes. Stir in the red pepper flakes and cook until fragrant, about 30 seconds. Add the dandelion leaves and sauté until wilted, 2 to 3 minutes.

Add the beans and their cooking liquid, reduce the heat to medium-low, cover, and cook for 10 to 15 minutes, until the beans are warmed through and the flavors have melded. Scoop ¼ cup of the cooking liquid into a small bowl, whisk in the miso until smooth, and stir it back into the beans.

Taste and add salt if needed. (The miso is salty, so you might not need any salt at all.)

Top with the chopped fennel and fronds and serve.

INDIAN RED KIDNEY BEANS

(RAJMA DAL)

My friend Udai Soni tells me that when he was growing up outside London, this dish was something all northern Indian families like his would cook every Sunday for lunch and then eat the leftovers for dinner. This recipe has his seal of approval—because it's from his mother, Neha. Serve with naan and/or rice or over toast for a snack. It will taste even better the next day when you reheat it.

Drain the beans. Combine them in a stovetop or electric pressure cooker with enough water to cover by 2 inches. Bring to high pressure, then reduce the heat to medium and cook for 10 minute if using a stovetop model or 15 minutes for electric. Let the pressure release naturally, then open. Drain the beans, reserving about 2 cups of the cooking liquid.

Puree the onions until smooth in a food processor.

In a large skillet, heat the oil over medium-high heat and stir in the pureed onions. Cook, stirring occasionally, until the onions start to dry out and brown on the bottom, about 20 minutes. Stir in the tomato puree, coriander, ginger, salt, chile powder, and turmeric. Cook until the mixture starts to brown on the bottom and the oil separates, about 10 minutes.

Transfer the onion mixture to the pressure cooker, add the drained beans and the reserved 2 cups of cooking liquid. Return to pressure over low heat and cook for 30 minutes if using a stovetop model or 40 minutes if using electric. Turn off the heat and let the pressure release naturally.

Garnish with the cilantro and serve hot, with naan bread or rice.

8 servings

1¼ cups dried red kidney beans (chitra rajma), washed and soaked overnight with 1 teaspoon kosher salt

Water

3 large red onions, cut into chunks

5 tablespoons sesame oil (not toasted) or other neutral vegetable oil

1 (15-ounce) can tomato puree

1 tablespoon ground coriander

1 teaspoon freshly grated ginger

1 teaspoon kosher salt, plus more to taste

½ teaspoon red chile powder (preferably Kashmiri)

½ teaspoon ground turmeric

½ cup lightly packed cilantro leaves, for garnish

TUNISIAN SOUP
(LABLABI) WITH CHICKPEAS, BREAD, AND HARISSA

This is a wonderfully fragrant and soothing soup, with a punch of harissa to keep things lively. I first made the traditional version from Anissa Helou's incredible book *Feast*, and I loved it for its depth of flavor and heartiness (from the bread). Still, I couldn't help but tweak it to my taste: I pureed some of the chickpeas and returned them to the soup, making it creamier, and added more roasted chickpeas on top for even more texture.

Combine the chickpeas with 5 cups water, 1 tablespoon of the olive oil, the bay leaves, and kombu in a Dutch oven or heavy stockpot over high heat. Bring to a boil, let boil for a few minutes, then reduce the heat to low, cover, and cook until the chickpeas are tender, about 1 hour.

Preheat the oven to 400°F.

While the chickpeas are cooking, cut the bread into thick slices, then tear the slices into bite-size pieces. Place the bread in one layer on a large rimmed baking sheet and toast until crisp and lightly browned on top, about 10 minutes. Remove from the oven and let cool in the pan.

Pour another 2 tablespoons of the oil into a large skillet over medium-high heat. When it shimmers, stir in the onion and garlic and sauté until tender and starting to brown, 6 to 8 minutes. Stir in 1 tablespoon of the cumin, the salt, and tomato paste and sauté until fragrant, about 30 seconds. Turn off the heat.

When the chickpeas are tender, remove and discard the bay leaves and kombu. Use a slotted spoon to transfer 2 cups of the chickpeas to a blender and a measuring cup to transfer ½ cup of the chickpea cooking liquid to the blender. Add the remaining ¼ cup of the olive oil and puree to combine. Return the puree to the soup and stir in the onion mixture from the skillet and as much of the pan juices as possible. If it seems too thick, add a little more water until it reaches your preferred consistency. Stir in 1 tablespoon of the harissa and the lemon juice. Taste and add more salt if needed.

To serve, divide the toasted bread pieces among soup bowls. Top each with a small dollop of harissa (more if you want things spicier), then ladle in the soup. Garnish with parsley, lemon zest, and roasted chickpeas, if desired. Serve hot.

The soup can be covered and stored, without the bread, in the refrigerator for up to 1 week or in the freezer for up to 3 months.

6 servings

1½ cups dried chickpeas, soaked overnight and drained

Water

¼ cup plus 3 tablespoons extra-virgin olive oil, plus more for serving

2 bay leaves

1 (3 by 5-inch) strip kombu (dried seaweed)

8 ounces hearty rustic bread

1 cup chopped onion

6 garlic cloves, chopped

2 tablespoons ground cumin, plus more for serving

1 teaspoon kosher salt

1 tablespoon tomato paste

2 to 3 tablespoons harissa

3 tablespoons fresh lemon juice

½ cup flat-leaf parsley leaves, chopped, for garnish

1 tablespoon finely grated lemon zest, for garnish

½ cup Crunchy Spiced Roasted Chickpeas (page 49; optional), for garnish

NEW ORLEANS RED BEANS AND RICE

8 servings

BEANS (MAKES 8 CUPS)

3 tablespoons extra-virgin olive oil

1 yellow or white onion, chopped

1 green bell pepper, chopped

1 celery stalk, chopped

2 teaspoons salt-free Creole seasoning

1 teaspoon Spanish smoked paprika (pimenton)

1 pound dried red kidney beans, soaked overnight, drained, and rinsed

5 cups Vegetable Broth (page 216), store-bought no-salt-added vegetable broth, or water, plus more as needed

1 bay leaf

1 (3 by 5-inch) strip kombu (dried seaweed)

2 teaspoons soy sauce or tamari, plus more to taste

2 teaspoons Tabasco or other favorite hot sauce, plus more to taste and for serving

1 teaspoon kosher salt, plus more to taste

RICE (MAKES 6 CUPS)

1 tablespoon grapeseed or other neutral vegetable oil

1 large yellow onion, diced

2 tablespoons unsalted vegan or dairy butter

1 bay leaf

1 teaspoon kosher salt

2 cups jasmine rice

3 cups Vegetable Broth (page 216), store-bought no-salt-added vegetable broth, or water

1 cup thinly sliced chives, for serving

Red beans and rice is a famous dish in NOLA. Dating to the 1700s and the arrival of French-speaking Haitians, this dish became a Monday tradition, according to bean company Camellia (which sells a stellar product worth seeking out), because that was laundry day, and laundry back then was much more involved than throwing clothes into a machine. Women got into the habit of tossing Sunday night's meat leftovers into a pot of red beans and cooking it slowly all day while they worked on the wash. Today, plenty of modern New Orleanians still celebrate red beans and rice Mondays. Emily and Alon Shaya of the restaurant Saba invite folks over just about every week and make two pots of beans—one with meat, the other without—and serve them with a salad. Emily's secrets to the plant-based version: a very flavorful vegetable broth, smoked paprika, and soy sauce. I add a little kombu to help soften the beans and some Creole seasoning.

To make the beans: Pour the olive oil into a Dutch oven or heavy stockpot over medium heat. When it shimmers, add the onion, bell pepper, and celery. Cook, stirring occasionally, until the onion just starts to turn translucent, 4 to 5 minutes. Stir in the Creole seasoning and paprika and cook until fragrant, about 1 minute.

Add the beans, broth (adding more if needed to cover the beans by 1 inch), bay leaf, and kombu. Increase the heat to high and bring to a boil. Reduce the heat to medium-high and let the beans boil for 10 minutes, then reduce the heat to low, cover, and cook until the beans are so tender they are almost falling apart, 4 to 5 hours, checking occasionally and adding more broth if needed to keep the beans covered.

Stir in the soy sauce, Tabasco, and salt. Taste and add more soy sauce, salt, and Tabasco if needed. If you want the beans to be a little creamier, use a wooden spoon or a potato masher to smash some against the side of the pot or use an immersion (handheld) blender to briefly—very briefly!—puree some of the beans in the pot. (You can also scoop out a cup or so, puree in a blender, and return to the pot.)

To make the rice: Pour the grapeseed oil into a saucepan over medium-high heat. Add the onion, butter, bay leaf, and salt and cook, stirring frequently, until the onion is soft, 6 to 8 minutes. Add the rice and stir to coat. Stir in the broth and bring the mixture to a boil. Reduce the heat to low, cover, and cook for 15 minutes. Turn off the heat and let the rice sit for at least 10 minutes, then uncover and fluff.

Serve the beans in bowls with a scoop of rice in the center and sprinkle the chives on top. Pass more Tabasco at the table.

BLACK BEAN SOUP

WITH MASA DUMPLINGS

6 servings

**MASA DUMPLINGS
(MAKES ABOUT
24 DUMPLINGS)**

1 cup instant masa harina, plus more as needed

½ teaspoon kosher salt

Hot water

3 tablespoons unsalted vegan or dairy butter, at room temperature

SOUP

3½ cups Salsa Madre black bean puree (page 35) or see Note opposite

1¾ to 2½ cups bean cooking liquid, Vegetable Broth (page 216), store-bought no-salt-added vegetable broth, or water

Kosher salt to taste (if needed)

1 large dried ancho chile

Flesh of 2 ripe avocados, cubed

1 cup Herb-Marinated Tofu Feta (page 217) or store-bought vegan or dairy feta, crumbled

½ cup lightly packed cilantro leaves

½ cup toasted pumpkin seeds (pepitas)

2 limes, cut into wedges

Yet another thing you can make with Salsa Madre (page 35): this stellar Mexican soup, from DC chef Christian Irabién, becomes super-hearty with the addition of easy-to-put-together masa dumplings, called chochoyotes. If you'd like, you can replace the dumplings with broken tortilla chips for a different texture.

To make the dumplings: Combine the masa harina and salt in the bowl of a stand mixer, fitted with the beater attachment. (Alternatively, you can use a large bowl and a hand mixer.) With the mixer on low speed, slowly pour in ¾ cup hot water until the mixture forms a dough. It should be moist and tacky but not sticky and not dry. If it's sticky, sprinkle in a little more masa harina and mix to combine; if it's dry, pour in a tablespoon or so more hot water and mix to combine. When the dough feels right, turn the mixer to medium-high speed and pinch off a small piece of butter and drop it into the dough, beating until it disappears before dropping in another piece. When all the butter is in the dough, turn the mixer to high and beat for another minute, until the masa dough is very fluffy. Check to see if it has remained slightly tacky but not sticky or dry; beat in more masa harina or water if needed to correct it.

Pinch off pieces of dough that are 1 scant tablespoon (or ½ ounce if you have a scale and want to be exact), roll them into balls, and use your thumb to make an indentation in the center of each one (this helps the masa harina cook more evenly).

Bring a medium saucepan of salted water to a boil, then reduce it to a simmer. (If the water is boiling, it will break up the dumplings.) Add the dumplings to the water and cook just until they float, about 2 minutes. Use a slotted spoon to scoop them into a bowl.

To make the soup: In a large saucepan over medium heat, whisk together the Salsa Madre and 1¾ cups of the bean cooking liquid. You want it to have the consistency of a creamy soup, not too thick and not too watery; add more bean cooking liquid as needed. Taste and add salt if needed (although you probably won't need any, since the Salsa Madre is salty). Reduce the heat to low and cover to keep warm.

In a small dry skillet over medium-high heat, place the ancho chile and cook for a minute or two on each side, until it puffs. Transfer to a plate, let cool, then remove the stem, tear it apart, discard the seeds, and crumble or tear the flesh into small pieces with your fingers.

To serve, divide the soup into six small serving bowls and top each with 4 dumplings, avocado cubes, feta, cilantro, pumpkin seeds, and dried ancho crumbles. Pass the lime wedges for squeezing.

NOTE

If you're in a hurry and don't have the Salsa Madre on hand, make the soup by sautéeing an onion and a clove or two of garlic in olive oil and adding three 15-ounce cans of black beans (drained and rinsed) plus 2 to 3 cups of vegetable broth, 1 teaspoon ground cumin, and kosher salt to taste; puree in a blender.

GARLICKY GREAT NORTHERN BEANS AND BROCCOLI RABE OVER TOAST

6 servings

2 cups dried great Northern beans (may substitute navy, cannellini, or other white beans), soaked overnight and drained

Water

1 onion, studded with 12 whole cloves

2 large carrots

1 (3 by 5-inch) strip kombu (dried seaweed)

3 bay leaves

3 tablespoons extra-virgin olive oil

1 large bunch of broccoli rabe, cut into 1-inch pieces

6 garlic cloves, finely chopped

1 teaspoon kosher salt, plus more to taste

¼ teaspoon freshly ground black pepper

6 thick slices rustic sourdough bread, lightly toasted

1 tablespoon chile oil (optional)

¼ cup vegan or traditional Parmesan, grated or shaved

My take on *Heartland* author and chef Lenny Russo's wonderfully satisfying bowl of beans and bitter greens amps up the garlic and uses the rich bean cooking liquid instead of stock. I love serving these beans over toast to make it a meal.

Combine the beans in a large pot with enough water to cover by 2 inches. Add the onion, carrots, kombu, and bay leaves, turn the heat to medium-high, and bring the beans to a boil. Let then boil for 5 minutes, then reduce the heat so the beans are at a bare simmer, cover, and cook until the beans are very tender, about 1 hour. (Alternatively, you can cook the beans, water, and aromatic vegetables in a stovetop or electric pressure cooker: Bring to high pressure and cook for 17 minutes if using a stovetop model or 20 minutes for electric. Let the pressure release naturally, then open.)

Discard the onion, carrots, kombu, and bay leaves and strain the beans, reserving all of the cooking liquid.

In a deep skillet, heat the olive oil over medium heat until it shimmers. Stir in the broccoli rabe and sauté until very tender, about 8 minutes. Stir in the garlic and cook until it starts to soften, about 2 minutes. Stir in the drained beans, 1½ cups of the reserved cooking liquid, and the salt. Cook just until the beans are hot and the flavors have melded, 2 to 3 minutes. Stir in the pepper, taste, and add more salt if needed.

Divide the toast among shallow serving bowls. Drizzle with the chile oil, if desired, and spoon the bean mixture and broth on top. Finish with the Parm and serve hot.

TEXAS-STYLE BOWL O' RED BEANS
(CHILE CON FRIJOLES)

4 to 6 servings

6 dried ancho chiles, rinsed

Hot water

2 tablespoons vegetable oil

1 large yellow onion, chopped

4 garlic cloves, finely chopped

1 teaspoon sea salt, plus more to taste

1 teaspoon freshly ground black pepper, plus more to taste

2 tablespoons dried oregano (preferably Mexican)

1 tablespoon ground cumin

1 teaspoon Spanish smoked paprika (pimenton)

8 ounces dried red kidney beans, rinsed

4 ounces dried black beans, rinsed

I was once a chili purist: one of those Texans who says that real chili is little more than chile peppers and meat, plus seasonings. That's why its original name is chile con carne. All that went out the window when I became vegetarian, and I embraced the anything-goes approach to chili making: beans, sure, but also sweet potatoes, and tomatoes, and corn, even jackfruit at one point or another. Then one day I found myself with a real hankering for that purist's chili again and thought, what if the only substitution I made were beans instead of meat? I dusted off my favorite Texas "bowl o' red" recipe—developed with the help of my brother, Michael—and got to work. With a combination of red kidney and black beans and seasoning that depends mostly on ancho chile peppers, this has the round flavors and slow-burning heat that I love, and I've made it for many a party. (And when I switched from my Dutch oven to a pressure cooker, the dish turned from an all-day to a weeknight recipe.) Serve with saltines or tortillas, grated cheddar cheese, chopped scallions, and sour cream, if you'd like.

Cut or tear the ancho chiles into 2-inch or so pieces, discarding the seeds and stems. Place in a dry skillet over medium heat and toast for about 5 minutes, just until fragrant, without allowing them to char. Transfer to a blender, add 5 cups hot water, and blend until smooth.

Heat the oil in a stovetop or electric pressure cooker, uncovered, over medium heat until it shimmers. Add the onion and garlic and cook, stirring frequently, until the onion turns translucent, about 5 minutes. Add the salt, pepper, oregano, cumin, and paprika and cook, stirring, until very fragrant, about 1 minute.

Stir in the red kidney and black beans, along with the ancho mixture, plus more water as needed to cover the beans by 1 inch. Lock on the lid, bring the cooker up to high pressure, and cook for 45 minutes if using a stovetop model or 55 minutes for electric. Let the pressure naturally release, then open. (Alternatively, you can make in a Dutch oven: cover and cook over low heat until the beans are very tender, up to 4 to 5 hours, stirring occasionally and adding water if the beans seem dry on top.)

Use a masher to lightly mash some of the beans in the pot, leaving some whole while thickening the chili. Stir in more water to loosen, if necessary, and add more salt and pepper to taste.

Serve warm, with the accompaniments of your choice.

CURRIED RED LENTIL STEW

WITH LIME AND HARISSA

It was one of those Instagram moments: I saw something so delicious and smart I had to direct-message the source. Thankfully, it was my old friend John Delpha, a New England chef always thinking up interesting dishes, even when he's cooking at home. What caught my eye was a red lentil shakshuka—how inspired to use creamy lentils instead of spicy tomato sauce for that classic Middle Eastern dish! Delpha actually made the dish with the leftovers from a stellar red lentil stew, bright with lime and with a kick from harissa and curry. I made the stew for a dinner party a few weeks later, where it was the undisputed star, then heated up the leftovers the next day, made a vegan twist on shakshuka—and posted it on Instagram, of course. Grits form a light skin over the top but stay creamy inside, a comforting complement to the spiced lentils.

Pour the olive oil into a Dutch oven or heavy stockpot over medium-high heat. When it shimmers, stir in the carrots, celery, onion, and garlic and cook, stirring occasionally, until the onion is translucent, about 10 minutes. Stir in the curry powder and cook, stirring, until fragrant and toasted, 1 to 2 minutes.

Add the lentils, 6 cups water, and salt. Add more water if needed to cover the lentils by 1 inch. Bring to a boil, then reduce the heat to low, cover, and cook until the lentils have softened but are not completely tender, about 10 minutes. Stir in the lime zest, lime juice, and agave and continue cooking, uncovered, until the lentils are soft and slightly creamy but not mushy, about 5 minutes. Remove from the heat and stir in the cilantro, harissa, and pepper. Taste and add more salt, harissa, and pepper if desired. Serve hot.

6 servings

2 tablespoons extra-virgin olive oil

2 carrots, finely chopped

2 celery stalks, finely chopped

1 yellow onion, finely chopped

10 large garlic cloves, finely chopped

¼ cup Madras curry powder

1 pound red lentils, picked over and rinsed

Water

1 teaspoon kosher salt, plus more to taste

1 tablespoon finely grated lime zest

½ cup fresh lime juice

2 tablespoons agave nectar

½ cup lightly packed cilantro leaves and tender stems, chopped

1 tablespoon harissa, plus more to taste

½ teaspoon freshly ground black pepper, plus more to taste

NOTE

To make vegan shakshuka, bring 3½ cups of water to a boil in a small saucepan over medium-high heat, add ½ teaspoon kosher salt, and whisk in 1 cup regular (not coarse or stone-ground) grits. Reduce the heat to very low and stir until the mixture thickens, 8 to 10 minutes. Pour the leftover red lentils into a deep sauté pan or saucepan. (Pick a size according to the amount of lentils you have so that they are at least 2 inches deep.) Whisk in water to loosen; the lentils will have thickened, and you want them the consistency of chunky tomato sauce. Turn the heat to medium. As soon as the liquid starts bubbling around the edges, make five wells in the lentils. Dollop about ½ cup grits into each well, cover, and cook on very low heat for about 5 minutes, until a light skin forms on top. Serve hot.

FRESH BABY LIMAS
WITH PRESERVED LEMON AND BUTTER

2 servings as a side dish

Water

2 cups fresh or frozen and thawed baby lima beans

1 tablespoon vegan butter (preferably cultured) or dairy butter

1 tablespoon Coconut-Cashew Yogurt (page 215) or store-bought coconut yogurt

¼ cup drained and finely chopped preserved lemon

Kosher or sea salt to taste (if needed)

A few generous grinds of black pepper

2 tablespoons chopped flat-leaf parsley leaves

The salty tang from yogurt and preserved lemon play beautifully with the creamy texture of quickly braised fresh or frozen lima beans. I first had this dish at a now-closed restaurant in my former neighborhood, Sally's Middle Name, and knew I'd try it at home. They used goat butter, but a combination of cultured vegan butter and coconut yogurt does the same trick.

In a medium skillet, bring ¾ cup water to a simmer over medium heat. Add the lima beans and return to a simmer, then reduce the heat to medium-low, cover, and cook until the beans are tender, 10 to 12 minutes.

Increase the heat to medium-high and cook, uncovered, until only a tablespoon or two of the liquid is left. Reduce the heat to low and stir in the butter, yogurt, and preserved lemon. Cook just until the butter melts and creates a sauce. Taste and add salt if needed.

Add the pepper and parsley and serve hot or at room temperature.

SIMPLY DELICIOUS MARINATED LIMA BEANS

It was an early fall Sunday afternoon in Hudson Valley, New York, and one of my favorite plant-based cooks, teachers, and authors, Amy Chaplin, was showing me just how satisfying a simple pot of pressure-cooked beans can be. She chose large lima beans from Rancho Gordo, a favorite of mine, too, that she had soaked overnight, pressure-cooked in water with a strip of kombu (just as I do—we're clearly culinary soul mates), and let the pressure release. Then the master strokes began. After salting the beans and letting them sit for about 10 minutes to absorb the seasoning, she quickly—and barely—drained the beans, returning them to the pot with some of their cooking liquid still clinging to them. "You don't really need anything more than that," she said when she tasted one. "It's so layered already." Still, she glugged in a little apple cider vinegar and olive oil, stirred in crushed red pepper flakes, added a little more salt to taste, and tossed in a handful of chopped parsley. And she stirred, and stirred, and stirred, creating a lightly tangy, rich sauce that turned little more than cooked beans into something, well, perfect. Spoon these over the grain of your choice, slather them on toast, or cool and eat over greens.

Combine the lima beans, kombu, bay leaves, and enough water to cover by 2 inches in a stovetop or electric pressure cooker with the lid off. Bring to a boil over medium-high heat, boil for 2 minutes, and skim off the extra foam. Lock on the lid, bring to high pressure, and cook for 18 minutes if using a stovetop model and 22 minutes if using electric. Let the pressure release naturally, then open. (Alternatively, you can cook these in a large pot on the stovetop for about 1 hour, until tender.)

Stir in the salt and let the beans sit for 10 minutes. Remove the kombu and bay leaves and quickly drain the beans; don't shake the colander or strainer and don't rinse the beans. Quickly return them to the pot so there is still some liquid clinging to them.

While the beans are still hot, stir in the vinegar, olive oil, and red pepper flakes. Taste and add more salt if needed. Vigorously stir for 30 seconds or so to create a creamy sauce. Stir in the parsley and serve.

6 servings

2 cups dried large lima beans, soaked overnight and drained

1 (3 by 5-inch) strip kombu (dried seaweed)

2 bay leaves

Water

2 teaspoons kosher salt

2 tablespoons apple cider vinegar

2 tablespoons extra-virgin olive oil

½ teaspoon crushed red pepper flakes

1 cup lightly packed flat-leaf parsley leaves, chopped

RED LENTIL FUL

WITH SUMAC-ROASTED CAULIFLOWER

6 servings

LENTIL FUL

1 tablespoon sunflower, safflower, or other neutral vegetable oil

¼ cup chopped white onion

1 garlic clove, minced

¼ cup chopped tomatoes

1 tablespoon ground cumin

1 teaspoon Moroccan spice (such as ras el hanout) or baharat spice blend

½ teaspoon ground coriander

1 teaspoon kosher salt, plus more to taste

½ teaspoon freshly ground black pepper

1 cup red lentils, picked over and rinsed

3 cups Vegetable Broth (page 216), store-bought no-salt-added vegetable broth, or water

2 cups cooked or canned no-salt-added chickpeas (from two 15-ounce cans), drained and rinsed

2 tablespoons unsalted vegan or dairy butter

2 tablespoons fresh lemon juice

2 tablespoons extra-virgin olive oil

ROASTED CAULIFLOWER

1½ pounds cauliflower, cut into florets

2 tablespoons sumac

½ teaspoon kosher salt

2 tablespoons extra-virgin olive oil, plus more for drizzling

Tahini, for drizzling

This hearty dish is a home-cook-friendly version of a multi-component wonder Rich Landau and company have served at V Street in Philly and Fancy Radish in DC. It's based on the classic Egyptian dish ful (aka foul), which is traditionally made with fava beans.

Preheat the oven to 450°F. Set a large rimmed baking sheet in the oven while it heats.

To make the lentil ful: Pour the vegetable oil into a Dutch oven or heavy stockpot over medium-high heat. When it shimmers, add the onion and garlic and sauté until it starts to brown, 4 to 6 minutes. Stir in the tomatoes, cumin, Moroccan spice, coriander, salt, and pepper and cook until the tomatoes break down, 2 to 3 minutes.

Stir in the lentils and broth, bring to a boil, reduce the heat to medium-low, and simmer until the lentils break down and become tender and the mixture becomes thick, 15 to 20 minutes. Stir in the chickpeas, butter, lemon juice, and olive oil and cook until the chickpeas are heated through, 2 to 3 minutes. Taste and add more salt if needed. Turn off the heat and cover to keep warm.

While the ful is cooking, make the roasted cauliflower: In a bowl, toss together the cauliflower, sumac, salt, and olive oil. Spread out on the heated baking sheet and roast until tender and browned, 15 to 20 minutes.

To serve, divide the ful among shallow serving bowls, top with the cauliflower, and drizzle with olive oil and tahini. Serve hot.

KABOCHA SQUASH, CHICKPEA, AND LEMONGRASS STEW

4 to 6 servings

2 tablespoons vegetable oil

1 large yellow onion, chopped

3 garlic cloves, chopped

1 jalapeño chile, stemmed, seeded, and chopped

2 tablespoons finely chopped lemongrass

½ teaspoon crushed red pepper flakes

1 teaspoon fine sea salt, plus more to taste

2 tablespoons freshly grated ginger

1¾ pounds kabocha or other dry-fleshed winter squash (see headnote), peeled, seeded, and diced into ½-inch pieces

1¾ cups cooked or canned no-salt-added chickpeas (from one 15-ounce can), drained and rinsed

1 (13.5-ounce) can full-fat coconut milk

1 cup Vegetable Broth (page 216) or store-bought no-salt-added vegetable broth, plus more as needed

2 teaspoons liquid aminos or coconut aminos (may substitute tamari), plus more to taste

4 cups lightly packed spinach leaves, chopped

½ cup chopped cilantro leaves, plus more for garnish

2 tablespoons fresh lime juice, plus more to taste

½ cup chopped roasted cashews

I became a fan of kabocha squash the first time I simmered it with coconut milk and curry paste. I love how its relative dry texture meant it absorbed liquid, which infused every bite of the squash with flavor. Here, it combines with the ever-versatile chickpeas in a fragrant stew packed with Southeast Asian flavors. If you can't find kabocha, try to substitute another dry-fleshed winter squash, such as acorn, hubbard, or turban.

Pour the oil into a large saucepan over medium heat. When it shimmers, add the onion, garlic, chile, and lemongrass and cook, stirring frequently, until the vegetables become soft, 5 to 6 minutes. Stir in the red pepper flakes, salt, and ginger and cook another minute or two, until the ginger becomes very fragrant.

Stir in the squash, chickpeas, coconut milk, broth, and aminos. Increase the heat to high to bring the liquid to a boil, then reduce it to a simmer, cover, and cook until the squash is tender, 10 to 15 minutes. Uncover and cook until it reduces and thickens, about 5 minutes. Stir in the spinach a cup at a time and cook, stirring, another minute or two, until the spinach has wilted. If the stew seems too thick, add a little more broth to loosen it.

Stir in the cilantro and lime juice. Taste and add more salt, aminos, and/or lime juice if needed. Top with the cashews and serve hot, on its own, or over rice or another grain of your choice, if desired.

LEBANESE-STYLE FUL MOUDAMMAS

Acclaimed Philly chef Michael Solomonov gave me this recipe, which he adapted from a Lebanese friend who ate it for breakfast, as is traditional. Don't skip the overnight soaking of the fava beans that is key to cooking them in a reasonable time, and make sure to look for small favas, which are harder to find but worth the trip to your favorite Middle Eastern market or onto the interwebs. Trust me on this: bigger ones will be a disaster, while these are perfect. Serve with flatbread, if you'd like.

Pour the olive oil into a Dutch oven or large stockpot over medium-low heat. When it shimmers, stir in the onion, garlic, and salt. Cook, stirring occasionally, until softened but not browned, 5 to 6 minutes. Stir in the cumin, coriander, caraway, pepper, and tomatoes and cook until the tomato has thickened slightly and the spices are well incorporated, about 2 minutes.

Add the fava beans and 6 cups water. Bring to a boil, then reduce the heat to low, cover, and cook until the beans are creamy and their skins have softened, 2 to 3 hours. Uncover, increase the heat to medium, and continue cooking until the liquid is slightly reduced and tastes very rich, 15 to 20 minutes.

To serve, spoon the beans into a bowl and top with the parsley and a squeeze of lemon.

4 to 6 servings

½ cup extra-virgin olive oil

1 yellow onion, thinly sliced

4 garlic cloves, thinly sliced

1 tablespoon kosher salt

1 tablespoon ground cumin

2 teaspoons ground coriander

2 teaspoons ground caraway

2 teaspoons freshly ground black pepper

¼ cup crushed tomatoes

2 cups dried whole mini fava beans, soaked overnight and drained

Water

½ cup chopped flat-leaf parsley leaves

1 lemon

BURGERS, SANDWICHES, WRAPS, TACOS & A PIZZA

This is the no-utensils chapter, the beans-on-bread (or other pick-up-able starch), the proof (as if you needed any) that beans are more than just dinner—they can be fun.

4

MUSHROOM-KIDNEY BEAN BURGERS

Ever since chef Brian Van Etten, then at Veggie Galaxy in Cambridge, Massachusetts (and now at Swillburger in Rochester, New York), showed me how he makes his great veggie burgers, I've tried many other recipes but keep coming back to his— or at least a version of them. The key to such good texture: mushrooms and beans, chopped and mixed by hand (the food processor can make things too mushy). I up the proportion of beans (of course) from his original, add walnuts for even more texture, and bake them first, let them cool, then fry or grill them. If you're short on time, you can fry them immediately after forming; they'll still be good, just not perfect.

Preheat the oven to 375°F. Line a large rimmed baking sheet with parchment paper.

Pour the olive oil into a large skillet over medium heat. When it shimmers, add the onion and garlic. Sauté until the vegetables are tender and lightly browned, 6 to 8 minutes. Stir in the chipotle, cumin, and salt and cook until fragrant, about 30 seconds. Add the cremini and shiitake mushrooms and cook, stirring occasionally, until the mushrooms exude their liquid and it evaporates and they start to brown, about 8 minutes. Transfer to a large bowl and let cool slightly.

Add the kidney beans, walnuts, aminos, chickpea flour, nutritional yeast, and lime juice and stir to thoroughly combine. Taste and add more salt if needed.

Lightly oil a ½-cup measure. Use it to scoop out six portions and use your wet hands to form them into large patties, about 5 inches across and ½ to ¾ inch thick. Place the patties on the lined baking sheet.

Bake the patties until firm and dry on the outside, about 30 minutes, flipping them over about halfway through. Transfer to a cooling rack to cool.

(At this point, you can wrap the patties in plastic wrap, seal them in zip-top bags, and refrigerate for up to 1 week or freeze for up to 6 months. Thaw them thoroughly before proceeding.)

Pour the vegetable oil into a large skillet over medium-high heat. When it shimmers, add as many patties as will fit without overcrowding. Fry until browned and crisp on the bottom, about 5 minutes, then carefully flip them over and fry until browned and crisp on the other side, about 4 minutes. Transfer to a platter.

Serve on buns with your preferred condiments and accompaniments.

Makes 6 burgers

2 tablespoons extra-virgin olive oil

½ large yellow onion, chopped

3 garlic cloves, chopped

1 teaspoon ground chipotle chile

2 teaspoons ground cumin

1 teaspoon kosher salt, plus more to taste

12 ounces cremini mushrooms, cut into ½-inch dice

4 ounces shiitake mushrooms, stems discarded and caps cut into ½-inch dice

1½ cups cooked or canned no-salt-added red kidney beans (from one 15-ounce can), drained, rinsed, and lightly mashed with a fork

½ cup walnuts, toasted and chopped

1 tablespoon liquid aminos, coconut aminos, or tamari

¾ cup chickpea flour

¼ cup nutritional yeast

1 tablespoon fresh lime juice

¼ cup vegetable oil, plus more for oiling the measuring cup

6 hamburger buns, lightly toasted

Condiments and accompaniments of your choice

BLACK-EYED PEA (ACCRA) BURGERS

Makes 12 burgers

1 pound dried black-eyed peas, soaked overnight and drained

Water

2 cups chopped yellow onion

1 tablespoon chopped jalapeño chile (seeds included)

3 tablespoons minced garlic

1 tablespoon kosher salt

Corn or vegetable oil, for frying

¾ cup Chickpea Aioli (page 214) or store-bought vegan or regular mayonnaise

⅓ cup hot pepper sauce, such as Tabasco, Louisiana, or Sriracha

12 soft burger buns, such as brioche or potato rolls, lightly toasted

12 leaves romaine or iceberg lettuce

2 to 3 large tomatoes, sliced

Flesh of 2 ripe avocados, sliced

When I told Valerie Erwin, self-described "recovering restaurateur," I was researching bean recipes, she had one immediate thought: accra, also known as akara, the black-eyed pea fritters native to Africa that she used to serve when she had Geechee Girl Rice Cafe in Philadelphia. I love their crispy-creamy texture. Getting the skins off the black-eyed peas can be a little tedious, but after you jump that hurdle, these are super-easy. They make a fabulous burger with your favorite toppings: I like to whisk a spicy pepper sauce with vegan mayo for the condiment and pile on a ripe tomato slice or two, a little avocado, and crunchy lettuce. For a party, you can serve these in appetizer portions, frying them in 2-tablespoon dollops and serving the pepper mayo as a dipping sauce.

To remove the skins of the black-eyed peas, transfer them to the bowl of a food processor, working in batches if necessary, and pulse them several times until they are slightly broken up. Transfer them to a large bowl, cover with water, and stir them vigorously with your hands. When the skins float to the top, pour the skins off with the water once the peas have settled to the bottom. Repeat several times to get rid of most of the skins.

Drain the black-eyed peas for about 15 minutes, then return them to the food processor, again working in batches if necessary, along with the onion, chile, garlic, and salt. Puree until smooth.

Transfer the batter into a fine-mesh strainer set over a bowl. Let the batter drain for 30 minutes. (At this point you can refrigerate it in an airtight container overnight or use it right away.)

Preheat the oven to 350°F. Have a large rimmed baking sheet at hand.

Pour ¼ inch of the oil into a large skillet over medium-high heat.

Using a ½-cup measure or large ice cream scoop, carefully drop ½ cup of batter into the skillet and use the back of a metal measuring cup to slightly flatten the patty to about a ½-inch thickness. Repeat with another patty or two, being careful not to overcrowd the skillet. Fry until the bottoms and edges are caramel brown, about 3 minutes, then use a spatula to carefully flip them over and fry until browned on the second side, about 3 minutes. Transfer the patties as they finish frying to the baking sheet.

When they are all fried, bake the patties until they are hot inside and register 180°F on an instant-read thermometer, about 15 minutes.

Whisk the aioli with the hot pepper sauce in a small bowl, then assemble the burgers: spread a little of the pepper mayo onto the cut sides of each bun, then stack a lettuce leaf, the black-eyed pea patty, tomato, and avocado between them. Serve warm.

BLACK BEAN–CHIPOTLE FALAFEL BURGERS

In the ongoing quest for the perfect veggie burger recipe, at a certain point a realization occurs: wasn't the perfect veggie burger created long ago—in falafel? Soaking but not precooking the beans, it turns out, is a good hedge against the curse of mushiness that befalls so many of this ilk. I grind the soaked beans with appropriate seasonings—chipotle and cilantro—along with the requisite onion and garlic, fold in some cooked sweet potato for extra binding power, and finish cooking in the skillet. The result boasts the crispy edges you love in falafel, plus a moist, but never mushy, interior.

Place the black beans in the bowl of a food processor. Add the onion, cilantro, garlic, salt, and chipotle and process until the mixture is the texture of very coarse cornmeal. Fold the sweet potato in by hand, just to combine.

Divide into eight portions (a heaping ⅓ cup apiece) and form by hand into patties about ½ inch thick. Cover in plastic wrap and refrigerate for at least 2 hours or overnight. (You can refrigerate them in an airtight container for up to 1 week.)

To fry the patties, heat the oil to a depth of ¼ inch in a large skillet over medium-high heat. Once it shimmers, add as many patties as will fit without overcrowding and cook until crisp and deeply browned, about 3 minutes per side. Transfer to paper-towel-lined plates to drain. Add more oil if needed and repeat with the remaining patties.

Serve on the burger buns, layered with the aioli and other condiments of your choice and with the lettuce, avocado, onion, and tomato.

Makes 8 burgers

1 cup dried black beans, soaked overnight and drained

½ cup chopped white onion

½ cup lightly packed chopped cilantro leaves and tender stems

4 garlic cloves, chopped

2 teaspoons kosher salt

2 teaspoons ground chipotle chile (may substitute 2 teaspoons adobo sauce from canned chipotles in adobo)

1 cup mashed cooked sweet potato

Vegetable oil, for frying

8 soft burger buns, such as brioche or potato rolls, lightly toasted

½ cup Chickpea Aioli (page 214) or vegan or traditional mayonnaise

Mustard, ketchup, or both (your choice)

8 leaves romaine or iceberg lettuce

Flesh of 2 ripe avocados, sliced

1 small red onion, thinly sliced

2 tomatoes, sliced

LENTIL, ZUCCHINI, AND CHERRY TOMATO SLOPPY JOES

6 servings

2 tablespoons extra-virgin olive oil

1 yellow onion, chopped

4 garlic cloves, chopped

1 tablespoon tomato paste

1 teaspoon ground ancho chile

1 teaspoon kosher salt, plus more to taste

½ teaspoon crushed red pepper flakes

2 pints cherry tomatoes, quartered

2 small zucchini, cut into ½-inch pieces

2 cups cooked brown lentils, drained and rinsed

1 teaspoon light or dark brown sugar

6 kaiser rolls or sturdy buns, warmed but not toasted

12 sour pickle slices

In my book *Eat Your Vegetables*, I wrote about how I don't tend to use much mock meat, preferring to cook—and eat—vegetables. But I conceded that when it came to a Sloppy Joe, chorizo-spiced seitan was a pretty good fit. Well, now I say to my 2013 self: what were you thinking, when you've got lentils around, just waiting to enrich that sauce with protein and earthy goodness? Always changing, always growing. I also know what not to change, namely, the textural interest that zucchini and cherry tomatoes bring and the zing of sour pickles.

Pour the olive oil into a large skillet over medium heat. When it shimmers, stir in the onion and garlic and sauté until they soften, about 8 minutes. Stir in the tomato paste, ground chile, salt, and red pepper flakes and sauté until fragrant, about 30 seconds.

Stir in the cherry tomatoes and zucchini and cook until the tomatoes collapse, 3 to 4 minutes. Stir in the lentils and brown sugar, increase the heat to bring the mixture to a boil, then reduce the heat to medium-low, cover, and cook until the squash is tender but not mushy and a thick sauce has formed. Taste and add more salt if needed. Let cool slightly.

Divide the bottom buns among six plates. Spoon the warm filling onto the buns, top with the pickles and the top buns, and serve.

CHICKPEA–TARRAGON SALAD SANDWICHES

6 sandwiches

3½ cups cooked or canned no-salt added chickpeas (from one 29-ounce can or two 15-ounce cans), drained and rinsed

1 celery stalk, thinly sliced

½ cup walnuts, toasted and chopped

¼ cup dried cherries

2 tablespoons tarragon leaves, chopped

¼ cup Chickpea Aioli (page 214) or vegan or traditional mayonnaise

2 tablespoons Coconut–Cashew Yogurt (page 215) or vegan or dairy yogurt

2 teaspoons fresh lemon juice

½ teaspoon salt, plus more to taste

¼ teaspoon freshly ground black pepper, plus more to taste

6 soft buns or 12 slices of sandwich bread

Here's the plant-based eater's answer to the luncheon staple of the 1980s, made popular by *The Silver Palate Cookbook*. It's rich and creamy, with bursts of sweetness and crunch. Serve on soft buns or sandwich bread, over greens, or with saltines.

In a large bowl, mash the chickpeas with a fork or potato masher, leaving some of them whole if desired. Add the celery, walnuts, cherries, and tarragon and toss to combine. Gently fold in the aioli, yogurt, lemon juice, salt, and pepper. Taste and add more salt and pepper if needed.

Scoop ½ cup of the salad onto the bottom half of one of the buns or one slice of bread. Place the top half of the bun or bread over the salad and repeat with the remaining ingredients.

GEORGIAN-STYLE BEAN-STUFFED BREAD

(KHACHAPURI LOBIANI)

If you've had khachapuri, you've probably had the cheesy, eggy, open-faced, boat-shaped version. But Georgia has many versions, including a much simpler one stuffed with red kidney beans (lobio) and nothing else, closed up like a large round calzone. I learned the traditional method at DC's Supra, but I add more seasonings, use store-bought pizza dough, and in a decidedly non-traditional touch, put in a little feta for a sharp, salty contrast. Serve as an appetizer or with salad as a main course.

Preheat the oven to 500°F.

Pour the oil into a large skillet over medium heat. When it shimmers, add the onion and sauté until tender but not browned, about 6 minutes. Stir in the fenugreek, Aleppo pepper, and salt and cook until fragrant, about 30 seconds. Stir in the kidney beans and cook until just warmed through, 2 to 3 minutes. Turn off the heat and use a fork to thoroughly mash the beans in the pan. Let cool.

Lightly flour your work surface. Divide the pizza dough in half and form each into a ball. Working with one ball at a time, stretch it to a 6-inch round. Scoop up half the cooled mashed beans and spread them into a 4-inch circle in the middle of the dough round. Sprinkle half the feta on top. Lift the dough from the edges, pull it around the top, over the beans and feta, pleating and pinching as you go, as if you're making a giant dumpling, and pinch all the pleats together in the center, making sure there are no holes. Press and/or roll it out to about a 9-inch round, trying to move the beans inside to the edges of the dough but being careful not to rip it. Poke a hole with your finger in the very center to allow steam to escape. Repeat with the second ball of dough.

Transfer the two khachapuri to a large rimmed baking sheet, brush the tops of both with the butter, and bake until firm and well browned, about 20 minutes.

Let the khachapuri rest for a few minutes, then use a sharp knife or pizza cutter to cut them into quarters and serve.

4 main-course or 8 appetizer servings

3 tablespoons sunflower oil

½ cup finely chopped yellow onion

1 teaspoon ground blue fenugreek (may substitute ¼ teaspoon ground fenugreek)

½ teaspoon Aleppo pepper (may substitute ground ancho chile)

1 teaspoon kosher salt, plus more to taste

2 cups cooked or canned no-salt-added red kidney beans (from two 15-ounce cans), drained and rinsed

Flour

1 pound store-bought pizza dough, thawed if frozen, and at room temperature for at least 1 hour

3 tablespoons Herb-Marinated Tofu Feta (page 217) or store-bought vegan or dairy feta, crumbled

2 tablespoons unsalted vegan or dairy butter, melted

FAVA, RICOTTA, AND LEMON PIZZA

4 servings

2 pounds fresh fava beans in their pods (may substitute frozen and thawed lima beans)

¾ cup lightly packed mint leaves, torn or roughly chopped

½ cup pistachios, toasted

2 garlic cloves, chopped

¼ cup plus 1 tablespoon extra-virgin olive oil, plus more for drizzling

1 tablespoon fresh lemon juice

¼ teaspoon crushed red pepper flakes

1 teaspoon plus a pinch of kosher salt

1 cup vegan or dairy ricotta

1 pound store-bought pizza dough, thawed if frozen and at room temperature

Flour, for dusting

Coarse cornmeal or grits

1 small lemon, sliced as thinly as possible

This pizza takes advantage of fresh fava beans, one of nature's prized gifts of spring, and pairs them with creamy vegan ricotta, lemon slices, and mint on a pizza crust. The fava beans show up two ways: in a rustic pesto and whole. The most work, of course, comes in prepping them: blanching the pods and peeling the beans, but it's worth it. (If you come across fava beans that are smaller than your thumbnail inside those pods, you can skip the peeling!)

Preheat the oven to 500°F. Arrange a rack 6 inches from the broiler element or flame. While the oven is heating, set a baking steel, stone, an overturned baking sheet, or overturned large cast-iron skillet on that rack and heat for at least 30 minutes (or up to an hour if using a stone).

Split open the fava pods and pop out the beans. Bring a large pot of water to a boil and add the fava beans. Cook for about 30 seconds, then scoop them out into a bowl of ice water. Cut a small slit in the peel of each bean and squeeze out the fava. You should have about 1 cup peeled fava beans.

Combine ½ cup of the favas with ½ cup of the mint, the pistachios, garlic, ¼ cup of the olive oil, the lemon juice, red pepper flakes, and 1 teaspoon of the salt in the bowl of a food processor and pulse until you have a chunky puree.

In a small bowl, whisk together the ricotta, a pinch of salt, and 1 tablespoon of the olive oil.

Lightly dust the pizza dough and your work surface with flour. Sprinkle a rimless cookie sheet or the back side of a large rimmed baking sheet with the cornmeal or grits; this will act as your pizza peel. Roll or stretch the dough to a 12-inch round, drizzle it with a little olive oil, and lay it on the cornmeal-covered baking sheet. (Jerk the sheet back and forth to make sure the dough will slide off; if it won't, pick it up where it's sticking and toss in more cornmeal or grits until it slides.) Dollop the dough with the ricotta and pesto, then add the lemon slices and the remaining fava beans.

Slide the dough directly onto the heated baking steel, stone, baking sheet, or skillet and bake until it starts to puff and lightly brown, about 3 minutes. Turn the oven off and turn on the broiler and broil until the toppings start to char and the dough is nicely puffed and browned, even charred in spots, 2 to 5 minutes, depending on the strength of your broiler. (Alternatively, you can keep baking the pizza until it's done, without using the broiler, 8 to 10 minutes.)

Use tongs and your "peel" to remove the pizza and transfer it to a cutting board. Sprinkle with the remaining mint leaves, add another drizzle of olive oil, cut into slices, and serve hot.

MOLLETES
WITH SHIITAKE BACON, FETA, AND ARUGULA

6 servings

SHIITAKE BACON

¼ cup extra-virgin olive oil

¼ cup maple syrup

1 tablespoon liquid aminos, coconut aminos, or tamari

1 teaspoon Spanish smoked paprika (pimenton)

½ teaspoon kosher salt

6 ounces shiitake mushrooms, stems discarded and caps cut into ¼-inch slices

REFRIED BEANS

1 tablespoon vegetable oil

1 small onion, chopped

3 garlic cloves, chopped

½ teaspoon ground cinnamon

½ teaspoon ground cumin

½ teaspoon ground ancho chile

1 teaspoon kosher salt, plus more to taste

¼ teaspoon freshly ground black pepper

3½ cups canned no-salt-added pinto or black beans (from one 29-ounce can or two 15-ounce cans) and their liquid

1 tablespoon fresh lime juice

3 large chewy, long rolls, such as Mexican bolillos or Italian-style sub rolls

¾ cup Herb-Marinated Tofu Feta (page 217) or store-bought vegan or dairy feta, crumbled

1½ cups arugula

2 tablespoons fresh lime juice

Flesh of 1 ripe avocado, sliced

½ cup Fastest-Ever Smoky Red Salsa (page 216) or your favorite store-bought salsa

After DC freelance writer Kara Elder introduced me to her mother's version of these Mexican open-faced bean toasts, I went looking for good versions of the homey dish on a trip to Mexico City—and came up disappointed. None were as good as Tami Elder's. Now they're one of my go-to meals, in addition to tacos and tostadas, whenever I have leftover refried beans (or leftover beans ready to refry!). I confess that I've taken to gilding the lily, adding chewy-crisp "bacon" made from shiitake mushroom caps and showering these with lime-dressed peppery greens. That's in addition to the requisite cheese, for which I use Herb-Marinated Tofu Feta (page 217).

Preheat the oven to 375°F.

To make the shiitake bacon: In a medium bowl, whisk together the olive oil, maple syrup, aminos, paprika, and salt. Add the mushrooms and toss to combine. Transfer to a large rimmed baking sheet and bake until the mushrooms turn a medium brown, firm and fairly dry, about 20 minutes. Remove the sheet from the oven and let the mushrooms cool on it; they will crisp up as they cool.

While the mushrooms are cooking, make the refried beans: Pour the oil into a large deep skillet over medium heat. When it shimmers, add the onion and garlic. Sauté until soft and lightly browned, about 10 minutes. Stir in the cinnamon, cumin, ground chile, salt, and pepper and cook until fragrant, about 30 seconds. Stir in the beans and their liquid, bring to a boil, reduce the heat to simmer, and cook, stirring occasionally, until the flavors meld, about 5 minutes. Use a potato masher or fork to mash the beans in the skillet. Stir in the lime juice. The beans should be thick and pourable, not dry; add a little water if needed to loosen. Taste and add more salt if needed.

Turn the oven to broil and arrange a rack 6 inches from the broiler element or flame.

Cut each roll in half lengthwise and arrange them on the baking sheet, cut sides up. Spread ½ cup of the refried beans on each of the rolls and scatter the feta on top. Broil until the beans are warmed through, the bread has darkened around the edges, and the cheese is just starting to brown, about 5 minutes.

In a small bowl, toss the arugula with the lime juice. Top the toasts with the shiitake bacon, avocado, salsa, and the dressed arugula and serve hot.

YELLOW BEAN AND SPINACH DOSAS

Priya Ammu has taught me so much about the South Indian staple on which she has built DC Dosa, a little stand inside Washington's Union Market with a fervent fan base. First, that there are many, many kinds of dosas. Like so many foods, they vary even from family to family, who use different lentils and other legumes, sometimes in combination with rice and with varying spices and fillings. Second, that you don't even have to fill them, serving them instead with a combination of chutneys and sambar, a legume-based stew. Third, and possibly most important, that I could make them myself. As with crepes, it takes practice to get the spreading technique right, but the worst thing that can happen is you end up with something less-than-perfectly formed. It will still taste as good—trust me.

Combine the moong dal, ginger, chiles, salt, and 1½ cups water in a blender (preferably a high-powered blender, such as a Vitamix) and puree until very smooth. The mixture should be the consistency of a pancake batter. Add a little more water if it is too thick. (If you use a conventional blender, you may need to add as much as ½ cup additional water.) Stir in the spinach. Taste and add more salt if needed.

Heat a large (preferably 11- to 12-inch) crepe pan or nonstick skillet over medium-high heat. If the pan is not nonstick, pour in 1 tablespoon of the oil and wipe it out.

With a ladle or heatproof measuring cup, scoop ⅓ cup of the batter into the center of the pan and then use the back of the ladle or cup to quickly spread the mixture from the center, working outward in rapid concentric circles. The goal is to get the dosa as thin—and large—as possible, making sure the batter is spread evenly and not too thick, especially at the edges. Use a little more batter if needed to patch small holes but resist the urge to keep smoothing any areas that seem too thick; just try to get it thinner the next time. It's fine if it's not perfect!

Working quickly, sprinkle about 2 tablespoons each of the onion and cilantro and a little of the chiles on the batter. Lightly sprinkle with some oil and use a spatula to press the toppings down into the batter.

8 to 10 servings

2 cups dried split mung beans (moong dal), soaked in water for 2 hours, drained, and rinsed

1-inch piece fresh ginger, peeled and chopped

2 small dried red chiles (preferably Kashmiri)

1 teaspoon kosher salt, plus more to taste

Water

1 cup packed baby spinach, finely chopped

1 to 2 tablespoons grapeseed or other neutral vegetable oil

½ yellow onion, finely chopped

1 cup chopped cilantro leaves and tender stems

1 to 2 jalapeño chiles, stemmed, seeded, and finely chopped

Cilantro-Sesame Chutney (page 136)

Tomato Peanut Chutney (page 137)

CONTINUED

Cook the dosa until the edges are golden brown, about 1 to 2 minutes. Use a spatula to loosen it if necessary, then flip the dosa over—using your fingers to pick it up on one side and flipping it with confidence. Use the spatula to help even it out if needed, then press with the spatula to sear the onions underneath the dosa and cook for another minute, then flip it again, transfer it to a plate, and fold it in half or in thirds like a business letter.

Serve the dosas immediately while hot (they lose some of their requisite crispy-edge-ness if they sit for long, especially if you stack them). Serve with the recipes that follow: Cilantro-Sesame Chutney, Tomato-Peanut Chutney, and Chickpea Sambar (page 138). Repeat with the remaining batter.

CILANTRO-SESAME CHUTNEY

This bright green, fiery sauce is an excellent traditional accompaniment to South Indian dosas, but it's is also perfectly at home on tacos or over rice.

Makes 2 cups

½ cup white sesame seeds	¼ cup chopped yellow onion
Water	1 tablespoon fresh lemon juice
3 cups packed cilantro leaves and tender stems, roughly chopped	½ to 1 habanero chile, stemmed and seeded
2 garlic cloves	½ teaspoon kosher salt, plus more to taste

Combine the sesame seeds and ½ cup water in a blender and pulse until the mixture is combined but the seeds are mostly still whole. Add an additional ½ cup water plus the cilantro, garlic, onion, lemon juice, chile, and salt and blend briefly, just until combined but not too smooth. (If you overblend, the sesame seeds can turn bitter.) Taste and add more salt if needed.

Serve immediately or refrigerate in an airtight container for up to 2 weeks.

TOMATO-PEANUT CHUTNEY

This vibrant, easy-to-make chutney was designed to accompany Priya's signature dish, but it is just as good spooned into tacos or over rice—or, depending on how thick you make it, as a fabulous dip.

Makes 2 cups

2 tablespoons extra-virgin olive oil

1 teaspoon black mustard seeds

1¼ pounds tomatoes, diced

1 jalapeño chile, stemmed, seeded, and chopped

2 tablespoons freshly grated ginger

Water

1 tablespoon sugar

¼ cup roasted unsalted peanuts

½ teaspoon kosher salt, plus more to taste

Pour the olive oil into a large skillet over medium heat. Add the mustard seeds and cook, shaking the pan frequently, until they start to pop, 1 to 2 minutes.

Stir in the tomatoes, chile, and ginger. Cook, stirring occasionally, until the tomatoes collapse and exude their juices and the juices thicken, 5 to 7 minutes. Stir in ½ cup water and the sugar. Cook, stirring occasionally, until the tomatoes are very soft, 8 to 10 minutes. Let the mixture cool slightly.

Scrape the tomato mixture into a blender, along with the peanuts and salt. Blend briefly until incorporated but still slightly chunky. Blend in up to ½ cup more water, as needed, to achieve a pourable but thick consistency.

Serve immediately, refrigerate in an airtight container for up to 1 week, or freeze for up to 3 months.

CHICKPEA SAMBAR

4 to 8 servings

2 cups chana dal (dried, split chickpeas), rinsed

Water

2 large Roma (plum) tomatoes, diced

½ yellow onion, thinly sliced

1 small turnip, peeled and cut into 1-inch dice

½ small green bell pepper, cut into 1-inch chunks

1 small to medium carrot, cut into ½-inch chunks

2 tablespoons tamarind concentrate

2 tablespoons sambar masala

1 teaspoon kosher salt, plus more to taste

1 tablespoon vegetable oil

2 small dried red chiles (preferably Kashmiri)

2 teaspoons black mustard seeds

⅛ teaspoon asafoetida (optional)

¼ cup packed cilantro leaves, chopped

This Indian soup is a traditional accompaniment to dosas, but it makes a satisfying light meal on its own. It's often made with red lentils, but my friend Priya Ammu of DC Dosa makes hers with chana dal, split chickpeas. Asafoetida (sometimes called hing or heeng) is a traditional addition, both for its unique umami enhancement and its ability to aid digestion.

In a large saucepan, combine the chana dal with 4 cups water, turn the heat to medium-high, and bring to a boil. Reduce the heat to medium-low, cover, and simmer until the chickpeas have started to soften but are still firm in the center, 20 to 30 minutes.

Add the tomatoes, onion, turnip, bell pepper, and carrots to the pan. Add more water if needed to cover. Increase the heat to medium-high and bring to a boil, then reduce the heat to medium-low, cover, and simmer until the chickpeas are soft but the vegetables are al dente, 7 to 10 minutes.

Stir in the tamarind, sambar masala, and salt and remove from the heat.

Pour the oil into a small sauté pan over medium heat. When it shimmers, add the chiles and mustard seeds and cook, shaking the pan occasionally, until the chiles darken and the mustard seeds pop, 3 to 4 minutes. Add the asafoetida, if desired, and immediately pour the oil mixture on top of the chickpea mixture and stir to combine. Taste and add more salt if needed. Divide among serving bowls, sprinkle the cilantro on top, and serve.

SMOKED JACKFRUIT, WHITE BEAN, AND MUSHROOM TACOS

WITH PINEAPPLE SALSA

Jackfruit has become the darling of the plant-based food world, and it's easy to understand why: the green (unripe) version of the fruit has meatlike strands and a slightly chewy texture that makes it a good stand-in for pulled pork. I like to pair it with beans for protein in one of my favorite preparations: with pineapple salsa in tortillas to evoke traditional Mexican al pastor tacos. Note: I like the jackfruit products of Upton's Naturals and the Jackfruit Company, both of which make fantastic smoked and plain versions. If you use the latter, you might want to add a little more ground chipotle. And if you can find neither but have access to an Asian supermarket, look for canned unripe jackfruit packed in water and add a little more ground chipotle to the mix to make up for the smokiness.

To make the filling: Heat a large cast-iron or other heavy-duty skillet over medium-high heat. Add the mushrooms to the dry skillet and sear, pressing them into the skillet with a spatula for a few seconds at a time, until they are browned, about 2 minutes, then scrape them up and turn over and repeat on the other side. Stir in the jackfruit and 3 tablespoons water. Sauté until the jackfruit is lightly browned, 4 to 5 minutes, breaking it up with the spatula as you cook it. Transfer from the skillet to a plate, scraping up as much of the pan bits and juices as possible.

Pour the olive oil into the skillet. When it shimmers, add the onion and garlic and sauté until tender, about 6 minutes. Stir in the chipotle, salt, and tomato paste and cook until fragrant, about 30 seconds. Stir in the beans, mushrooms, and jackfruit, along with any of the pan bits and juices from the plate, and cook just to warm through, about 30 seconds. If the mixture seems too dry, add water, 2 tablespoons at a time, until it's moist but not saucy. Taste and add more salt if needed. Cover to keep warm.

To make the salsa: In a small bowl, combine the pineapple, cilantro, shallots, chile, lime juice, and salt. Taste and add more salt if needed. (This makes enough for this recipe, but if you have some left over, it keeps for about 3 days in an airtight container in the refrigerator, but it's best eaten fresh.)

Warm the tortillas in a dry skillet over medium-high heat for a few seconds on each side, then transfer them as they're heated to a packet of foil.

To serve, divide the filling among the warm tortillas and top with the salsa.

Makes 12 tacos

FILLING

8 ounces oyster mushrooms, trimmed and cut into bite-size pieces (may substitute creminis)

1 (10-ounce) package smoked jackfruit

Water

2 tablespoons extra-virgin olive oil

1 small yellow or white onion, chopped

2 garlic cloves, chopped

½ teaspoon ground chipotle chile

½ teaspoon kosher salt, plus more to taste

2 tablespoons tomato paste

1¾ cups cooked or canned no-salt-added white beans (may substitute cannellini, navy, or great Northern beans), drained and rinsed

PINEAPPLE SALSA (MAKES ABOUT 1 CUP)

1 cup fresh pineapple chunks, cut into ½-inch cubes

2 tablespoons fresh cilantro, chopped

2 large shallots, finely chopped

1 jalapeño chile, stemmed, seeded, and chopped

2 tablespoons fresh lime juice

½ teaspoon kosher salt, plus more to taste

12 (6-inch) corn tortillas

KIDNEY BEAN AND POBLANO TACOS
WITH QUICK-PICKLED ONIONS

Makes 6 tacos

PICKLED ONIONS

¼ cup fresh grapefruit juice

¼ cup fresh orange juice

¼ cup fresh lime juice

¼ cup white distilled vinegar

1 red onion, thinly sliced

FILLING

2 tablespoons extra-virgin olive oil

2 poblano peppers, stemmed, seeded, and cut into ½-inch slices

1 small yellow onion, chopped

2 large garlic cloves, chopped

½ teaspoon ground cumin

½ teaspoon ground cinnamon

½ teaspoon Spanish smoked paprika (pimentón)

½ teaspoon kosher or sea salt, plus more to taste

½ teaspoon freshly ground black pepper, plus more to taste

1¾ cups cooked or canned no-salt-added red kidney beans (from one 15-ounce can), drained but not rinsed

6 (6-inch) corn tortillas

½ cup Fastest-Ever Smoky Red Salsa (page 216) or your favorite store-bought salsa

½ cup Herb-Marinated Tofu Feta (page 217) or store-bought vegan or dairy feta, crumbled

Toasted pumpkin seeds (pepitas)

As much as I love pinto and black beans in tacos, this recipe proves that kidney beans, with their beautiful crimson color and hearty texture, belong in them, too. I like to pair them with thick slices of mild poblano pepper, whose hint of heat and bitterness sets off the beans' creaminess. And nothing beats the addition of pickled onions; you'll have more than you need for this recipe, but they will keep for weeks in the refrigerator.

To make the pickled onions: Combine the grapefruit juice, orange juice, lime juice, and vinegar in a small saucepan over medium heat. Bring to a boil, turn off the heat, and add the red onion. Let cool in the pan. (To store what you don't need for this recipe, transfer them to a quart-size Mason jar and refrigerate for up to 3 weeks.)

To make the filling: Pour the olive oil into a large skillet over medium heat. When it shimmers, add the poblanos, onion, and garlic and cook, stirring frequently, until the vegetables start to soften, about 4 minutes. Sprinkle in the cumin, cinnamon, paprika, salt, and pepper and cook for another minute or two, until the spices are very fragrant. Stir in the beans, reduce the heat to medium-low, and cook just until warmed through. Taste and add more salt and pepper if needed. Turn off the heat and cover to keep warm.

Warm the tortillas in a dry skillet over medium-high heat for a few seconds on each side, then transfer as they're heated to a packet of foil.

To assemble the tacos, lay out the tortillas and top each with some of the bean-poblano mixture. Top each with a spoonful of the salsa, feta, pumpkin seeds, and a few slices of pickled onions and serve hot.

PUFFY PINTO BEAN TACOS

Makes 8 tacos

SHELLS

1 cup instant masa harina

Water

¼ teaspoon kosher salt, plus more to taste

Grapeseed or other neutral vegetable oil, for frying

FILLING

2 tablespoons extra-virgin olive oil

1 small yellow onion, chopped

4 garlic cloves, finely chopped

1 teaspoon Spanish smoked paprika (pimenton)

1 teaspoon ground cumin

½ teaspoon ground cinnamon

½ teaspoon kosher salt, plus more to taste

¼ teaspoon freshly ground black pepper

1¾ cups cooked or canned no-salt-added pinto beans (from one 15-ounce can), drained but not rinsed (reserve the bean liquid)

1 tablespoon fresh lime juice

½ cup Herb-Marinated Tofu Feta (page 217), or store-bought vegan or dairy feta, crumbled

½ cup Fastest-Ever Smoky Red Salsa (page 216) or your favorite store-bought salsa

Flesh of 1 ripe avocado, sliced

If you've never had one of these Tex-Mex specialties, which are native to San Antonio, now's your chance to make things right. Rather than frying tortillas until they get crispy (or using a prefried taco shell), you start with masa dough, press it as if you're going to make a tortilla, and slip it right into the oil. It flutters and puffs and gets crisp, and you end up with a taco shell that borders on the ethereal. I use the technique described by my favorite source of Tex-Mex recipes, cookbook author and *Homesick Texan* blogger Lisa Fain, with whom I've been happy to have shared plates of enchiladas, beans and rice, and sips—okay, perhaps they were gulps—of margaritas in our home state. The only trick here is in the shaping, which takes a little practice, but even if they don't come out quite right, you can always use them as flat tostadas—or break them up into chips and scoop up the filling as a dip. The eating is messy but delicious.

To make the shells: In a medium bowl, stir together the masa harina, ¾ cup water, and salt until it forms a soft ball the consistency of moist Play-Doh. If it's too dry, add more water, a tablespoon at a time.

Form the dough into a large disk, then use a sharp knife to cut it like a pie into eight equal wedges. Form each one into a ball, then use a tortilla press (lined with plastic wrap) or roll it out with a rolling pin between layers of parchment paper or plastic wrap to a 5- or 6-inch circle. (It's okay if the edges are ragged.) Keep the pressed circles in one layer on a large rimmed baking sheet and cover them with a clean, damp cloth.

Line a large plate with paper towels.

Pour the oil to a depth of 2 inches in a large saucepan set over medium-high heat. Heat the oil until it reaches 350°F on an instant-read thermometer. Use a heatproof spatula to gently lay a tortilla in the oil; it should sink but quickly start to puff and float. After about 10 seconds, use two wooden spoons or spatulas to gently lift each side a bit from underneath to encourage the tortilla to slightly fold into a V-shape. You can also use the pan to help, by pressing the tortilla against it while lifting on one side to encourage the folding. (If the tortilla is puffing up too much on top, try holding one side up with one spoon or spatula while gently pressing in the middle with the other.) Don't try to fold too much, or you won't leave room for fillings. Hold it while it fries for another 20 seconds or so, until light brown and crisp, turning it over in the oil as needed. Use tongs to gently lift it from the oil, letting the excess drip off, and transfer to the paper-towel-lined plate. Repeat with the remaining tortillas.

To make the filling: Pour the olive oil into a large skillet over medium-high heat. When it shimmers, stir in the onion and garlic and sauté until tender, 6 to 8 minutes. Stir in the paprika, cumin, cinnamon, salt, and pepper and sauté just until fragrant, about 30 seconds. Stir in the beans and 1 cup of the reserved bean liquid (add some water if you don't have enough bean liquid) and cook until the beans are heated through and the flavors meld, about 3 minutes. Mash with a fork or potato masher and cook until the beans are thick, 1 to 2 minutes. Turn off the heat and stir in the lime juice. Taste and add more salt if needed.

To serve, spoon the filling into the taco shells and top with the feta, salsa, and avocado slices.

SUPER-GREEN FAVA BEAN FALAFEL

Makes about 40 falafel

1 yellow onion, cut into chunks

1½ cups chopped flat-leaf parsley leaves

1½ cups chopped cilantro leaves and tender stems

1½ cups chopped fresh chives

⅓ cup garlic cloves

1 pound dried split fava beans, soaked overnight and drained

1 tablespoon fine sea salt, plus more to taste

1½ tablespoons ground cumin

1½ tablespoons paprika

1 tablespoon ground coriander

2 teaspoons crushed red pepper flakes

Peanut, sunflower, or other neutral oil, for frying

The Egyptian way with falafel packs them with herbs for something fabulously moist, fluffy, and green inside a crisp brown shell. Serve these stuffed into pita with tahini, hummus, and pickled vegetables, on salads or grains, or as appetizers with the dip of your choice. I adapted this from a fun Egyptian-cooking-lesson day with chef-owner Dina Daniel and her sous chef, Elmer Ramos, at the wonderful Fava Pot in Falls Church, Virginia.

Combine the onion, parsley, cilantro, chives, and garlic in a large bowl.

Combine about one-third of the onion-herb mixture and one-third of the fava beans in the bowl of a large food processor. Process for 10 seconds or so, until the fava beans are about the size of broken grains of rice; the mixture should be very moist and hold together when you squeeze a little into a ball. Stop and scrape down the food processor as needed while you process the mixture. Transfer the mixture to a bowl and repeat two more times with equal parts of the onion-herb mixture and the fava beans.

Add the salt, cumin, paprika, coriander, and red pepper flakes to the bowl and stir to combine.

Set a cooling rack over a large rimmed baking sheet.

Pour the oil into a large deep saucepan or Dutch oven to a depth of 3 inches and set it over medium-high heat. When the oil is hot enough that a little pinch of the falafel mixture bubbles back up to the surface when you drop it in, reduce the heat to medium and start shaping and frying the falafel. Use your hands to make golf-ball-size falafel that are oblong and slightly flattened. (If they are perfectly round, they may not cook through before they are crispy on the outside.)

Working in batches to avoid overcrowding, carefully drop the falafel into the oil and fry, stirring occasionally with a slotted spoon or skimmer to keep them moving, until they are dark brown all over, 5 to 6 minutes. Transfer them to the cooling rack and continue with the remaining falafel. Serve hot.

CHICKPEA AND QUINOA CHORIZO

Makes 5 cups

1 cup dried red quinoa

Water

2¼ teaspoons kosher salt

¾ cup walnuts

2 dried ancho chiles

1 tablespoon ground chipotle chile

1 teaspoon freshly ground black pepper

1 teaspoon dried oregano

1 teaspoon ground cumin

1 teaspoon ground coriander

½ teaspoon whole cloves or ¼ teaspoon ground cloves

1¾ cups cooked or canned no-salt-added chickpeas (from one 15-ounce can), drained and rinsed

½ cup panko-style or other dry bread crumbs

4 garlic cloves, minced

¼ cup apple cider vinegar

⅔ cup grapeseed oil

For years, I've made my version of a tofu "chorizo" recipe by vegan cookbook author Roberto Martin that's so fantastic it has even fooled friends who hail from Mexico. It proved to me that so often the tastes carnivores love—which they think is about the meat—is really about the seasonings. When I set out to make a chorizo using chickpeas, though, I just couldn't get it to work right; the beans have so much moisture and starch in them that it took far too long to get them crumbly; by that point, they were really sandy more than anything. Then I realized that a veggie burger recipe I had been struggling with because it tends to crumble might hold the key. Brooks Headley's recipe for the namesake dish at his hit Superiority Burger joint in Manhattan relies on a combination of chickpeas, red quinoa, and walnuts, and even though the patties are so delicate they are a little vexing to cook, the crispy-edged texture—mainly from the quinoa—is so magical I decided a mash-up was in order. I took the main ingredients in Headley's recipe, left out most of the rest (including onions, carrots, and his own seasonings), and swapped in Martin's flavors (chiles, warming spices, and apple cider vinegar). My new favorite "chorizo" was born: spicy, a little tart, crumbly, chewy (in a good way), and crispy. This recipe uses a good amount of oil, but I think that's a requirement; pork-based chorizo (from what I remember, anyway) is plenty fatty, and that's part of the appeal. This is not health food, but you don't need to eat much at a time. Use it on tacos (my favorite combination is with potatoes, thinly sliced cabbage, and salsa), in burritos, grain bowls, or salads—anywhere you want a punch of flavor.

Combine the quinoa, 1½ cups water, and ¼ teaspoon of the salt in a small saucepan over medium-high heat. Bring to a boil, then reduce to medium-low, cover, and cook until fluffy, about 35 minutes.

While the quinoa is cooking, toast the walnuts: Scatter them into a dry large skillet over medium heat and cook until fragrant and lightly browned, 5 to 6 minutes, shaking the pan occasionally to prevent scorching. Cool, then crush or chop.

Use scissors to cut open the ancho chiles, discarding the stems and seeds. Cut them into ½-inch pieces and transfer them to a food processor (the smaller, the better) or dedicated spice grinder. Add the chipotle, pepper, oregano, cumin, coriander, and cloves and process until finely ground.

In a large bowl, mash the chickpeas with a potato masher or fork. When the quinoa is ready, scrape it into the bowl with the chickpeas and let cool for a few minutes. Stir in the chile-spice mixture, the walnuts, the remaining 2 teaspoons salt, the bread crumbs, garlic, and vinegar and mix until well incorporated. (You might want to use your hands.)

In a large cast-iron or other heavy-duty skillet, heat ⅓ cup of the oil over medium-high heat. Once it shimmers, add half the chickpea mixture. Cook, stirring frequently, for a few minutes until the mixture absorbs most of the oil. Spread it out in the pan and let it cook for a minute or two undisturbed, then stir, scoop, and spread it out again. Repeat until the mixture has turned dark brown and gone from a soft mash to crispy crumbles, about 10 minutes. (The quinoa will pop; that's okay.) Scoop it into a bowl and repeat with the remaining ⅓ cup of the oil and the remaining chickpea mixture.

Use immediately, refrigerate in an airtight container for up to 1 week, or freeze for up to 3 months.

CASSEROLES, PASTA, RICE & HEARTY MAIN COURSES

Beans and grains are inseparable. It has something to do, obviously, with the fact that beans don't have quite all the amino acids that make up a "complete" protein, and neither do grains, but together they do. That's why cultures the world over have paired them—even though we now know that you can combine these complementary proteins over the course of a day rather than in the same dish or even meal, and get the same benefits. But what fun is that? They're great apart and even better together. Not every main-course bean dish needs the combination, of course: set a whole roasted cauliflower on a bed of creamy hummus, and you'll see what I mean.

RATATOUILLE CASSOULET

Two great tastes in one bubbling pot. It was part accident, part inspiration, part recovery: I wanted to see how dried flageolet beans would handle being baked in a tomato sauce underneath layers of thinly sliced summer vegetables. You know, as an addition to the type of ratatouille served at the end of the movie *Ratatouille* that, if you're a purist, is not technically ratatouille at all, but a dish called a tian. I started with one of my favorite, simplest ratatouille recipes, from Deb Perelman's *Smitten Kitchen*. But I diverged in a few key ways: I made the tomato sauce layer extra-soupy, and I covered the pot as it baked, imagining that both those changes would help the beans cook. I added my favorite spice blend, the completely inauthentic za'atar, too. After an hour, when I realized the beans weren't quite done and the whole affair was looking too watery, I took off the lid and kept on baking to evaporate some liquid—but not before adding a layer of bread crumbs, which made a crust that reminded me of that great (but meaty) bean dish from another part of France, and so, ratatouille cassoulet was born. And a glorious birth it was. The za'atar adds welcome depth without being identifiable, so you can feel free to omit mention of it if you have any French diners at your table. This dish takes some time in the oven, making it perfect for those lazy Sundays. And trust me, you want to be home when it's cooking, because the aromas that waft into your house are divine. (If you're hosting a real estate open house, forget chocolate chip cookies: this is what you should put in the oven to evoke comfort and drive a bidding war.)

Preheat the oven to 375°F.

Pour 2 tablespoons of the olive oil into a large, deep ovenproof skillet or flameproof casserole (that has a lid) over medium heat. Add the onion and garlic and cook, stirring occasionally, until tender, about 8 minutes. Stir in the za'atar, ½ teaspoon of the salt, and ¼ teaspoon of the pepper and cook until fragrant, about 30 seconds. Pour in the tomatoes and beans, stir to incorporate, increase the heat to medium-high, and bring to a boil. Turn off the heat.

CONTINUED

6 servings

3 tablespoons extra-virgin olive oil

1 onion, chopped

5 garlic cloves, chopped

3 tablespoons za'atar

1 teaspoon kosher salt

½ teaspoon freshly ground black pepper

1 (28-ounce can) crushed tomatoes, preferably fire-roasted

4 ounces (about ⅔ cup) dried flageolet beans (may substitute cannellini beans or other small white bean), soaked overnight and drained

1 (8-ounce) eggplant (or half a larger eggplant), thinly sliced

1 (8-ounce) zucchini, thinly sliced

1 (8-ounce) yellow summer squash, thinly sliced

1 red bell pepper, thinly sliced

½ cup panko-style or other dry bread crumbs

Starting at the outer edge of the skillet and working your way around, arrange alternating slices of the eggplant, zucchini, and summer squash in concentric circles on top of the tomato-bean mixture, tightly overlapping them. Continue working your way toward the center of the dish and make sure to completely cover the tomato-bean mixture. Arrange the bell pepper on top.

Drizzle the vegetables with the remaining 1 tablespoon oil and sprinkle with the remaining ½ teaspoon salt and ¼ teaspoon pepper.

Cover the skillet and bake for 1 hour; the ratatouille will look soupy, and the beans won't be quite tender. Uncover it, sprinkle with the bread crumbs, return to the oven, uncovered, and bake for another hour, until the bread crumbs are browned, the liquid is thickly bubbling around the edges, and the beans on the bottom layer are very tender.

Let cool for at least 15 minutes before serving. Serve hot, with bread and/or the grain of your choice.

ROOT VEGETABLE, WHITE BEAN, AND MUSHROOM CASSOULET

At his legendary former restaurant Heartland in St. Paul, Minnesota, and now at the Hotel Landing in nearby Wayzata, Lenny Russo has been a locavore's dream chef, cooking with the produce of the upper Midwest even through the winter. "Here, it takes up a good chunk of the year," he says. That means that he's a fellow bean lover. No other plant-based food stores as well as dried beans. Russo combines heirloom beans with other winter storage crops—carrots, celery root, turnip—for a cassoulet that captures the depth and heartiness of the French original with a midwestern American spin. I streamlined (and veganized, of course) his version, keeping intact the backbone of warming spices and root vegetables and, naturally, the white beans that star. Cook them twice—once fairly simply (see Techniques, pages 14–19) and then again with the spices and vegetables. My favorite touch of Russo's: use the starchy bean cooking liquid from round one to cook the other ingredients in round two—and to thicken the stew. You could substitute canned beans and water, but it won't be the same.

Preheat the oven to 375°F.

Pour the olive oil into a Dutch oven or other large pot over medium-high heat. When it shimmers, add the onion, celery, and garlic and sauté until the vegetables are soft, about 6 minutes. Stir in the tomato paste, miso, paprika, salt, nutmeg, cayenne, and cloves and cook until fragrant, about 30 seconds. Stir in the wine and cook, deglazing (scraping the bottom of the pan), for about 1 minute.

Add the carrots, celery root, and turnip and stir to coat. Stir in the tomatoes, beans, and bean cooking liquid, adding more bean liquid and/or water to cover, if needed. Taste and add more salt if needed. Bring to a boil, then turn off the heat.

Scatter the mushrooms on the bean mixture and sprinkle the bread crumbs on top. Drizzle with a little olive oil.

Cover and bake for 45 minutes, until the stew is bubbling around the edges and the root vegetables are tender. Uncover and continue baking until the bread crumbs are browned and the vegetables are very tender, about 45 more minutes. (If you'd like, you can turn the oven to broil for a few minutes to get extra browning on the bread crumb crust.)

Serve hot.

4 to 6 servings

3 tablespoons extra-virgin olive oil, plus more for drizzling

1 large sweet yellow onion, diced into ½-inch pieces

2 celery stalks, diced into ½-inch pieces

2 garlic cloves, sliced

2 tablespoons tomato paste

1 tablespoon red miso

1 teaspoon Spanish smoked paprika (pimentón)

1½ teaspoons kosher salt, plus more to taste

¼ teaspoon ground nutmeg

¼ teaspoon cayenne pepper

¼ teaspoon ground cloves

1 cup dry white wine

3 carrots, diced into ½-inch pieces

1 small celery root, peeled and cut into ½-inch dice

1 medium turnip, peeled and cut into ½-inch dice

2 Roma (plum) tomatoes, chopped

4 cups cooked or canned no-salt-added cannellini, navy, great Northern, or flageolet beans (from three 15-ounce cans) drained (reserve the cooking liquid) and rinsed

2½ cups bean cooking liquid, Vegetable Broth (page 216), store-bought no-salt-added vegetable broth, or water, plus more as needed

12 ounces cremini mushrooms, sliced

1 cup panko-style or other dry bread crumbs

LENTIL–MUSHROOM FARMER'S PIE
WITH TURMERIC–CAULIFLOWER MASH

6 servings

1 cup dried brown or green lentils, picked over and rinsed

Water

2 tablespoons extra-virgin olive oil

1 large onion, chopped

2 carrots, diced

1 pound cremini mushrooms, quartered

2 tablespoons flour

1½ teaspoons kosher salt

½ teaspoon freshly ground black pepper

2 teaspoons chopped thyme leaves

2 tablespoons tomato paste

1 cup Vegetable Broth (page 216) or store-bought no-salt-added vegetable broth

2 tablespoons red wine vinegar

1 cup frozen corn

1 pound Yukon gold potatoes, scrubbed and cut into 1-inch cubes

1 small head cauliflower, cut into florets

1 teaspoon ground turmeric

¼ cup unsalted vegan or dairy butter

Why call this a farmer's pie? Because a shepherd's pie was originally named for the inclusion of ground lamb, and this one uses lentils. (Even though, honestly, a shepherd could just as easily have been interested in consuming vegetables as in consuming members of the flock, don't you think?) Anyhow, I've kept all the comforts of the classic intact, while punching them up here and there. I think any farmer would be proud to serve it, whether he or she grows lentils—or raises sheep.

Combine the lentils and 2½ cups water in a small saucepan over medium-high heat. Bring to a boil, reduce the heat, cover, and simmer until the lentils are tender, 20 to 30 minutes. Drain.

While the lentils are cooking, pour the olive oil into a large skillet over medium heat. Stir in the onion and carrots and sauté until they start to soften, 8 to 10 minutes. Increase the heat to medium-high and stir in the mushrooms. Cook, stirring occasionally, until the mushrooms soften and exude their liquid and it mostly evaporates, about 10 minutes. Stir in the flour, 1 teaspoon of the salt, the pepper, and thyme and cook, stirring, until fragrant, about 30 seconds.

Whisk the tomato paste into the broth and stir it into the mushroom mixture, along with the cooked lentils. Stir in the vinegar and bring the mixture to a gentle boil, then turn off the heat and stir in the corn. Transfer the mixture to a 9 by 13-inch baking dish.

Preheat the oven to 400°F.

Set up a steamer basket over medium-high heat, add the potatoes and cauliflower, and steam until very tender, about 25 minutes. Transfer to a large bowl, add the turmeric, the remaining ½ teaspoon salt, and the butter and mash with a potato masher until smooth and fluffy.

Spread the cauliflower mixture on top of the lentil-mushroom mixture in the dish and bake until the filling is bubbly and the topping starts to brown on the edges, 25 to 30 minutes. Serve hot.

NOTE

You can make the two components—the lentil-mushroom mixture and the cauliflower-potato topping—up to 1 week ahead of time, refrigerate them separately, and then assemble and bake the night you're ready to eat. Bring to room temperature before baking, or add an extra 10 to 15 minutes of baking time.

RAVIOLI E FAGIOLE

This twist on pasta "fazool" takes advantage of fresh shell beans, but you can easily substitute canned or cooked-from-dried beans—just cook them long enough to warm them through. I like to make the dish thick and stewy instead of brothier and soupy. Ravioli instead of small pasta gives it extra heartiness, but feel free to substitute short rigatoni or macaroni.

Pour the olive oil into a Dutch oven or heavy stockpot over medium heat. When it shimmers, add the onion, garlic, bell pepper, and carrot. Sauté until the vegetables start to soften, about 4 minutes. Stir in the salt, paprika, and red pepper flakes and cook, stirring, until fragrant, about 30 seconds.

Stir in the spinach and cook just until wilted, about 30 seconds. Add the tomatoes, 4 cups water, and the beans, increase the heat to medium-high, and bring to a boil. Reduce the heat to low, cover, and cook until the beans are very tender, 30 to 40 minutes.

Uncover, increase the heat to medium, and add the ravioli. Cook for the time suggested on the package, until the pasta is just tender, usually 4 to 6 minutes for small ravioli. Stir in the pepper and Parmesan. Taste and add more salt if needed. Serve hot.

4 servings

1 tablespoon extra-virgin olive oil

1 yellow onion, chopped

4 garlic cloves, thinly sliced

1 red bell pepper, diced into ½-inch pieces

1 carrot, diced into ½-inch pieces

½ teaspoon sea salt, plus more to taste

1 teaspoon Spanish smoked paprika (pimenton)

½ teaspoon crushed red pepper flakes

2 cups baby spinach

1 (28-ounce) can diced or crushed tomatoes, preferably fire-roasted

Water

1 cup fresh cranberry/borlotti, lima, or other shell beans

1 (8- or 9-ounce) package vegan or traditional cheese ravioli

½ teaspoon freshly ground black pepper

¼ cup finely grated vegan or traditional Parmesan

SUCCOTASH RAVIOLI
WITH CHERRY TOMATO-BUTTER SAUCE

Makes about 32 ravioli

FILLING

3 ears corn, husks intact

2 tablespoons extra-virgin olive oil

1 small onion, chopped

2 garlic cloves, chopped

1 red bell pepper, finely chopped

2 cups fresh lima beans (may substitute frozen)

1 teaspoon kosher salt, plus more to taste

½ teaspoon freshly ground black pepper

Water

8 ounces vegan or dairy cream cheese

SAUCE

1 cup unsalted vegan or dairy butter

1 pint Sungold or other cherry tomatoes, halved

¼ cup lightly packed basil leaves, chopped, plus more for garnish

1 teaspoon finely grated lemon zest

2 tablespoons fresh lemon juice

½ teaspoon kosher salt, plus more to taste

Pinch of sugar (optional)

Egg-free wonton/dumpling wrappers (look for Hong Kong–style)

Succotash is one of the defining dishes of summer, a southern classic that celebrates the season's bounty—including corn, bell peppers, tomatoes, and fresh shell beans such as limas. After I saw my friend Cathy Barrow post a photo of cheese ravioli stirred into succotash, I decided to stuff the succotash (or most of the components anyway) into ravioli instead. What a success! The side dish became an elegant main course, with a simple, delectable butter sauce made colorful with cherry tomatoes, basil, and a hit of lemon. If you can't find fresh limas or other shell beans, you may substitute frozen limas; don't bother thawing them before adding—they'll cook long enough to thaw in the pan.

To make the filling: Run water over the corn cobs in their husks and microwave on high for 5 to 7 minutes, until steaming hot. Let cool slightly, then use your fingers to feel where the row of kernels ends on the wide end of the cob (opposite the silk end) and use a sharp knife to cut through those last kernels and through the cob. Holding the silk end, squeeze each cob out of the husk from that end; it should pop out clean and slightly cooked. Rinse if needed to get more of the silks off. Cut each cob in half crosswise, then stand one half at a time on a cutting board, cut side down, and slice off the kernels.

Pour the olive oil into a large deep skillet over medium-high heat. When it shimmers, add the onion, garlic, and bell pepper and sauté until tender, about 6 minutes. Stir in the corn, lima beans, salt, pepper, and ¼ cup water. Reduce the heat to medium, cover, and cook until the beans are tender, 15 to 20 minutes.

Transfer the vegetable mixture to a large bowl and let cool to room temperature. Stir in the cream cheese, taste, and add more salt if needed. Cover and transfer to the freezer to firm up while you make the sauce.

To make the sauce: Rinse and dry the skillet, set it over medium heat, and melt the butter. Add the tomatoes and cook, stirring occasionally, until they collapse and release their juices into the butter, about 5 minutes. Stir in the basil, lemon zest, lemon juice, and salt. Taste and add more salt and a pinch of sugar if desired. Cover to keep warm.

CONTINUED

SUCCOTASH RAVIOLI WITH CHERRY TOMATO-BUTTER SAUCE

CONTINUED

To form the ravioli, set as many wrappers as will fit on a large rimmed baking sheet and place a small dish of water and the cooled ravioli filling nearby. Scoop a heaping tablespoon of the filling into the center of half the wrappers. (I like to use a #40 disher, one of my prized cookie-making implements, which measures out 1½ tablespoons.) Working with 3 or 4 wrappers at a time, dip a finger into the water and use it to paint around the edge of the wrappers with filling on them. Put a second wrapper on top of each and press around the edges to seal, trying to avoid trapping any big air bubbles inside. Turn the wontons over as you work and press around the edges again on the second side. Repeat until you have used all of the filling.

To cook the ravioli, bring a medium pot of salted water to a boil. Reheat the sauce if needed, and keep it covered over low heat. Carefully transfer 4 ravioli into the pot and cook until slippery and translucent, about 3 minutes. Use a slotted spoon to carefully remove the ravioli as they are finished to serving plates. Repeat until all of the ravioli are cooked.

To serve, spoon the sauce over the ravioli on the plates. Sprinkle with more of the chopped basil and serve hot.

CHINESE-STYLE NOODLES
WITH BLACK BEANS AND SHIITAKES

This is a riff on a riff on Chinese zha jiang mian, noodles with pork and fermented bean sauce, that I spied in Milk Street founder Christopher Kimball's cookbook *Milk Street: Tuesday Nights*. Kimball's shortcut involves using prepared black bean garlic sauce instead of the traditional fermented bean paste, while my interpretation replaces the pork with—what else?—black beans. I knew they'd go perfectly, given their presence in the prepared sauce (which you can find in the Asian section of large supermarkets). I also like leaving the mushrooms in bigger pieces for more texture and using thick rice noodles (the hollow ones are like rice bucatini!) instead of Chinese wheat noodles, such as udon, although those work well, too.

Bring a large pot of water to a boil. Add the noodles and cook according to the package instructions, until al dente. Reserve 1 cup of the cooking water, then drain the noodles and rinse under cold water until cold. Drain well.

Pour the oil into a 12-inch skillet over medium-high heat. When it shimmers, add the mushrooms and cook until softened and browned, 6 to 8 minutes.

Stir in the beans and cook for 1 minute, just to heat through. Stir in about three-quarters of the scallions (saving the remaining one-quarter for garnish) and all of the garlic and red pepper flakes and cook until fragrant, about 30 seconds. Stir in the mirin and cook until evaporated. Stir in the reserved cooking water, the black bean sauce, hoisin, and tamari. Bring to a boil, reduce the heat to medium, and simmer, stirring occasionally, until the sauce has thickened and reduced slightly, 4 to 5 minutes. Remove from the heat and stir in the vinegar.

Add the noodles to the skillet and use tongs to toss and coat them with the sauce.

To serve, divide the noodles among serving bowls, spoon any remaining sauce over them, and top with the cucumber and the remaining scallions.

3 to 4 servings

12 ounces thick rice noodles (may substitute udon)

2 tablespoons safflower, grapeseed, or other neutral vegetable oil

8 ounces shiitake mushrooms, stems discarded and caps diced into ½-inch pieces

1½ cups cooked or canned no-salt-added black beans (from one 15-ounce can), drained and rinsed

4 scallions, thinly sliced

4 large garlic cloves, chopped

½ teaspoon crushed red pepper flakes

½ cup mirin (Japanese rice wine)

3 tablespoons black bean garlic sauce

1 tablespoon hoisin sauce

1 tablespoon low-sodium tamari

2 tablespoons unseasoned rice vinegar

½ English cucumber, cut into matchsticks

CREAMY PASTA FAGIOLE

6 servings

1¼ cups extra-virgin olive oil, plus more for drizzling

2 carrots, diced into ½-inch pieces

3 celery stalks, diced into ½-inch pieces

1 yellow onion, diced into ½-inch pieces

1 teaspoon tomato paste

2 cups dry white wine

½ pound dried cannellini beans, soaked overnight and drained

6 cups Vegetable Broth (page 216) or store-bought no-salt-added vegetable broth

1 teaspoon kosher salt, plus more to taste

1 (3 by 5-inch) piece kombu (dried seaweed)

2 bay leaves

2 garlic cloves, smashed

1 sprig of rosemary

½ pound small dried rigatoni, macaroni, or other pasta shapes

Freshly ground black pepper

I had never tasted this classic Italian dish of pasta with beans quite like the one I had at Officina, chef-restaurateur Nick Stefanelli's three-story restaurant and market on DC's Wharf. Creamy, almost silky, and with a super-deep flavor, it was a stunner. When I asked him how he made it, I suppose I shouldn't have been surprised at the answer: he blends some of the cannellini beans with a lot—a lot—of very good extra-virgin olive oil and returns it to the soup. There were some other tricks that he showed me, and I was hooked. I'll never make it another way again. If you want to add even more interest, try stirring in cooked bitter greens such as broccoli rabe, escarole, or mustard greens.

Pour ¼ cup of the olive oil into a Dutch oven or heavy stockpot over medium heat. Stir in the carrots, celery, and onion and cook until the vegetables are very soft, about 10 minutes. Stir in the tomato paste and cook until fragrant, about 30 seconds. Increase the heat to medium-high, pour in the wine, stirring and scraping any bits from the bottom of the pan, and cook for about 10 minutes, until the wine reduces slightly.

Add the beans, broth, salt, kombu, and 1 of the bay leaves. Bring to a boil, then reduce the heat to a simmer, cover, and cook until the beans are tender, about 1 hour. (Alternatively, you can bake them in a 300°F oven until the beans are tender or cook them in a pressure cooker for 18 minutes at high pressure, then let the pressure naturally release.)

While the beans are cooking, in a small saucepan over medium-low heat, combine the remaining 1 cup olive oil, the remaining bay leaf, the garlic, and rosemary. Cook just until the garlic starts to sizzle, 5 to 6 minutes, then remove the pan from the heat and let cool to room temperature.

When the beans are ready, look to see that you have roughly equal parts liquid and beans; if you need more liquid, add more stock or water.

Use a slotted spoon to strain out 1 cup of the cooked beans, reserving all the liquid, and transfer them to the bowl of a food processor or blender. Strain the rosemary, garlic, and bay leaf out of the oil, then pour the oil into the food processor or blender and puree with the beans until smooth.

Return the puree to the pot of beans and set the heat to medium. Bring to a simmer, then add the pasta. Taste and add more salt if needed. Cook the pasta gently (don't rapidly boil), following the suggested time listed on the pasta package, until al dente.

To serve, divide the soup among bowls, drizzle a little olive oil (why not?), and sprinkle with the pepper.

CANNELLINI CANNELLONI

I confess: this is a cart-before-the-horse recipe. That is, I came up with the name first, because I love wordplay, and the technique and combinations second. (Ask me sometime about Romanesco cauliflower with romesco sauce.) But I also knew that white beans would bring an earthy creaminess to the filling for this dish of baked pasta tubes, taking the place of the common ricotta and reuniting with their old friend, Swiss chard. This is one of those bubbly, cheese-topped, comfort-food, cold-night dishes. Oh, and don't fret if you can't find cannelloni shells; manicotti work just as well, even if "Cannellini Manicotti" doesn't have quite the same ring.

Preheat the oven to 400°F.

Pour 2 tablespoons of the olive oil directly into the can of tomatoes. Add ½ teaspoon of the salt, ¼ teaspoon of the pepper, and the oregano and stir to combine.

Strip the chard leaves off the stems. Thinly slice the stems and chop the leaves, keeping them in separate piles.

Pour the remaining 2 tablespoons of the olive oil into a large skillet over medium heat. When it shimmers, add the chard stems, onion, and garlic and cook, stirring frequently, until tender, about 8 minutes. Stir in the remaining ½ teaspoon salt, the remaining ¼ teaspoon pepper, and the red pepper flakes and cook for 30 seconds. Stir in the chard leaves and cook, stirring, until they are tender, about 2 minutes. Turn off the heat, stir in the beans, taste, and add more salt if needed. Use the back of a wooden spoon, a fork, or a potato masher to lightly mash some of the beans.

Transfer the mixture to a bowl and let it cool slightly.

Lightly grease a 9 by 13-inch baking dish with olive oil. Spread 1 cup of the tomato sauce on the bottom of the dish.

Use a teaspoon (a long-handled iced tea spoon with a narrow bowl works particularly well) and your fingers to fill the dried pasta shells with the bean mixture, stuffing them as full as possible. Place the shells in the baking dish as you fill them, packing them tightly.

Pour the remaining tomato sauce over the shells, spreading it so it evenly covers the shells. Sprinkle on the mozzarella and Parmesan, cover the dish with aluminum foil, and bake until the sauce is bubbly and the pasta is tender, about 30 minutes. Uncover and bake until the cheese is lightly browned, about 10 minutes. Serve hot.

4 to 6 servings

4 tablespoons extra-virgin olive oil, plus more for greasing the baking dish

1 (28-ounce) can crushed tomatoes

1 teaspoon sea salt, plus more to taste

½ teaspoon freshly ground black pepper

2 teaspoons dried oregano

2 bunches of Swiss chard

1 onion, chopped

3 garlic cloves, chopped

1 teaspoon crushed red pepper flakes

1¾ cups cooked or canned no-salt-added cannellini beans, drained but not rinsed

1 package (12 pieces) dried cannelloni or manicotti shells

8 ounces grated vegan or traditional part-skim mozzarella

2 ounces finely grated vegan or traditional Parmesan

ENFRIJOLADAS
WITH SWEET POTATOES AND CARAMELIZED ONIONS

Makes 8 enfrijoladas

1½ large onions

5 tablespoons extra-virgin olive oil

1 teaspoon kosher salt, plus more to taste

Water

1 pound sweet potatoes, cut into 1-inch cubes

1 chipotle chile in adobo sauce, plus 1 tablespoon of the sauce, plus more to taste

3½ cups cooked or canned no-salt-added pinto, pinquito, or black beans (from two 15-ounce cans), drained but not rinsed (reserve the liquid)

8 (6-inch) corn tortillas

Flesh of 2 ripe avocados

1 pint cherry tomatoes, quartered

1 cup thinly sliced cabbage, sauerkraut, or curtido

½ cup Herb-Marinated Tofu Feta (page 217), or store-bought vegan or dairy feta (optional)

I was destined to write a bean cookbook years ago, after I became so enamored of the traditional Mexican dish of enfrijoladas—tortillas coated in a bean puree and covered with fresh, crunchy toppings—that I couldn't stop making them. When my dear friend Pati Jinich, star of PBS's *Pati's Mexican Table*, suggested I try rolling them around fillings, much like enchiladas, well, it was obvious my enfrijolada obsession wouldn't end anytime soon. These are a little messy to make but so comforting and satisfying. This is a multi-component recipe, but you can prepare elements in advance: the caramelized onions, the potatoes, the bean puree. Then when it's time to serve, just reheat everything, dip, stuff, roll, top, and serve. You may have some bean puree left over, but you'll be glad you did: it's fabulous in tacos, smeared on tostadas, as a sandwich condiment, or instead of the refried beans in Molletes (page 132).

Thinly slice the whole onion (you should have 3 to 4 cups) for caramelizing and chop the half onion for making the bean puree.

To caramelize the onions, pour 2 tablespoons of the olive oil into a large skillet over medium-high heat. Once it shimmers, add the sliced onion and use tongs to toss them for a few minutes, until they wilt. Stir in ½ teaspoon of the salt, reduce the heat to low, and cook, tossing or stirring occasionally, until they are browned, very soft, and sweet, up to 1 hour.

Meanwhile, bring a Dutch oven or heavy stockpot of salted water to a boil. Add the sweet potatoes and cook until fork-tender, about 10 minutes. Drain.

Rinse out the Dutch oven or stockpot, set it back over medium heat to make the bean puree, and pour in 1 tablespoon of the oil. Add the chopped onion and cook until tender, 8 to 10 minutes. Stir in the remaining ½ teaspoon salt and the chipotle and sauce and cook, stirring, until the chipotle darkens, about 30 seconds. Stir in the beans, 1 cup of their cooking liquid (if you don't have enough liquid, add water), and 1 cup water. Increase the heat to medium-high to bring to a boil, then reduce the heat to low, cover, and simmer until the beans are very soft and the flavors have melded, about 10 minutes. Transfer to a blender or

CONTINUED

use an immersion (handheld) blender to puree until smooth. (You should have about 4 cups.) Add more bean liquid or water until the puree is thick but pourable. Taste and add more salt if needed. Turn off the heat and cover to keep warm.

When the onions are caramelized, scrape them into a bowl and return the skillet to medium heat. Add the cooked sweet potatoes and sauté, stirring occasionally, until the sweet potatoes are starting to brown, about 8 minutes. Stir in the caramelized onions and cook for another minute or so to warm through. Turn off the heat and cover to keep warm.

In another small skillet, heat the remaining 2 tablespoons oil over medium heat. Quickly heat the tortillas in the oil one at a time, for just a few seconds on each side, then let the excess oil drip off and transfer them to a plate lined with paper towels, stacking them as they are ready. (If you have super-fresh tortillas that are soft and pliable, you can instead char them in spots by holding them with tongs over the flame of a gas burner for a few seconds on each side, adding a smoky note to the dish.)

Spoon about ¼ cup of the sweet potato and onion filling in each tortilla, then fold the tortilla around it and move to a serving plate, giving each guest one or two enfrijoladas. Spoon the bean puree generously over the filled tortillas and top with avocado, tomatoes, cabbage, and feta, if desired. Serve hot.

> **NOTE**
>
> If you have super-fresh tortillas that can fold or roll without breaking, you can skip the step of heating them in the oil before assembling the enfrijoladas.

ARROZ NEGRO

You know a recipe is worth publishing when your tester says, "I may eat this every day for the rest of my life. No joke." In Spain, the dish by this name is colored with squid ink and includes seafood, but in parts of Mexico, it refers to a simple preparation of rice cooked in the liquid from a pot of black beans. (This is where you want to make sure not to soak those beans, keeping the liquid inky black rather than paler gray.) I like to add black garlic for its sweet, nutty, slightly fermented flavor and pop of noncolor. Serve with white beans, if you'd like, for a flipped version of black beans and white rice.

In a small saucepan, heat the olive oil over medium-high heat until it shimmers. Stir in the onion and garlic and cook, stirring, until the onion is translucent, about 4 minutes. Stir in the rice and cook, stirring, until it changes color, 2 to 3 minutes. Stir in the salt and bean liquid, bring to a boil, then reduce the heat to low, cover, and cook for 15 minutes.

Turn off the heat, let the rice sit for 10 minutes, then uncover and fluff. Taste and add more salt if needed. Serve hot.

4 servings

1 tablespoon extra-virgin olive oil

½ cup chopped yellow or white onion

4 cloves black garlic, thinly sliced (may substitute regular garlic)

1 cup basmati rice

½ teaspoon kosher salt, plus more to taste

2 cups black bean cooking liquid (from home-cooked beans, not canned)

RIGATONI E CECI

4 servings

3 cups cooked chickpeas, drained and liquid reserved

4 tablespoons extra-virgin olive oil

2 garlic cloves, chopped

1 teaspoon chopped fresh rosemary, plus more for garnish

½ teaspoon kosher salt, plus more as needed

¼ teaspoon freshly ground black pepper, plus more to taste

8 ounces dried rigatoni

There's something so natural about the combination of pasta and legumes, such as in the classic soupy pasta e fagiole, but this might be its apotheosis: half the chickpeas are left whole, and half are pureed with some of their cooking liquid to create a creamy sauce. The rigatoni are sized perfectly for allowing whole chickpeas to slip right inside, and rosemary adds just the right grassy counterpoint. I first published a version of this recipe when I wrote a review about its source, *The Silver Spoon: Quick and Easy Italian Recipes.* When I came back to it years later, it was after a reader told me that he had been playing with its proportions over the years, increasing the amount of chickpeas and liquid to get something much saucier than the original. Good move. Serve with lemon-dressed arugula and fennel, sliced tomatoes and celery, or another crisp, raw salad.

Combine half the chickpeas, 1 cup of their cooking liquid, and 1 tablespoon of the olive oil in the bowl of a food processor or blender and process until smooth.

Heat the remaining 3 tablespoons olive oil in a large deep skillet over medium heat. Add the garlic and rosemary and cook, stirring frequently, until the garlic is lightly browned and soft, 2 to 4 minutes.

Add the pureed chickpeas and the reserved whole chickpeas to the skillet, stir in the salt and pepper, reduce the heat to low, cover, and cook, stirring occasionally until the flavors meld, about 5 minutes. Taste and add more salt and pepper if needed. Reduce the heat to very low to keep warm while the pasta cooks.

Meanwhile, bring a large saucepan of salted water to a boil. Add the rigatoni and cook according to the package directions, until al dente. Drain and then stir the pasta into the chickpea sauce, which will quickly thicken.

Pour the pasta into warm serving dishes, garnish with chopped rosemary, and serve.

NOTE ───────────────────────────────────

It takes 8 ounces of dry chickpeas to yield 3 cups of cooked. You can make this with canned chickpeas and vegetable broth instead of cooked-from-dried and the cooking liquid, but it simply won't be as flavorful.

ORECCHIETTE
WITH BORLOTTI BEANS, BITTER GREENS, AND LEMONY BREAD CRUMBS

I got the idea for this dish from chef Michelle Fuerst, who called the combination of pasta, beans, and bread crumbs her "triple carb threat." Bread crumbs are an essential element of so many great pasta dishes, adding that irresistible crunch that here balances the creamy borlotti (aka cranberry) beans and the al dente pasta. I like using orecchiette for this, because the beans and bread crumbs seem to find themselves nestling in those little ear-shaped cups, but you could use any shape you like. An unorthodox addition is a little red miso, which provides the salt and umami you'd get from, say, anchovies.

Bring a large pot of salted water to a boil.

While the water is heating, pour 2 tablespoons of the olive oil into a medium skillet, preferably nonstick, over medium-high heat. Add the bread crumbs and cook, stirring frequently, until browned, 3 to 5 minutes. Transfer to a small cup and stir in the lemon zest and salt.

Add the pasta to the boiling water and cook according to the package directions, until al dente.

While the pasta is cooking, pour the remaining ¼ cup of the oil into a large deep skillet with a lid or a Dutch oven over medium heat. Add the onion and garlic and sauté until soft, about 6 minutes. Add the greens, cover, and cook, tossing occasionally, just until wilted, 3 to 4 minutes. Uncover and stir in the beans. Turn off the heat and cover to keep warm.

When the pasta is cooked, drain it in a colander, reserving 1 cup of the cooking water.

In a small bowl, whisk the miso with a little of the pasta cooking water and stir it into the bean mixture. Add the pasta, tossing and stirring it into the beans and greens. Add more of the cooking water and/or bean cooking liquid as needed to moisten the pasta and create a little sauce. Stir in one-third of the bread crumbs and the pepper. Taste and add more salt if needed.

Transfer the pasta to a large serving platter or individual shallow bowls or plates and top with the remaining bread crumbs. Drizzle (or squeeze) the lemon juice over the top and sprinkle with the red pepper flakes, if desired. Serve hot.

6 servings

¼ teaspoon kosher salt, plus more as needed

¼ cup plus 2 tablespoons extra-virgin olive oil

1 cup panko-style or other dry bread crumbs

2 tablespoons fresh lemon zest

1 pound dried orecchiette or other pasta shape

1 yellow onion, chopped

3 garlic cloves, chopped

6 cups lightly packed baby bitter greens, such as baby kale, arugula, mizuna, radicchio, or a mix

2 cups cooked borlotti (cranberry) beans, drained and liquid reserved

1 tablespoon red miso

½ teaspoon freshly ground black pepper

1 tablespoon fresh lemon juice

½ teaspoon crushed red pepper flakes (optional)

PENNE
WITH CICERCHIE IN ROSEMARY-SCENTED TOMATO SAUCE

4 servings

1½ cups dried cicerchie, soaked overnight and drained (may substitute chickpeas)

Water

3 tablespoons extra-virgin olive oil, plus more (optional) for drizzling

1 yellow onion, chopped

3 garlic cloves, smashed

½ teaspoon crushed red pepper flakes

1 sprig rosemary

½ teaspoon kosher salt, plus more to taste

1 (28-ounce) can diced tomatoes, preferably fire-roasted

12 ounces dried penne, rigatoni, or other tubular pasta

2 teaspoons finely grated lemon zest

Cicerchie, wild chickpeas that are an ancient staple of southern Italian cooking, look like misshapen corn hominy and taste particularly nutty and intriguing. They are best soaked overnight before cooking, with the soaking water discarded to rid them of compounds that can be toxic—but only if you eat the unsoaked beans every day for months. The idea for the pasta approach came my way from Tuscany-based author, teacher, and tour leader Judy Witts Francini, who said the twice-cooked-beans approach to a pasta sauce is *very* Tuscan. This dish also proves the magical powers of pasta water: the sauce seems too rustic and grainy, but the pasta water pulls it together and smooths it out. The sauce turns a gorgeous rosy orange color reminiscent of a vodka sauce. Look for cicerchie in good Italian markets or by mail-order (see Sources, page 222), or you can substitute chickpeas.

Combine the cicerchie in a large pot with enough water to cover by 3 inches. Bring to a boil, then reduce the heat to simmer, cover, and cook until the cicerchie are tender, 60 to 90 minutes. (Alternatively, you can cook the cicerchie in a pressure cooker for 25 minutes at high pressure, then let the pressure naturally release.)

Pour the olive oil into a large deep skillet with a lid or a Dutch oven over medium heat. Once it shimmers, stir in the onion and garlic and sauté until the onion is translucent, about 5 minutes. Stir in the red pepper flakes, rosemary, and salt and cook until fragrant, about 30 seconds.

Stir in 2 cups of the cicerchie and cook for a minute or two, then stir in the tomatoes. Increase the heat to medium-high to bring the mixture to a boil, then reduce it to low, cover, and simmer until the tomatoes have broken down and thickened into a sauce and the chickpeas are very soft, about 30 minutes.

Fish out the rosemary and use an immersion (handheld) blender to puree the sauce. Stir in the remaining ½ cup cicerchie, reduce the heat to low, cover, and let it keep cooking while you boil the pasta.

Bring a large pot of salted water to a boil and cook the pasta according to the package directions, until al dente. Reserving 2 cups of the cooking water, drain the pasta into a large warmed serving bowl or bowls. Stir 1 cup of the hot pasta water into the cicerchie sauce and add more if needed to loosen and smooth it out. Stir in the lemon zest, taste, and add more salt if needed.

Spoon the sauce over the pasta and drizzle with more olive oil, if desired.

FUSILLI
WITH WHITE BEANS, CHERRY TOMATOES, AND CORN SAUCE

I've been making this simple, summery pasta dish in some form or another for many years, ever since I first realized that the southern technique for "creamed" corn—pulling the natural milky juices out of the cobs rather than adding cream—would make for a perfect pasta sauce. I've taken to tossing in cherry tomatoes for a little color and pop of tartness. My latest addition: southern lady cream peas, beautiful pale little beans in the cowpea family that I buy from Camellia beans of Louisiana. Feel free to substitute black-eyed peas or another variety of cowpea or any white bean of your choice. Note: If you have any Crunchy Spiced Roasted Chickpeas (page 49) around, blitz some of those in the food processor to use instead of bread crumbs, to combine with the nutritional yeast instead of the Parmesan.

Bring a large pot of salted water to a boil. Cook the pasta according to the package directions, until al dente, and drain, reserving 1 cup of the pasta cooking water.

Meanwhile, shuck the corn and rinse the cobs under running water, using your hands to remove as much of the silk as you can.

Set a box grater over a bowl and run 4 of the cobs across the coarse side of the grater. (You should have about 1½ cups "milk" and pulp.) Cut the remaining cobs in half crosswise, then stand one half at a time on a cutting board, cut side down, and slice off the kernels. Keep the whole kernels (about 3 cups) separate from the "milk" and pulp.

Heat the olive oil in a large deep skillet over medium heat. Add the onions and garlic; sauté until lightly browned, about 5 minutes. Reduce the heat to medium-low and continue cooking, stirring occasionally, until the onions are very soft and sweet, about 10 minutes. Increase the heat to medium and add the corn kernels and tomatoes. Sauté until the corn brightens and softens slightly, about 2 minutes. Stir in the lady cream peas and cook until heated through, about 3 minutes.

Add the pasta to the skillet, along with the reserved corn "milk" and pulp. Toss to combine, adding the reserved pasta water a little at a time if the sauce needs loosening. Stir in the Parmesan, plus the salt and pepper. Taste and add more salt and pepper if needed. Stir in the basil, divide the pasta among serving bowls, and serve hot.

8 servings

½ teaspoon kosher salt, plus more as needed

Water

1 pound whole-wheat fusilli, farfalle, or other curly pasta

8 ears fresh corn

2 tablespoons extra-virgin olive oil

2 yellow onions, chopped

4 garlic cloves, thinly sliced

1 pint cherry tomatoes, halved

2 cups cooked and cooled lady cream peas (may substitute cooked or canned no-salt-added navy beans or black-eyed peas, from one 29-ounce can or two 15-ounce cans), drained and rinsed

¼ cup finely grated vegan or traditional Parmesan, or a combination of 2 tablespoons toasted bread crumbs and 2 tablespoons nutritional yeast

½ teaspoon freshly ground black pepper, or more as needed

½ cup packed basil leaves, chopped

PERUVIAN BEANS AND RICE
(TACU TACU)

2 to 4 servings

SALSA CRIOLLA

½ small red onion, thinly sliced

Water

2 tablespoons chopped cilantro leaves

2 tablespoons fresh lime juice

¼ teaspoon aji amarillo paste (may substitute 1 teaspoon Tabasco or other pepper sauce)

¼ teaspoon kosher salt

TACU TACU

3 tablespoons grapeseed, safflower, or other neutral vegetable oil

½ small red onion, chopped

2 garlic cloves, chopped

½ teaspoon kosher salt, plus more to taste

1 teaspoon aji amarillo paste (may substitute 2 teaspoons Tabasco or other pepper sauce)

2 cups cooked or canned canary beans (from two 15-ounce cans), drained and rinsed

1 cup cold (preferably day-old) cooked white rice

1 tablespoon chopped flat-leaf parsley leaves

1 tablespoon chopped fresh oregano

1 lime, cut into wedges

In Peru, this pancake of leftover rice and creamy canary (aka mayacoba or Peruano) beans often comes topped with steak and/or a fried egg, but it's delicious and hearty on its own, especially with a crunchy onion salsa. Some cooks fry individual portions in the oblong shape of an omelet, but I prefer one large cake, which you can divide and serve as you please. Look for aji amarillo paste (made from Peru's favorite chile pepper) at Latin grocery stores or online, or substitute Tabasco.

To make the salsa: Combine the onion with enough cold water to cover, and let sit for at least 10 minutes, then drain. Toss with the cilantro, lime juice, aji amarillo, and salt.

To make the tacu tacu: Pour 1 tablespoon of the oil into a 10-inch nonstick skillet over medium-high heat. Stir in the onion and garlic and sauté until lightly browned, 5 to 6 minutes. Stir in the salt and aji amarillo, and scrape the mixture into the bowl of a food processor. Wipe out the skillet.

Add 1 cup of the canary beans to the food processor and puree briefly until mostly smooth but still chunky. Scrape them into a large bowl. Add the remaining 1 cup canary beans (left whole), the rice, parsley, and oregano to the bowl and stir to thoroughly combine. Taste and add more salt if needed.

Set the skillet back over medium heat and pour in another 1 tablespoon of the oil. Add the rice-and-bean mixture and use a spatula to spread it around evenly and lightly pack it down. Cook until deeply browned on the bottom, about 7 minutes. Remove from the heat, invert a plate (preferably with no rim) on top of the skillet, and carefully flip both over to land the bean-and-rice cake bottom-side up onto the plate. Set the skillet back over medium heat, pour in the remaining 1 tablespoon oil, and slide the cake back into the skillet. Cook for another 7 minutes, or until deeply browned on the other side, then invert the plate and flip the skillet over again to land the cake onto the plate. If the cake cracks or breaks apart, just pat it back together.

Top with the salsa and serve hot with lime wedges.

LENTIL MEATBALLS IN TOMATO SAUCE

**Makes about
32 meatballs**

MEATBALLS

¼ cup plus 2 tablespoons
extra-virgin olive oil

2 tablespoons white or black
chia seeds, ground in a spice
grinder

Water

1 cup large dried brown or
green (not small French) lentils,
picked over and rinsed

1 yellow onion, chopped

4 garlic cloves, chopped

1 teaspoon dried oregano

½ teaspoon Spanish smoked
paprika (pimenton)

1½ teaspoons kosher salt, plus
more to taste

3 cups fresh bread crumbs
(may substitute 1½ cups
panko-style or other dry bread
crumbs)

2 tablespoons nutritional yeast

1 tablespoon fresh lemon juice

TOMATO SAUCE

¼ cup extra-virgin olive oil

2 garlic cloves, smashed

1 teaspoon kosher salt, plus
more to taste

½ teaspoon freshly ground
black pepper

¼ teaspoon crushed red
pepper flakes

2 (28-ounce) cans crushed
tomatoes

6 large basil leaves, shredded

These tender meatless meatballs get their earthy taste from lentils and their lightness from the addition of fresh bread crumbs. I was inspired to make them after I tried my friend Domenica Marchetti's great recipe for eggplant "meatballs" in *The Glorious Vegetables of Italy*. They are even better the next day. Serve over pasta of your choice or with crusty bread and a salad.

Preheat the oven to 350°F.

To make the meatballs: Pour ¼ cup of the olive oil into a large rimmed baking sheet and set it in the oven while it heats.

Combine the chia seeds and 6 tablespoons water in a small bowl and whisk to combine. Let them sit while you continue making the meatballs; the mixture needs at least 10 minutes to fully gel.

Meanwhile, combine the lentils in a small saucepan with 3 cups water over medium-high heat. Bring to a boil, reduce the heat to medium-low, cover, and simmer until tender, about 15 minutes. Drain and let cool.

Pour the remaining 2 tablespoons olive oil into a large deep skillet over medium-high heat. When it shimmers, add the onion and garlic. Sauté until tender, about 6 minutes, then stir in the oregano, paprika, and salt and cook until fragrant, about 30 seconds.

Transfer the onion mixture (including any oil in the pan) to the bowl of a food processor, along with the bread crumbs, nutritional yeast, lemon juice, cooked lentils, and chia "eggs." Pulse until the mixture comes together but leave the texture chunky. Taste and add more salt if needed.

Set a small bowl of water at your work station. Wet your hands and scoop up golf-ball-size portions of the lentil mixture and roll them into balls. When they're all formed, slightly flatten them with your hands. Remove the baking sheet from the oven (being careful not to slosh out any of the hot oil) and transfer the slightly flattened balls to the sheet. Return to the oven and bake until the meatballs are dark brown on the bottom, about 30 minutes. Carefully turn the meatballs over with a spatula and cook until the other side is dark brown, about 20 minutes. Remove the meatballs from the sheet, transfer to a platter, and let cool for 10 to 15 minutes to firm them up on the inside.

While the meatballs are baking, make the tomato sauce: set the same skillet you used to cook the onion mixture for the meatballs over medium-low heat and pour in the olive oil. Add the smashed garlic cloves and warm them in the oil, pressing down on them with a spoon to release their flavor. Cook until the garlic begins to sizzle, 2 to 3 minutes; do not let them brown. Stir in the salt, pepper, and red pepper flakes and cook until fragrant, about 30 seconds. Carefully stir in the crushed tomatoes. Bring to a boil, then reduce the heat to medium-low and cook, stirring occasionally, until the sauce darkens and thickens and the oil has started pooling on the surface, 20 to 25 minutes. Taste and add more salt if needed. Remove from the heat and stir in the basil. Cover to keep warm.

When the meatballs are finished baking, transfer them to the sauce, gently turning them to coat, and return the pan to medium heat. Cover and cook for a few minutes until heated through. Serve hot, with bread or over the pasta of your choice.

BLACK BEAN CHILAQUILES

2 servings

Vegetable oil, for frying

4 (6-inch) corn tortillas, stacked and cut into 8 wedges

½ teaspoon kosher salt

1 cup Salsa Madre black bean puree (page 35) or see Note below

Water

1 tablespoon extra-virgin olive oil

½ cup Quick and Simple Charred Salsa Verde (page 217) or store-bought salsa verde, plus more for serving

Flesh of 1 ripe avocado, cubed

2 scallions, thinly sliced

½ cup Herb-Marinated Tofu Feta (page 217), store-bought vegan or dairy feta, or other vegan cheese, shredded

I've had two styles of chilaquiles, the Mexican breakfast dish of tortillas, salsa, and (sometimes) eggs: one baked into a casserole, making it almost like deconstructed enchiladas, and the other, more popular (and, frankly, better) version, a skillet affair that keeps the tortilla chips crisp. This is the latter, and it is a very casual, adaptable dish, often made for just one or two servings. To me, the key is to not use so much salsa that the chips get soggy. Some of my favorite versions, at the Red Tree House bed-and-breakfast in Mexico City and at DC chef Christian Irabién's restaurant Amparo Fondita, start with a base of pureed black beans.

In a large cast-iron or other heavy-duty skillet over medium-high heat, pour the vegetable oil to a depth of ½ inch. Once it shimmers, fry the tortilla wedges—working in batches to avoid overcrowding—until crisp, about 2 minutes, turning halfway through. Use a slotted spoon to transfer them to a paper-towel-lined plate. Sprinkle with the salt. Pour out the oil, cool it, and strain for another use.

In a small saucepan over medium heat, spoon in the black bean puree and whisk in ½ cup water to combine. Bring to a simmer, then turn off the heat and cover to keep warm.

Set the skillet back over medium heat and pour in the olive oil. When it shimmers, pour in the salsa verde, swirl to coat the bottom of the pan, then quickly add the fried tortilla wedges. Use a spatula to scoop them up and turn them over a time or two to coat in the salsa. Turn off the heat.

Divide the black bean puree among two shallow bowls or plates. Top with the tortillas and salsa from the skillet. Add the avocado, scallions, feta, and a few more dollops of fresh salsa. Serve hot.

NOTE ———

If you're in a hurry and don't have any Salsa Madre on hand, combine in a blender 1½ cups cooked or no-salt-added canned black beans, rinsed and drained, with ¼ teaspoon kosher salt, ½ teaspoon ground cumin, and just enough water or bean cooking liquid to help the blender blades turn; blend until smooth.

TOFU MIGAS
WITH BLACK BEANS AND NOPALES

I have such fond memories of migas from my college days in Austin. Back then, no self-respecting Tex-Mex joint would throw the black beans right into the mix of scrambled eggs, tortillas, salsa, and cheese but instead kept the beans on the side. But with all that already going on, why not? I make them this way all the time now. My other upgrade is to add nopales (cactus paddles), after my friend Pati Jinich, star of PBS's *Pati's Mexican Table*, showed me how easy they are to work with—especially if you can find them in a Latin grocery where they've already been scraped of their thorns. If you can't, it's a bit of a messy process—dare I say thorny?—but worth it. (Tip: Use plastic gloves to protect your hands.) I love using nopales in tofu migas, because their gelatinous aspect comes in handy: it makes the migas creamier!

Rinse the cactus paddle under cold water, being careful to avoid the small thorns on its surface. Using a vegetable peeler or small sharp knife, peel away the thorns and the darker bumps where thorns grow but try not to peel off too much of the dark green skin. Trim off about ¼ inch around the edge of the paddle and ½ inch off the thick base. Dice into ½-inch squares.

Pour the oil into a large skillet over medium heat. Add the tortilla pieces and cook, stirring occasionally, until they turn crisp. (Work in batches if necessary.) Scoop the pieces out onto a plate.

Pour a little more oil into the pan if needed, add the diced cactus paddle, onion, and garlic and cook, stirring occasionally, until the cactus turns from bright to khaki green and the onion and garlic are soft, about 10 minutes. Add the tomato and cook until it softens, 4 to 5 minutes. Stir in both types of tofu, turmeric, salt, cumin, and paprika and cook, stirring frequently, until the tofu is completely colored yellow and is heated through, about 2 minutes.

Stir in the fried tortilla pieces, beans, salsa verde, and cheese and cook, stirring, until the cheese melts. Remove from the heat, taste, and add more salt if needed. Stir in the cilantro and serve immediately.

4 to 6 servings

1 cactus paddle (may substitute 2 poblano chiles, stemmed, seeded, and diced)

2 tablespoons grapeseed or other neutral vegetable oil, plus more as needed

4 (6-inch) corn tortillas, cut or torn into bite-size pieces

1 small onion, cut into ¼-inch dice

4 garlic cloves, finely chopped

1 Roma (plum) tomato, chopped

7 ounces medium or firm water-packed tofu, drained (but not pressed) and crumbled

7 ounces silken tofu, drained and mashed (preferably in a shelf-stable aseptic package, not packed in water and refrigerated)

1 teaspoon ground turmeric

1 teaspoon kosher salt, plus more to taste

½ teaspoon ground cumin

½ teaspoon Spanish smoked paprika (pimentón)

1 cup cooked or no-salt-added canned black beans (from one 15-ounce can), drained and rinsed

½ cup Quick and Simple Charred Salsa Verde (page 217) or store-bought salsa verde

½ cup grated vegan or traditional cheddar cheese

¼ cup lightly packed cilantro leaves

PAELLA
WITH CHICKPEAS, GREEN BEANS, AND SHISHITO PEPPERS

Ever since the first time I traveled to Spain and followed expert advice to go to a paella restaurant south of Valencia, I've been making the dish at home fairly regularly. It's such a perfect dinner party centerpiece: it feeds—and wows—a crowd, can be made ahead and served at room temperature, and you really need only a salad, a good wine, and perhaps some nice crusty bread to complete the meal. Unlike popular misconception, paella doesn't require seafood, and there are many, many versions, including plenty that are all veg. Since Spain is also in love with chickpeas, I like to add them to my paellas; in this instance, with green beans and shishito peppers, but you can sub in any of your favorite seasonal vegetables. I learned the techniques for a good paella from the late cookbook author Penelope Casas; now I improvise to my heart's content. If you don't have a large paella pan, use two of your biggest skillets.

Preheat the oven to 400°F.

In a saucepan, combine the broth and saffron over medium-high heat, bring to a boil, then reduce the heat to low and cover while you assemble the paella.

Set a box grater over a bowl and run the cut side of the tomatoes across the coarse side of the grater, continuing until you are left with just the skin.

Heat a 17- to 18-inch paella pan over two or three burners or heat two 10- to 11-inch cast-iron skillets over medium-high heat. Pour in the olive oil and when it shimmers, add the shishitos, searing each side for a minute or two, then use tongs to transfer them to a plate.

Stir in the onion, garlic, and bell peppers and cook, stirring frequently, until the vegetables are soft, 6 to 8 minutes. Stir in the paprika, cumin, and salt and cook until fragrant, about 30 seconds. Stir in the green beans and cook, stirring frequently, until they lose a little of their crunch.

Stir in the tomato pulp and parsley and cook for about 30 seconds, then stir in the rice, coating it well with the pan mixture. Stir in the broth, chickpeas, and spinach, taste, and add more salt if needed. Cook, stirring and rotating the pan occasionally, until the mixture is no longer soupy, but the rice is still covered by liquid, about 5 minutes.

Nestle the shishitos on the rice and transfer the pan to the oven. Bake, uncovered, until the rice is al dente, 12 to 15 minutes. Remove, cover with aluminum foil, and let it sit for 10 minutes, until the rice is fully cooked.

Serve hot, with the aioli on the side.

8 to 10 servings

6 cups Vegetable Broth (page 216) or store-bought no-salt-added vegetable broth

¼ teaspoon crumbled saffron threads

2 tomatoes, halved

½ cup extra-virgin olive oil

24 small shishito peppers, stemmed but left whole

1 large yellow onion, chopped

6 garlic cloves, chopped

2 red bell peppers, chopped

2 teaspoons Spanish smoked paprika (pimenton)

1 teaspoon ground cumin

1 teaspoon kosher salt, plus more to taste

1 pound fresh green beans, cut into 1-inch pieces

¼ cup finely chopped flat-leaf parsley leaves

3 cups imported Spanish rice, preferably Calasparra (may substitute Arborio)

3 cups cooked or canned no-salt-added chickpeas (from one 29-ounce can or two 15-ounce cans), drained and rinsed

2 cups spinach, chopped

1 cup Chickpea Aioli (page 214) or store-bought vegan or traditional mayonnaise, mixed with 1 finely chopped garlic clove

CHICKPEA AND MUSHROOM PUTTANESCA
WITH CRISPY POLENTA

4 to 6 servings

POLENTA

Water

1½ teaspoons kosher salt, plus more to taste

1 cup coarse-ground polenta or yellow cornmeal

2 tablespoons vegan or dairy butter

PUTTANESCA

2 tablespoons extra-virgin olive oil

1 yellow onion, chopped

4 garlic cloves, chopped

½ teaspoon kosher salt, plus more to taste

½ teaspoon freshly ground black pepper

1 teaspoon crushed red pepper flakes

8 ounces cremini mushrooms, chopped

1¾ cups cooked or canned no-salt-added chickpeas (from one 15-ounce can), drained and rinsed

1 (28-ounce) can crushed tomatoes, preferably fire-roasted

½ cup pitted oil-packed olives, chopped

¼ cup salt-packed capers, soaked in warm water for at least 15 minutes and drained

¼ cup lightly packed flat-leaf parsley leaves, chopped

2 tablespoons fresh lemon juice

2 tablespoons extra-virgin olive oil, plus more for oiling the dish

To me, there are few things tastier than a puttanesca sauce, that Italian workhorse that may or may not have been named for prostitutes who wanted something quick to serve their clients. It takes humble pantry ingredients and elevates them into something far greater than its parts: a tangy, spicy, slightly sweet sauce that's meant for pasta—but here goes wonderfully with pan-fried polenta squares. Consider the pan-frying optional, since you can ladle the puttanesca over the warm, creamy grain—or easier still, over pasta or even roasted sweet potatoes (I know it's heresy, but trust me).

To make the polenta (using Marcella Hazan's method): Combine 4 cups water and the salt in a small saucepan over medium-high heat and bring to a boil. Add the polenta in a thin stream while whisking. Reduce the heat to medium and continue whisking for 1 minute. Reduce the heat to low, cover the pan, and cook gently for 45 minutes, stirring with a wooden spoon for a minute or so every 10 minutes. Remove from the heat and whisk in the butter. Taste and add more salt if needed.

While the polenta is cooking, make the puttanesca: Pour the olive oil into a Dutch oven or heavy stockpot set over medium-high heat. Add the onion and garlic and sauté until soft, 6 to 8 minutes. Stir in the salt, pepper, and red pepper flakes and sauté until fragrant, 30 seconds. Stir in the mushrooms and cook until they collapse, 2 to 3 minutes. Add the chickpeas, tomatoes, olives, and capers. Stir to combine, bring to a boil, then reduce the heat to low, cover, and simmer until the sauce darkens and the flavors meld, about 15 minutes. Stir in the parsley and lemon juice, taste, and add more salt if needed. Keep covered over very low heat to keep warm while you fry the polenta.

When the polenta is finished, lightly oil a 9 by 13-inch glass Pyrex dish, pour in the polenta and refrigerate, uncovered, until set, about 30 minutes. (If you want to make this ahead, cover with plastic wrap at this point and refrigerate for up to 5 days.)

Turn the polenta out onto a work surface and cut into 8 equal squarish pieces.

Heat a large nonstick skillet over medium-high heat, pour in the olive oil and once it shimmers, add as many polenta squares as will fit without overcrowding. Fry until crisp and browned, 6 to 8 minutes per side. (Use a splatter screen, if necessary, to avoid the popping oil from the moist polenta.)

Transfer to serving plates and top with the puttanesca.

MOONG DAL KHICHDI
WITH SPINACH

Khichdi is Indian home cooking at its most comforting, as the lentils and rice cook together to become very soft and almost porridgelike. Seemingly every family in India has its own version. This one, from Priya Ammu of DC Dosa, adds baby spinach for extra color and nutrition. Look for asafoetida in Indian markets; it is sometimes called heeng or hing.

Combine the rice and mung beans in a fine-mesh strainer and rinse with water over a bowl until the water runs mostly clear. Turn out the rice and beans into a bowl, add water to cover by at least 2 inches, and soak for 2 hours. Drain and rinse.

Pour the oil into a Dutch oven or heavy stockpot over medium-high heat. Once it shimmers, add the cumin seeds, bay leaves, and cardamom and cook, stirring, until the spices darken and the oil becomes very fragrant, about 30 seconds. Stir in the onion, ginger, garlic, and asafoetida and cook, stirring frequently, until the onion turns golden brown, 6 to 8 minutes. Stir in the spinach and cook just until wilted.

Add the drained rice and mung beans and cook, stirring, until they are well coated in the oil, about 2 minutes. Add 4 cups water, the turmeric, and salt and bring to a boil. Reduce the heat to low, cover, and simmer until the water is fully absorbed, 10 to 12 minutes. Remove from the heat and let sit, covered, for 10 minutes, then taste, stir in more salt if needed, and serve hot.

4 servings

1 cup basmati rice

1 cup dried split mung beans (moong dal)

Water

3 tablespoons vegetable oil

2 teaspoons cumin seeds

2 bay leaves

2 black cardamom pods

½ yellow onion, thinly sliced

3 tablespoons freshly grated ginger

3 garlic cloves, chopped

½ teaspoon asafoetida

2 cups packed baby spinach, chopped

½ teaspoon ground turmeric

2 teaspoons kosher salt, plus more to taste

SHOW-STOPPING WHOLE ROASTED CAULIFLOWER

4 to 6 main-course servings with sides or 8 appetizer or side-dish servings

¼ cup extra-virgin olive oil, plus more for drizzling

4 garlic cloves, finely chopped

1 tablespoon finely grated lemon zest

1 teaspoon sea salt

1 large head cauliflower

⅓ cup tahini

3 tablespoons za'atar

1 teaspoon black sesame seeds

2 cups Black Chickpea Hummus with Black Garlic and Preserved Lemon (page 42) or other hummus of your choice

Crunchy Spiced Roasted Chickpeas (page 49), extra cooked black chickpeas, baby spinach leaves, and/or chopped preserved lemon (for optional garnishes)

Tahini and za'atar give this cauliflower a burnished, flavor-packed crust. I like to serve it over a bed of hummus—particularly the super-nutty Black Chickpea Hummus on page 42, although you can use any of the hummi in the book (or your own favorite) if you'd like. Scatter roasted chickpeas around for extra texture.

Preheat the oven to 400°F.

In a small bowl, stir together the olive oil, garlic, lemon zest, and salt.

Place the cauliflower, stem side up, on a cutting board. Using a sharp paring knife, cut out the tough stem, core, and leaves while being careful to leave the head and florets intact and connected.

Turn the cauliflower over and set it in a large cast-iron skillet or on a large rimmed baking sheet. Use your hands to rub it all over (including underneath) with the oil mixture.

Cover the skillet tightly with aluminum foil and roast for 30 minutes. Remove the foil and continue roasting, uncovered, for 20 minutes. Remove the skillet from the oven, carefully tilt it to one side, and use a tablespoon to baste it with the oil from the pan.

If the tahini is particularly thick, microwave it in a small bowl on high until pourable, 20 to 30 seconds. Drizzle or brush the cauliflower with the tahini, coating the cauliflower completely, and sprinkle with 2 tablespoons of the za'atar and ½ teaspoon of the sesame seeds. Continue roasting until the cauliflower is browned and tender all the way through when pierced with a skewer, 20 to 30 minutes, basting occasionally.

To serve, spread the hummus on a platter. Set the cauliflower on top and sprinkle the whole platter with the remaining 1 tablespoon za'atar and the remaining ½ teaspoon sesame seeds. Drizzle it with a little olive oil. Garnish with the chickpeas, spinach, and/or preserved lemon, as desired.

CRISPY HOPPIN' JOHN
WITH SMOKED TOFU

8 servings

BLACK-EYED PEAS

3 tablespoons vegetable oil

8 ounces smoked tofu, cut into ½-inch cubes

1 cup chopped yellow onion

1 carrot, chopped

2 celery stalks, chopped

2 teaspoons kosher salt

1 teaspoon freshly ground black pepper

1 tablespoon dried thyme

1½ cups dried black-eyed peas, rinsed

Water

RICE

Water

1½ cups jasmine rice

½ teaspoon kosher salt

1 tablespoon extra-virgin olive oil

HOPPIN' JOHN

Kosher salt to taste (if needed)

2 tablespoons vegetable oil

Flat-leaf parsley leaves, for garnish

Hot sauce, for serving

This recipe turns hoppin' John—a fluffy pilaf of black-eyed peas and rice—into a crispy cake. It's an inspired interpretation from Philly chef Valerie Erwin, who served this (with ham instead of my smoked tofu) when she had Geechee Girl Rice Cafe. The trick is in making sure your black-eyed peas and your rice are cold, which is a problem for me, because I always want to eat some of the peas immediately. The solution? Don't resist: feel free to take a cup or two of the peas and eat or serve them over a cup or two of the rice. The next day, mix equal parts of the black-eyed pea mixture and rice and make the cake.

To cook the black-eyed peas: Pour 2 tablespoons of the oil into a large skillet over medium heat. When it shimmers, add the tofu cubes and fry, turning them frequently, until crispy on all sides, about 10 minutes. Use a slotted spoon to transfer them to a paper-towel-lined plate.

Pour the remaining 1 tablespoon oil into the skillet, still over medium heat. When it shimmers, add the onion, carrot, and celery and sauté until tender, about 10 minutes. Stir in the salt, pepper, and thyme and cook until fragrant, about 30 seconds. Stir in the black-eyed peas and 4 cups water, bring to a boil, then reduce the heat to medium-low and cook, uncovered, until the black-eyed peas are tender, 35 to 45 minutes, adding more water if needed to keep the peas covered. Stir in the fried tofu cubes. Let cool to room temperature and then refrigerate in an airtight container for up to 1 week.

While the black-eyed peas are cooking, make the rice: Combine 3 cups water, the rice, salt, and olive oil in a medium saucepan over medium-high heat. Bring to a boil, reduce the heat to low, cover, and cook for 15 minutes. Turn off the heat, let sit for 15 minutes, then uncover and fluff with a fork. Let cool to room temperature and then refrigerate in an airtight container for up to 1 week.

Preheat the oven to 500°F.

To make the Hoppin' John: Measure out the cold rice and transfer it to a large bowl. Use a slotted spoon to scoop out the same amount of the black-eyed pea mixture and add it to the rice in the bowl, leaving the liquid behind. (You can save the liquid to drink as a delicious broth.) Mix well. Taste and add more salt if needed.

Pour the oil into a large ovenproof skillet, preferably nonstick, over medium heat. When it shimmers, scoop in the black-eyed pea–rice mixture and pat it to an even thickness. Transfer to the oven and bake until deep brown around the edges, 20 to 30 minutes. Remove from the oven and let it rest for 10 minutes. If you've used a nonstick skillet, slide the cake onto a large platter, then invert another platter over it and turn it over so the crispy bottom of the hoppin' John is now on top. If you've used a regular skillet, you'll probably want to scoop it out of the pan in pieces—it won't look quite as polished but will be just as tasty.

Garnish with the parsley and serve with the hot sauce.

THREE SISTERS MINI TAMAL PIES

8 servings

FILLING

8 ounces peeled and seeded winter squash (see headnote), cut into ½-inch cubes

1 tablespoon extra-virgin olive oil, plus more for oiling the ramekins

¾ teaspoon kosher salt, plus more as needed

½ teaspoon freshly ground black pepper

3 cups cooked or canned no-salt-added red kidney beans (from one 29-ounce can or two 15-ounce cans), drained and rinsed

½ teaspoon ground cumin

½ teaspoon Spanish smoked paprika (pimenton)

MASA

½ cup plus 1 tablespoon vegetable shortening

¼ teaspoon kosher salt

Water

¾ teaspoon baking powder

12 ounces (a scant 2½ cups) instant masa harina

2⅔ cups Vegetable Broth (page 216) or store-bought no-salt-added vegetable broth

½ cup Herb-Marinated Tofu Feta (page 217) or store-bought vegan or dairy feta, crumbled, plus more for optional garnish

1 cup Quick and Simple Charred Salsa Verde (page 217) or store-bought salsa verde

Cilantro leaves, for garnish

These special-occasion-worthy tamales, inspired by the Native American gardening philosophy called "three sisters" (the coplanting of squash, beans, and corn), were the product of one of my Saturday cooking sessions with buddy and public-television star Pati Jinich, designed for one of my Weeknight Vegetarian columns in the *Washington Post*. When Pati told me she sometimes likes to layer tamales into ramekins instead of wrapping them in corn husks, I was excited to try it. My contribution: to suggest that we turn the tamales out of the ramekins for serving, onto a pool of salsa, to show off all the layers. They pop out so easily! Feel free to play around with the winter squash variety—delicata, butternut, acorn, or another (except spaghetti, whose texture won't work)—or sub in sweet potatoes, carrots, or even roasted cauliflower. The beans, too, are flexible; try black, pinto, or really anything you like. You'll need eight 6-ounce ramekins.

Preheat the oven to 375°F.

To make the filling: Toss together the squash, olive oil, ½ teaspoon of the salt, and the pepper on a large rimmed baking sheet. Roast until the squash is fork-tender, 15 to 20 minutes; leave the oven on.

Combine the beans, cumin, the paprika, and the remaining ¼ teaspoon salt in a large bowl. Taste and add more salt as needed.

To make the masa: Spoon the shortening into the bowl of a stand mixer fitted with the paddle attachment; beat on medium-high speed until lightened, about 1 minute. Add the salt and ¾ teaspoon cold water; continue to beat until the mixture is white and spongy, about 2 minutes. Reduce the speed to low, sprinkle in the baking powder and add about ½ cup of the masa, then gradually increase the speed to medium-high and beat until the masa is incorporated.

Again reduce the speed to low, then add about ½ cup of the broth; gradually increase the speed to medium-high and beat until well incorporated. Repeat, alternating between the masa and the broth, until both are incorporated, then increase the speed to high and continue beating until the dough is very fluffy, 3 to 6 minutes. Test to see if it's ready by dropping ½ teaspoon of the dough into a cup of cold water; if it floats, the masa is ready. If not, continue beating.

When ready to assemble, lightly oil the eight 6-ounce ramekins.

Use a spoon to drop ¼ cup of masa dough into the bottom of each ramekin, then spread it evenly. Top with a few tablespoons of squash, ¼ cup beans, and 1 tablespoon feta. Spoon ¼ cup of masa dough onto the top of each ramekin and spread it evenly, smoothing the top.

Spray the shiny side of eight pieces of heavy-duty aluminum foil with cooking spray and use the pieces to tightly cover the ramekins, shiny side down. Transfer the ramekins to a large rimmed baking sheet and bake until the tops are slightly puffed, firm, and dry to the touch when you check under the foil, about 1 hour. Leave covered and let cool slightly, then uncover. Run a knife around the edges to loosen and invert onto small plates to unmold.

To serve, spoon about 2 tablespoons of the salsa verde around and over each tamal. Top each portion with a little feta, if desired, and some cilantro leaves. Serve warm.

NOTE

The roasted squash and spiced beans can be refrigerated in an airtight container for up to 1 week. The assembled pies can be refrigerated for up to 3 days before baking. The baked pies can be refrigerated for up to 3 days; let them come to room temperature and reheat in a 200°F oven.

YOU NAME IT GALETTE

This open-faced tart is my homage to Shirley Caesar, whose "beans, greens, potatoes, tomatoes" sermon got sampled into a video song—punctuated by her cries of "You name it!"—that went viral. I was also inspired by food writer and pastry chef Polina Chesnakova's gorgeous galette dough, which is so easy to handle and adaptable for any sweet or savory filling. Inside is a base of ricotta and cheese, topped with sautéed kale and onions, tomato sauce–coated potato slices, and red kidney beans. Feel free to sub in your favorite seasonal vegetables—you name it!—but keep the ricotta base, which protects the bottom crust from getting soggy.

To make the dough: Combine the flour, cornmeal, sugar, and salt in the bowl of a food processor. Pulse a few times to combine. Add the cubed butter and pulse or process briefly until the mixture resembles coarse meal.

Mix 2 tablespoons ice water and the yogurt in a small cup, then drizzle it into the mixture while pulsing to combine. The dough should be hydrated but not sticky; when you pinch it into clumps, it should hold together. Add more water a little at a time if needed. Transfer the dough to the countertop, gather it into one mass, and form it into a disk. Wrap it in plastic wrap and freeze it while you make the filling. (If desired, you can refrigerate for up to 1 hour or overnight.)

To make the filling: In a medium bowl, stir together the shredded cheese, ricotta, and za'atar. Prick the potatoes with a fork and microwave on high for 2 minutes, then let cool.

Pour the olive oil into a large skillet over medium-high heat. When the oil shimmers, add the onion and garlic and sauté until tender, 6 to 8 minutes. Stir in the red pepper flakes and salt and sauté briefly, just until fragrant. Add the kale and sauté until it is tender, about 10 minutes, then stir in the beans. Increase the heat to high to cook off as much of the remaining liquid as possible, being careful not to scorch the kale. Turn off the heat, taste, and add more salt if needed. Let cool.

When the potatoes have cooled, cut them into very thin slices, using a mandoline if necessary.

CONTINUED

4 to 6 servings

DOUGH

1 cup flour, plus more as needed

¼ cup medium- or fine-ground cornmeal

1 teaspoon sugar

½ teaspoon kosher salt

½ cup cold unsalted vegan or dairy butter, cut into cubes

Ice water

2 tablespoons Coconut–Cashew Yogurt (page 215) or store-bought vegan or dairy yogurt

FILLING

¼ cup shredded vegan or dairy cheese, plus more for sprinkling

1 cup vegan or dairy ricotta

2 tablespoons za'atar

6 ounces small red potatoes, scrubbed

2 tablespoons extra-virgin olive oil, plus more for drizzling

1 small onion, thinly sliced

3 garlic cloves, thinly sliced

½ teaspoon crushed red pepper flakes

½ teaspoon kosher salt, plus more to taste

6 ounces kale, stripped from its stems and chopped

1¾ cups cooked or canned no-salt-added red kidney beans (from one 15-ounce can), drained and rinsed

½ cup oil-packed sun-dried tomatoes, drained and chopped

1 tablespoon nondairy or dairy milk

When the filling is finished, lightly flour a work surface. Line a baking sheet with parchment paper. Roll out the disk of dough into a 13-inch circle, about ⅛ inch thick, and transfer to the baking sheet.

Spread the ricotta filling on the galette dough, leaving a 2-inch border around the edges. Arrange the potato slices in overlapping, concentric circles. Scatter the sun-dried tomatoes on top. Scoop the kale-bean mixture over everything and use a spatula to spread it evenly.

Fold the edges of the galette dough partially over the filling (resist the urge to stretch), pleating the dough as needed. Brush the exposed galette dough with the milk and sprinkle with more shredded cheese. Refrigerate for 20 to 30 minutes.

Preheat the oven to 375°F.

Bake until the dough is golden brown and crisp, about 1 hour, rotating the pan halfway through. Remove and let cool slightly, then drizzle with olive oil and serve warm or at room temperature.

CURRIED CHICKPEA PANCAKE
WITH MUSHROOMS

This is my riff on the Italian chickpea pancake called farinata. After I made a recipe by Los Angeles chef Tal Ronnen that included butternut squash right in the mix, I started thinking about what else I could do, and before I knew it, I had turned this toward India and its own chickpea crepes called pudla, which I also love. I sautéed mushrooms and chickpeas, added Madras curry to the batter before pouring it on top, and came up with something pretty great, IMHO. Be sure to let the batter rest for an hour or two before making this; it helps keep it from being gritty. Serve with a salad or other greens of your choice.

In a medium bowl, whisk together 1½ cups of the chickpea flour and 2 cups water until smooth. Add 3 tablespoons of the oil, the cilantro, curry powder, salt, and pepper, whisking until the mixture has the consistency of thin pancake batter; add some or all of the remaining chickpea flour as needed. Taste and add more salt if needed. Cover and let stand at room temperature for 1 to 2 hours.

Preheat the oven to 425°F.

Pour the remaining 2 tablespoons oil into a 10-inch cast-iron or other ovenproof heavy-duty skillet over medium heat. When it shimmers, add the onion and sauté until tender but not browned, about 6 minutes. Stir in the mushrooms and cook until they release their liquid, about 5 minutes, and continue cooking another 2 to 3 minutes until the liquid mostly evaporates. Stir in the chickpeas and butter and cook until the butter melts and the chickpeas are heated through.

Whisk the batter again to bring it back together. Make sure the mushroom-chickpea mixture is spread evenly in the skillet, then pour the rested batter over them. Carefully transfer the skillet to the hot oven and bake until the edges are browned and pulling away from the sides of the pan, about 30 minutes. Remove from the oven and cool in the pan for 10 minutes.

To serve, flip the pancake onto a cutting board and cut into eight wedges or cut the wedges out of the pan (turning them over so the filling is on top when you serve). Squeeze a little lime juice over the top and garnish with cilantro.

8 servings

1½ to 2 cups chickpea flour

Water, at room temperature

5 tablespoons vegetable oil

½ cup chopped cilantro leaves and tender stems, plus more for garnish (may substitute parsley or mint)

½ teaspoon Madras curry powder (may substitute another curry of your choice or garam masala)

1 teaspoon kosher salt, plus more to taste

¼ teaspoon freshly ground black pepper

½ large yellow onion, chopped

8 ounces cremini mushrooms, chopped

1½ cups cooked or canned no-salt-added chickpeas (from one 15-ounce can), drained and rinsed

2 tablespoons vegan or dairy butter

1 lime

DRINKS & DESSERTS

This is the surprise: beans can work so well in less-expected places—less expected, that is, if you're not familiar with the wide use of little red adzuki beans in Asian sweets, the navy bean pie of American Muslim communities, the old diet trick of black bean brownies, and more. It makes perfect sense: beans can replace some or all of the flour in baked goods; they can help bind like eggs; and they can be crunchy like nuts. You can even blend them into smoothies and use aquafaba—the liquid from a can of chickpeas—to make foamy cocktails.

COCONUT CREAM BEAN PIE

This pie was inspired by the iconic navy bean pie of the nation of Islam, members of which followed longtime leader Elijah Muhammad's divine instruction: "Allah (God) says that the little navy bean will make you live, just eat them." I learned how to make the traditional bean pie from Imani Muhammad, who sells eight hundred of them a week from her Chicago bakery. I had read that she is the queen of the Chicago bean pie, so I ordered some to be shipped to me, loved what I tasted, and called her for the recipe. She told me that she had grown up eating them, learned to bake them for a project for her home-schooled children, and got so many requests that she decided to go into business selling them. "We were taught that as far as nutrition goes, everything you need is inside that navy bean," she says. Traditionally, the pies include pureed navy beans, eggs, milk, sugar, butter, flour, and spices, and when they bake, a little layer of butter rises to the top and browns, giving the pie its distinctive look. To me, they taste like a cross between a sweet potato pie, with the warming spices of nutmeg and cinnamon, and a southern chess pie. For my veganized version, I veered from the script, lost the spices, and turned it into another favorite pie: coconut cream, with its crisp crust, two types of creamy filling, and crunchy toasted coconut. I dare say that no recipient of this pie would detect the navy beans, but why hide them? Shout from the rooftops the glories of the navy bean!

To make the crust: Combine the flour, butter, and salt in a medium bowl. Use your fingers to pinch the butter pieces into the flour. Sprinkle in ¼ cup ice water and use a fork to combine, adding another 1 tablespoon ice water at a time until the dough holds together when you pick up a piece and squeeze it together. Form it into a disk, wrap it in plastic wrap, and refrigerate it while you make the filling and topping.

To make the filling: Combine the coconut milk, beans, granulated sugar, tapioca, and vanilla in a blender and blend until smooth. Pour into a small saucepan set over medium heat and cook, stirring constantly, until the mixture starts to thicken, 4 to 5 minutes. Transfer to a bowl and cover with plastic wrap, pressing it directly onto the surface to prevent a skin from forming. Cut a few vent holes in the plastic with a sharp paring knife. Refrigerate until cold, at least 2 hours or overnight.

Makes one 9-inch pie

CRUST

1½ cups flour, plus more for dusting

7 tablespoons cold unsalted vegan or dairy butter, cut into small pieces

1 teaspoon kosher salt

Ice water

FILLING

1 (13.5-ounce) can full-fat coconut milk

1 cup cooked or canned no-salt-added navy beans (from one 15-ounce can), drained and rinsed

¾ cup granulated sugar

6 tablespoons tapioca starch

1 teaspoon vanilla extract

TOPPING

2 (13.5-ounce) cans full-fat natural coconut milk (without guar gum or other stabilizers), refrigerated in the can overnight

2 tablespoons confectioners' sugar

1 teaspoon vanilla extract

1½ cups unsweetened large-flake dried coconut

CONTINUED

To make the topping: Carefully open the cans without shaking and use a spoon to scoop the solidified cream into a bowl, leaving the thinner coconut water behind. (Use it for smoothies or in soups.) Use a handheld electric mixer or a stand mixer fitted with the whisk attachment to beat the coconut cream until light and fluffy. Add the confectioners' sugar and vanilla and beat to combine.

Set a large skillet over medium heat and scatter in the coconut flakes. Cook, stirring frequently, until the flakes start to brown, 3 to 4 minutes. Transfer them to a bowl to cool.

Dust your countertop and rolling pin with flour. Roll the disk to about 11 inches in diameter and lay it in a 9-inch glass or ceramic pie plate, being careful not to stretch it. Trim and crimp the edges. Prick the bottom of the pastry all over with a fork, cover with plastic wrap, and freeze for 30 minutes. (If making this ahead, you can refrigerate the crust for up 3 days.)

When you're ready to bake the pie, preheat the oven to 425°F.

Remove the plastic wrap from the crust, line the crust with a piece of aluminum foil, and fill with coins, beans, or other pie weights. Bake the crust for 15 minutes, then remove the foil and pie weights and continue baking until the crust is golden brown and crisp all over, 20 to 25 minutes. Let cool.

When the filling is cold and set, scrape it into the baked pie shell and smooth the top. Swirl the topping over the filling and add the toasted coconut flakes. Serve immediately or refrigerate, covered, for up to 5 days.

JULIA'S DEEP, DARK CHOCOLATE MOUSSE

What would Julia Child think of this veganized version of the classic chocolate mousse recipe she included in *Mastering the Art of French Cooking*? Well, she didn't always have nice things to say about vegetarians, so if I could go back in time and serve it to her, I think I would have kept it a secret until she tasted, and then I know she would have been happy—and, once I broke the news to her, curious. Mousse is perhaps the highest and best use of aquafaba—the liquid from a can of chickpeas—and I bet she would have been fascinated at the magical way it can imitate egg whites. Be sure to use the best chocolate you can find; for vegan chocolate, I like Theo 70 percent cacao. As David Lebovitz wrote in his own adaptation of the original, you can use decaf or black tea instead of the coffee here and a teaspoon of vanilla instead of the rum. I like to add raspberries and some slivered almonds or walnuts for a little crunch, and if you'd like, you can dollop on some whipped coconut cream, but know that it's perfectly wonderful unadorned.

8 servings

6 ounces bittersweet vegan or traditional chocolate, chopped

¾ cup unsalted vegan or dairy butter, cut into small pieces

⅔ cup plus 1 tablespoon sugar

¼ cup dark-brewed coffee, cooled

2 tablespoons dark rum

½ cup aquafaba (from 1 can no-salt-added chickpeas, see page 18)

½ teaspoon cream of tartar

Pinch of salt

½ teaspoon vanilla extract

Raspberries, for garnish

Toasted slivered almonds or walnut pieces, for garnish

Fill a large bowl with ice water.

Set a medium bowl (large enough to fit into the bowl of ice water) over a saucepan of barely simmering water. Add the chocolate, butter, ⅔ cup of the sugar, the coffee, and rum. Stir until smooth. Remove the bowl from the heat and set it in the bowl of ice water. Whisk until cool and thick.

Pour the aquafaba into the bowl of a stand mixer fitted with the whisk attachment (or into a deep bowl for using a handheld electric mixer). Beat on medium-high speed until frothy, then add the cream of tartar and salt and continue beating until the aquafaba starts to hold its shape. Add the remaining 1 tablespoon sugar and continue to beat until the mixture holds stiff peaks, then beat in the vanilla.

Fold one-third of the beaten aquafaba into the chocolate mixture, then fold in the remainder of the aquafaba just until incorporated. Be careful not to overfold or the mousse won't keep its airy volume.

Transfer the mousse to a large serving bowl or divide it among eight ½-cup ramekins, mounding it if needed. Cover with plastic wrap and refrigerate until firm, at least 4 hours.

Remove the mousse from the refrigerator about 30 minutes before you're ready to serve so it softens a little. Garnish with raspberries and toasted almonds and serve.

FIVE-SPICE PUMPKIN–OAT MUFFINS

Makes 12 jumbo muffins

2¼ cups flour

¾ cup rolled oats

1½ tablespoons baking powder

4 teaspoons Chinese five-spice powder (may substitute a mixture of cinnamon, star anise, black pepper, ground fennel, and cloves)

½ teaspoon kosher salt

1 (15-ounce) can 100% pumpkin puree (not pumpkin pie mix)

1 (15-ounce) can no-salt-added navy beans, drained and rinsed

1 cup maple syrup

¾ cup sunflower or other neutral vegetable oil

3 tablespoons molasses

1 teaspoon vanilla extract

1¼ cups chopped toasted walnuts

½ cup chopped crystallized ginger

½ cup turbinado sugar

These hearty, not-too-sweet muffins get their deeply spiced flavor not from a ho-hum pumpkin-spice blend but from Chinese five-spice powder, which typically includes my favorite star anise in the profile. They were inspired by a recipe from one of my favorite chef-authors, Isa Chandra Moskowitz of Brooklyn's Modern Love restaurant. I couldn't help but add navy beans for their magical protein, while chopped crystallized ginger, oats, walnuts, and coarse turbinado sugar give sparks of flavor and texture.

Preheat the oven to 450°F. Lightly grease two 6-muffin (jumbo) tins.

In a medium bowl, whisk together the flour, oats, baking powder, five spice powder, and salt.

In a food processor, puree the pumpkin, beans, maple syrup, oil, molasses, and vanilla until smooth. Pour into the bowl with the dry ingredients, add the walnuts and crystallized ginger, and stir just until combined, being careful not to overmix.

Divide the batter among the muffin tins. Sprinkle the tops with the sugar. Bake for 5 minutes, then reduce the oven temperature to 375°F and bake for another 13 to 15 minutes, until a toothpick inserted in the center comes out clean and dry.

Remove from the oven and cool in the tins for a couple minutes, then remove the muffins and cool completely on a cooling rack.

PLANTAIN, BLACK SESAME, AND WHITE BEAN QUICK BREAD

The best banana bread I've ever tasted was at Tandem Coffee in Portland, Maine, where a crater of black sesame and coarse sugar coats the top of a moist, sweet bread. Heaven. I took that idea and applied it to the best banana bread I've ever made, a recipe from *Cook's Illustrated*—and a vegan adaptation in America's Test Kitchen book *Vegan for Everybody*. I proved two things to myself: yes, white beans can give a nice protein boost and go completely unnoticed in banana bread, and, yes, super-ripe plantains can be even better than bananas. If you have easier access to bananas than to plantains, feel free to use them instead. But don't skimp on the black sesame: it makes everything that much better.

Preheat the oven to 350°F. Grease and flour a 9 by 5 by 3-inch loaf pan and tap to remove any excess.

Toast the walnuts on a small rimmed baking sheet until fragrant, 6 to 8 minutes. Remove and chop.

In a large bowl, whisk together the flour, granulated sugar, baking soda, salt, and 2 tablespoons of the sesame seeds. When the walnuts are cool, stir them in.

Combine the oil, plantains, yogurt, beans, lemon juice, and vanilla in the bowl of a food processor and process until mostly smooth (small lumps of plantain are fine).

Pour the wet mixture into the dry mixture and gently fold until just combined. Scrape the batter into the greased and floured loaf pan and smooth the top. Use a butter knife to drag an indentation lengthwise through the middle of the top of the batter and sprinkle the remaining 2 tablespoons sesame seeds along that indentation, followed by most of the turbinado sugar, sprinkling the rest of the turbinado sugar lightly over the rest of the top of the batter.

Bake until the top is firm and deep golden and a toothpick inserted into the bread comes out clean, about 1 hour (rotate the pan halfway through baking).

Let the bread cool in the pan for 10 minutes. Use a butter knife to loosen it around the edges, remove the bread from the pan, and let it cool on a cooling rack for at least 30 minutes to serve warm or for 3 hours to serve at room temperature.

Makes 1 loaf

6 tablespoons grapeseed or other neutral vegetable oil, plus more for greasing the pan

2 cups flour, plus more for dusting the pan

1½ cups walnut halves

¾ cup granulated sugar

1 teaspoon baking soda

½ teaspoon kosher salt

4 tablespoons black sesame seeds

3 large ripe (yellow with plenty of black spots) plantains, peeled and mashed

½ cup Coconut–Cashew Yogurt (page 215), store-bought plain almond or coconut milk yogurt, or your favorite plain dairy yogurt

1 cup canned no-salt-added cannellini, navy, or great Northern beans, drained and rinsed

1 tablespoon fresh lemon juice

2 teaspoons vanilla extract

2 tablespoons turbinado sugar

RED BEAN ICE CREAM

Makes about 3½ cups

SWEET RED BEANS
½ cup dried adzuki beans

Water

1 (3 by 5-inch) strip kombu (dried seaweed)

⅔ cup sugar

ICE CREAM
2 cups raw cashews, soaked for at least 2 hours (or as long as overnight) and drained

Water

½ cup sugar

¼ cup plain vegan or dairy cream cheese

2 tablespoons cornstarch

2 tablespoons light corn syrup

¼ teaspoon kosher salt

This is a classic ice cream flavor in Asia, where adzuki beans are sweetened and made into countless other desserts, including buns, ices, sweet soups, and so many more. This is loosely based on recipes by *A Common Table* author Cynthia Chen McTernan and ice cream entrepreneur Jeni Britton Bauer.

To make the sweet red beans: Combine the beans, 4 cups water, and kombu in a small saucepan over medium-high heat. Bring the water to a boil, then reduce the heat until the water is barely bubbling, cover, and cook until the beans are so tender you can easily smash one between your fingers, 60 to 90 minutes. (Check the water level from time to time and add more if needed to keep the beans submerged.)

When the beans are soft, remove and discard the kombu. Make sure there is enough water to cover, stir in the sugar, increase the heat to medium, and bring to a boil. Cook until the water forms a syrup, 10 to 15 minutes. Let cool and divide in half, reserving the cooking liquid/syrup.

To make the ice cream: Combine the cashews and 1½ cups water in a high-powered blender, such as a Vitamix, and blend until smooth. You should have 3 cups or so; blend in a little more water if needed to get to that volume. Add the sugar, cream cheese, cornstarch, corn syrup, and salt and blend until very smooth, scraping down the sides of the blender as needed.

Pour the mixture into a storage container with a lid and stir in half the sweetened red beans and their syrup. Refrigerate, covered, for at least 2 hours (and preferably overnight), until very cold then process according to the manufacturer's instructions for your ice cream maker. Return to the storage container and freeze until firm, about 2 hours.

Scoop into bowls and top with the remaining sweet red beans.

NOTE

Making ice cream takes planning: If you're not already storing your ice cream maker canister in the freezer, make sure to put it in the coldest part of your freezer for at least 24 hours before making ice cream. Allow time for chilling the ice cream "batter"—overnight if possible—before churning and at least 2 hours to freeze after churning. Nondairy ice creams can freeze firmer than dairy ones, so if this becomes too firm to scoop, just let it thaw a little, break it up into pieces, transfer the pieces to the bowl of a food processor, and pulse until they are broken down into pellet-size balls. Return them to the storage container and use a spoon or spatula to smooth them out, then scoop.

CARDAMOM, LIME, AND WHITE BEAN BUNDT CAKE

12 to 16 servings

FILLING/TOPPING

½ cup unsalted vegan or dairy butter, plus more for greasing the pan

½ cup packed light brown sugar

3 cups cooked or canned no-salt-added navy beans (from one 29-ounce can or two 15-ounce cans), drained and rinsed

1 cup roasted unsalted pistachios, chopped

1 cup unsweetened small-flake dried coconut

BATTER

1¼ cups granulated sugar, plus more for dusting the pan

3 cups flour

2 teaspoons baking soda

1 teaspoon kosher salt

½ teaspoon baking powder

1 tablespoon ground cardamom

⅔ cup safflower oil

1 cup fresh lime juice

1 cup light coconut milk

2 teaspoons vanilla extract

3 tablespoons finely grated lime zest

ICING

¼ cup fresh lime juice

2 cups confectioners' sugar

¼ cup refined coconut oil, melted

1 teaspoon lemon extract (optional)

I make—and love—cakes in which beans are pureed into the batter. But when I wanted one that showcased the beans a little more, I turned to Fran Costigan, queen of vegan baking, for some brainstorming. I knew I wanted to start with a riff on her amazing Big Orange Bundt Cake, and Fran suggested: why not add the beans as part of a filling between layers of batter? Brilliant. I swapped in some of my favorite ingredients, flavoring her Bundt with lime juice, coconut milk, and cardamom and then candying navy beans, pistachios, and coconut for the filling. A lime icing completes the picture. You use barely half the filling, so you can save the other half for serving with the finished cake.

To make the filling/topping: In a small saucepan, combine the butter and brown sugar over medium heat and cook until melted. Add the beans and cook, stirring occasionally, until the mixture is thick and the beans darken slightly all over, 6 to 8 minutes. Stir in the pistachios and coconut, remove from the heat, and let the mixture cool. (If you want to speed up the cooling, transfer the mixture to a small rimmed baking sheet, spread it out, and refrigerate.)

Preheat the oven to 400°F. Position a rack in the middle of the oven. Grease a 10- to 12-cup Bundt pan thoroughly and dust it with the granulated sugar.

To make the batter: In a medium bowl, whisk together the granulated sugar, flour, baking soda, salt, baking powder, and cardamom.

In a separate bowl, whisk together the oil, lime juice, coconut milk, vanilla, and lime zest until well combined. Pour this into the dry mixture and stir with a whisk until the batter is smooth.

Pour a little more than half of the batter into the prepared pan. Dollop the filling evenly around the batter and pour in the remaining batter. The pan should be about three-quarters full. (If you have more batter than that, perhaps a cup or so, bake it in one or two 1-cup baking ramekins or custard cups.) Smooth the top of the batter with a small spatula. Rotate the pan to level the batter and tap it lightly on the counter to eliminate any air bubbles.

Bake for about 55 minutes, or until the cake is golden brown and springs back near firm at the center when touched lightly, and a tester inserted in a few spots near the center of the cake comes out clean or with only a few crumbs.

Remove the cake from the oven and cool in the pan on a rack for 15 minutes. Place another wire rack on top of the cake and turn the pan upside down. Shake the pan gently to release the cake. Cool the cake completely before glazing and serving.

To make the icing: Combine the lime juice, confectioners' sugar, coconut oil, and lemon extract, if desired, in the bowl of a food processor and puree until smooth. Use immediately, if possible, or if waiting for the cake to cool, refrigerate until ready to use. Microwave very briefly to re-liquefy the icing if it has solidified, but make sure it cools to room temperature before icing the cake.

When the cake is completely cool, transfer it to a serving platter and drizzle with the icing. Spoon the remaining filling around the cake and serve.

MINT CHOCOLATE CHIP AND WHITE BEAN–OAT COOKIES

Makes about 24 cookies

1½ cups no-salt-added canned navy beans (from one 15-ounce can), with their liquid (aquafaba; see page 18)

½ cup vegan or dairy butter, at room temperature, or refined coconut oil

½ cup plus 2 tablespoons packed light brown sugar

¼ cup almond milk

1 teaspoon peppermint extract

1 teaspoon vanilla extract

2 cups rolled oats

1 teaspoon kosher salt

½ teaspoon baking soda

½ teaspoon baking powder

½ cup semisweet dairy-free or traditional chocolate chips

These are a mash-up of two of my favorite cookies—mint chocolate chip and oatmeal—with the added boost of white beans, which play their background part almost invisibly. They're crisp-chewy, which is my ideal cookie texture. Be strong and resist eating them when they're warm, because they'll be too crumbly. Once they cool, they're perfect.

Preheat the oven to 350°F. Set two oven racks in the upper middle and lower middle positions. Lightly grease two large baking sheets.

Drain the beans, reserving 3 tablespoons of the aquafaba (the liquid from the can). Rinse the beans and mash them thoroughly with a fork.

In a small bowl, using an electric handheld mixer on medium speed (or whisking by hand), beat the aquafaba for about 2 minutes, until thickened. Transfer to a large bowl or the bowl of a stand mixer fitted with the paddle attachment, add the butter and brown sugar, and beat at medium speed for about a minute, until smooth. Add the almond milk and peppermint and vanilla extracts and beat for another 30 seconds. Add the beans and beat until smooth, about 1 minute.

Add the oats, salt, baking soda, baking powder, and chocolate chips and mix on low speed just until combined. Refrigerate the dough, covered with plastic wrap (or a plate), for at least 30 minutes and as long as overnight.

Scoop about 2 tablespoons of dough onto the cookie sheets in rounded spoonfuls, leaving at least 2 inches between cookies. Flatten slightly with the back of a spatula. Bake until the bottoms are deeply browned, about 25 minutes, rotating the baking sheets top to bottom and front to back halfway through.

Let the cookies cool on the sheets for about 5 minutes, then use a spatula to carefully transfer them to cooling racks to finish cooling.

CHOCOLATE CHICKPEA SPREAD

Dennis Friedman, chef-partner at the wonderful DC fast-casual mini-chain Shouk, makes this for his young children as a way to sneak some nutrition into something sweet and delicious. Use this the way you would Nutella or any other chocolate or chocolate-nut spread: with fruit as a dip/snack, on a sandwich with bananas and peanut or almond butter, or slathered onto biscuits, croissants, or toast with jam.

Combine the chickpeas, ⅔ cup water, maple syrup, cocoa, vanilla, salt, and sugar in a blender and blend until smooth. (If you have a high-powered blender such as a Vitamix, it will get smoother, but this comes together fine in a regular blender or a food processor; it will be a little grainier but tastes great.) Taste and add more salt if needed.

For the most spreadable results, refrigerate for at least 2 hours so the mixture will stiffen. Refrigerate in an airtight container for up to 1 week.

Makes 3 cups

3 cups cooked or canned no-salt-added chickpeas (from one 29-ounce can or two 15-ounce cans), drained and rinsed

Water

½ cup plus 2 tablespoons maple syrup

½ cup Dutch-process cocoa

1 teaspoon vanilla extract

½ teaspoon kosher salt, plus more to taste

2 tablespoons sugar

CHOCOLATE, RED BEAN, AND ROSE BROWNIES

If black bean brownies could be a thing—and believe me, they are a thing—then why not red bean brownies, based on the little adzuki (aka azuki) beans that are so beloved across Asia for their versatility in sweets? I started with a pretty killer gluten-free recipe from Dana Shultz's Minimalist Baker site and set to tinkering. In went the adzuki beans, out went the black. In went aquafaba—the liquid from a can of chickpeas, not the adzukis, because the flavor is milder—and out went a flax egg. In went a little chickpea flour for extra structure. The master stroke, based on a suggestion from my friend and cookbook author Tess "The Blender Girl" Masters: rose water, which takes these from everyday-American-take-to-work good to special-occasion-Middle-Eastern great. They're very fudgy and dense on the inside, a little chewy on the outside—and easy enough to make whenever you want.

Preheat the oven to 350°F. Lightly grease one 6-muffin (jumbo) tin. Dust with flour and tap out the excess.

In the bowl of a food processor, combine the butter, flour, adzuki beans, aquafaba, cocoa, salt, rose water, vanilla, sugar, and baking powder and process until very smooth, 2 to 3 minutes, scraping down the sides of the bowl as needed.

Divide the batter evenly among the prepared muffin cups and smooth the tops with a spoon. If using, sprinkle on the chocolate chips, nuts, and/or rose petals.

Bake until the tops are dry and the edges start to pull away from the sides, 20 to 25 minutes. Remove from the oven and let cool for 30 minutes before using a fork to remove them from the pan. They are meant to be very fudgy inside, so don't worry if they seem too moist.

Store in an airtight container at room temperature for up to 3 days or freeze for up to 3 months.

6 servings

3 tablespoons vegan or dairy butter or coconut oil, melted, plus more for greasing the muffin tin

½ cup plus 1 tablespoon chickpea flour, plus more for dusting (may substitute all-purpose flour)

1 (15-ounce) can no-salt-added adzuki beans, drained and rinsed

⅔ cup aquafaba (the liquid from a shaken can of no-salt-added chickpeas; see page 18)

¾ cup Dutch-process cocoa powder

½ teaspoon kosher salt

1 tablespoon rose water

1 teaspoon vanilla extract

⅔ cup sugar

1½ teaspoons baking powder

2 tablespoons dairy-free or traditional semisweet chocolate chips (optional)

2 tablespoons chopped walnuts or pistachios (optional)

2 teaspoons crushed dried organic rose petals (optional)

CHICKPEA PRALINES

(PICTURED ON PAGE 204)

Makes 18 to 24 pralines

1½ cups roasted chickpeas (roasted as on page 49 but with a neutral vegetable oil and without salt or spices)

1½ cups granulated sugar

¾ cup packed light brown sugar

½ cup full-fat coconut milk (do not use light)

6 tablespoons vegan or dairy butter

½ teaspoon kosher salt

1 teaspoon vanilla extract

For most of my youth, I didn't know what I was missing when it came to southern-style pralines. I mistakenly equated all pralines with those hard, gritty things I'd sometimes pick up on the way out of Tex-Mex restaurants in San Angelo, Texas. It wasn't until my sister Teri took me to a fabulous candy shop in Savannah, Georgia, where I tasted them freshly made—still warm, the simple butter-and-sugar candy barely holding together a mound of toasted pecans—that I knew the truth. I never made them at home, though, until I saw Emma Christensen's perfect recipe on The Kitchn a few years back, and I shouldn't have been surprised at how well it worked. But then I challenged myself: could I make two major changes—veganize the candy and use roasted chickpeas instead of pecans—and still love them? The answers came as quickly as this combination of two types of sugars, coconut milk, and vegan butter can reach 238°F: yes and yes. You'll need an instant-read thermometer at hand or a candy thermometer that can clip to the side of your saucepan.

Set out a piece of parchment for the pralines, plus two soup spoons: one for dropping the candies onto the parchment and a second for helping scrape the candies off the first one.

In a medium saucepan (at least 4 quarts), combine the chickpeas, granulated sugar, brown sugar, coconut milk, butter, salt, and vanilla over medium-high heat. Cook, stirring occasionally, until the mixture comes to a boil, then start stirring constantly. Let it boil until the syrup registers 238° to 240°F on the thermometer, about 3 minutes.

Remove the pan from the heat immediately and begin stirring more vigorously and constantly, as the mixture will become creamy, cloudy, and start to thicken. When you notice it starting to get just a touch grainy, the syrup is ready.

Drop spoonfuls of the pralines onto your parchment. Work quickly, since the syrup starts to set as it cools. Let the pralines cool and harden for at least 10 minutes before eating. They will keep for several days in an airtight container, but they're best eaten within the first 24 hours.

WHITE BEAN SMOOTHIES
WITH MANGO, COCONUT, MINT, AND GINGER

This pale green smoothie, a twist on a mango lassi, is a little tart and a little spicy-cool from the mint-ginger twofer, and it gets extra fiber and creaminess from white beans, which fade into the background. This is a good use for canned beans, which have all the nutrition but less flavor than those you cook at home from dried with aromatic vegetables added. Note: If you use frozen mango cubes, first try this without any ice, then add some to the blender if needed.

In a high-powered blender, such as a Vitamix, combine, in this order, the beans, mango, coconut milk, mint, agave, ginger, lime juice, turmeric, salt, if desired, and ice. (Make sure to end with the ice on top for better blending.) Blend until smooth and serve immediately.

Makes 4 cups

1 cup canned no-salt-added cannellini or other white beans, drained and rinsed

Flesh of 1 large mango, cubed

1 (13.5-ounce can) full-fat coconut milk

¼ cup lightly packed mint leaves

3 tablespoons agave nectar

2 tablespoons freshly grated ginger

2 tablespoons fresh lime juice

½ teaspoon ground turmeric

¼ teaspoon kosher salt (optional)

2 cups ice

CHOCOLATE CHICKPEA TART

Makes 1 (10-inch) tart

8 ounces gingersnap cookies, broken into pieces

8 dried figs, roughly chopped

5 tablespoons unsalted vegan or dairy butter, at room temperature

¼ teaspoon fine sea salt

1 (15-ounce) can no-salt-added chickpeas, drained (reserve the cooking liquid/aquafaba; see page 18) and rinsed

Water

¼ cup fresh orange juice

¼ cup Grand Marnier or Cointreau

2 tablespoons sugar

2 ounces bittersweet chocolate (preferably 70% cacao or higher), melted and cooled

¼ cup Dutch-process cocoa powder

¼ teaspoon vanilla extract

1 tablespoon orange zest

2 tablespoons coconut oil, melted

½ cup aquafaba (from the chickpea liquid reserved above)

Raspberries, for garnish

You know you've hired the right recipe tester when she not only makes great tweaks to your recipes, finds missing ingredients and/or instructions, and generally saves your ass, but when she sends you a recipe she developed that's so perfect for your book, you pretty much want to cry tears of joy. Kristen Hartke was looking for a no-bake dessert to make for a dinner party and started playing around with the idea of trendy chocolate hummus in tart form. Here, a touch of orange three ways—juice, zest, and liqueur—marries with the dark chocolate, while the chickpeas and their liquid add body and take the place of any dairy or eggs. This is very rich, so if you want to make it in a smaller tart pan, be sure to cut your pieces that much smaller. Serve with raspberries.

Put the cookie pieces in the bowl of a food processor and process until finely ground. Add the figs, butter, and salt and pulse until combined. Press the crust into the bottom and up the sides of a 10-inch tart pan with a removable bottom and chill in the refrigerator while you make the filling. Rinse and dry the food processor bowl, blade, and lid.

Working over a bowl, gently massage the chickpeas in your hands, picking them up a handful at a time, to help all the skins slip off when you heat them.

Add the chickpeas (skins and all) to a small saucepan and add enough water to cover by 3 inches. Bring it to a boil over high heat, then turn off the heat. With a slotted spoon or small sieve, skim away and discard any of the skins that have floated to the top. Stir vigorously to get more skins to rise and keep skimming. Pop any other skins off by hand, if you have the patience. (Aim to remove a heaping ½ cup of skins.) It's impossible to get all the skins, but the more you remove, the smoother the tart filling will be.

Drain the chickpeas thoroughly and return them to the saucepan over medium-high heat. Add the orange juice, Grand Marnier, and sugar and bring to a simmer, stirring occasionally. Reduce the heat to medium and let the liquid reduce until it becomes thick and syrupy, 10 to 15 minutes. Let cool to room temperature.

Transfer the chickpea mixture to the bowl of the food processor. Add the chocolate, cocoa powder, vanilla, orange zest, coconut oil, and 2 tablespoons of the aquafaba. Pulse a few times to combine, then process on high speed until very smooth. With the motor running, drizzle in the remaining aquafaba and continue processing, scraping down the sides of the bowl as needed.

Pour the chocolate-chickpea filling into the chilled prepared crust, smoothing the top evenly with an offset spatula. Refrigerate, uncovered, until set, 1 to 2 hours. (If you are refrigerating for longer, cover with plastic wrap after it has set and refrigerate for up to 3 days.)

To serve, remove the tart from the refrigerator and let it sit at room temperature for at least 10 minutes before popping the tart out of the tart ring. Cut it into slices, top with raspberries, and serve.

SALTY MARGARITA SOUR

1 serving

1½ tablespoons (¾ ounce) aquafaba (from one 15-ounce can no-salt-added chickpeas; see page 18)

¼ teaspoon fine sea salt

Ice

2 tablespoons (1 ounce) fresh lime juice

3½ tablespoons (1¾ ounces) tequila, preferably blanco or reposado

1 tablespoon (½ ounce) Cointreau

1 tablespoon (½ ounce) agave nectar

Finely grated lime zest, for garnish (optional)

One of my favorite margaritas in the world is served at Oyamel, José Andrés's Mexican restaurant in DC. I always order my margaritas without the salted rim, because I find that the very salty crunch distracts from the appeal of the tequila-lime-orange-liqueur combination I so adore. At Oyamel, they've solved my issue: instead of a salt-rimmed glass, they top the margaritas with a foamy layer of "salt air," which adds just the right briny touch—and gives you a fun foam mustache, if you're into that sort of thing. Given that José & Co. are kings of Spanish modernist cooking, I figure that their "air" involves some alchemy I wouldn't have access to at home, but I do have plenty of aquafaba, which bartenders are using for egg-free takes on such foamy cocktails as fizzes, flips, and sours. Classic cocktails have you shake the egg or egg white with the rest of the ingredients, and a layer of foam rises to the top. But I wanted to keep that saltiness confined to the top layer. So after shaking up my go-to margarita—a slightly sweeter version of the one in Robert Simonson's *A Proper Drink*—I simply whisked a little aquafaba with some salt until it was foamy, dolloped it on top, drank up, and flipped.

Whisk the aquafaba and salt together in a small bowl until it turns white and foamy and expands in volume.

Fill a cocktail shaker with ice, then add the lime juice, tequila, Cointreau, and agave. Seal and shake vigorously for 15 seconds, then strain into a cocktail glass.

Spoon the aquafaba mixture on top, garnish with the lime zest, if desired, and drink.

CONDIMENTS & OTHER PANTRY RECIPES

These are not recipes that use beans; they are recipes for some extra touches that can make your bean dishes that much more special.

CHICKPEA AIOLI

Makes about 1 cup

1 garlic clove

¼ cup aquafaba (from one 15-ounce can of no-salt-added chickpeas; see page 18)

2 tablespoons cooked or canned no-salt-added chickpeas

¾ teaspoon Dijon mustard

½ teaspoon kosher salt, plus more to taste

¾ cup grapeseed or other neutral vegetable oil

1 tablespoon fresh lemon juice, plus more to taste

News flash: You don't need eggs to make mayonnaise, now that we've got aquafaba, the cooking liquid from chickpeas, which behaves much like egg whites. When I first tried it, I liked the results—but the mayo needed a little body, I thought. What better than a small amount of chickpeas to help thicken it up? Turns out I wasn't the only one onto such an idea. My friends at Little Sesame in Washington, DC, told me they were doing the same thing. Great minds and all that. Note that it's easiest to make it in a mini food processor or small bullet-style blender because larger machines often require more volume than this to work effectively, but you can also use an immersion (handheld) blender, especially if you have a jar with an opening big enough for the blender to fit into.

Cut open the garlic and remove any green sprout inside; that will keep the garlic from being too bitter when eaten raw.

In a mini food processor or small bullet-style blender, puree the garlic, aquafaba, chickpeas, mustard, and salt until smooth. With the processor running, drizzle in the oil, starting slowly and then feeling free to speed up once it starts thickening. (If using an immersion blender, you may need to blend for several minutes before the mixture will thicken.) When you've poured in all the oil and the aioli is thick, add the lemon juice and whir a few seconds just to combine. Taste and add more salt and lemon juice if needed.

This will keep in an airtight container in the refrigerator for up to 1 week.

COCONUT–CASHEW YOGURT

A small amount of cashews helps this plant-based yogurt thicken nicely. Use it wherever you want a touch (or more) of creamy tartness: drizzle it onto tacos, stir fruit and granola into it for breakfast, use it in recipes such as Chickpea-Tarragon Salad Sandwiches (page 128) and Plantain, Black Sesame, and White Bean Quick Bread (page 197).

Combine the cashews and coconut milk in a blender and blend until very smooth. Pour into a clean, sterilized quart-sized Mason jar. Open the probiotic capsule, sprinkle the contents into the coconut mixture, and stir gently.

Cover the jar with a clean tea towel or piece of cheesecloth, then use a rubber band or just the ring of a Mason jar lid to secure the cloth. (Do not use a lid on the mixture, which needs to breathe during the first fermentation.)

Set the jar in a warm place for 24 hours, then taste to see if it has started to become tart. If it hasn't, leave it for another 24 hours and taste again. When it tastes a bit tart, put on a tight lid and transfer the jar to the refrigerator, where it will keep for up to 1 week. (If it has started to separate, shake the tightly covered jar to combine before refrigerating.)

Once it has chilled, it will thicken further—and it may separate again. Depending on how thick the solids are, you may wish to scoop them out into a bowl and whisk them, perhaps with a little bit of the liquid as needed to get the consistency you desire.

Makes 1 quart

½ cup raw cashews, soaked for at least 2 hours (or as long as overnight), drained

2 (13.5-ounce) cans full-fat coconut milk (do not substitute light coconut milk)

1 probiotic capsule

FASTEST-EVER SMOKY RED SALSA

Makes about 2 cups

1 (14.5-ounce) can diced tomatoes, preferably fire-roasted

¼ cup packed cilantro leaves and tender stems, chopped

1 large garlic clove, halved

1 chipotle in adobo, plus more to taste

½ teaspoon salt, plus more to taste

1 tablespoon fresh lime juice, plus more to taste

This used to be what I made whenever I wanted a tasty salsa for tacos, tostadas, or grain bowls but didn't have time to actually cook. Then I started making it every week or two even if I had a little time, because it's just that good. You really may never buy salsa again; that's how easy this is. Tip: You can also start with any leftover tomato pasta sauce instead of canned tomatoes, turning it from Italian to Mexican in a flash.

Combine the tomatoes, cilantro, garlic, chipotle, salt, and lime juice in the bowl of a food processor or blender and puree until combined but still slightly chunky. Taste and add a little more adobo sauce from the chipotle, salt, and/or lime juice as needed.

VEGETABLE BROTH

Makes about 12 cups

Water

2 yellow or white onions, cut into 1-inch chunks

1 head of celery, cut into 1-inch chunks

2 large carrots, cut into 1-inch chunks

1 head of fennel, fronds included, cut into 1-inch chunks

2 star anise pods

2 tablespoons coriander seeds

4 bay leaves

2 teaspoons crushed red pepper flakes

1 lemon, halved

1 head of garlic, peeled

I often make a quick vegetable broth from scraps and vegetable trimmings I store in my freezer until I have enough. But when I want something with a little more depth of flavor, I make this recipe from Emily Shaya of the New Orleans restaurant Saba. A few spices and a little lemon make it especially good for New Orleans Red Beans and Rice (page 106), her favorite use for it, but it's also good in soups, stews, and rice dishes (such as Paella with Chickpeas, Green Beans, and Shishito Peppers, page 177) or anytime you want something as thin as water—but with much more going on.

Combine 1 gallon water, the onions, celery, carrots, fennel, star anise, coriander, bay leaves, red pepper flakes, lemon, and garlic in a large stockpot over medium-high heat and bring to a boil. Reduce the heat to medium-low and cook, uncovered, for at least 30 minutes and up to 2 hours. (The broth will be more concentrated the longer you cook it.) Strain, discarding the solids.

Use what you need immediately and pour the rest into jars and refrigerate for up to 5 days. Or pour it into ice cube trays, freeze, transfer the cubes to a gallon-size zip-top bag, and freeze for up to 6 months.

QUICK AND SIMPLE CHARRED SALSA VERDE

Some recipes for Mexican salsa verde have you boil the tomatillos and add onion, cilantro, and oil. But this quick take from DC chef Christian Irabién packs in tons of flavor with just a few ingredients. The key is the charring.

Pour the oil into a large skillet over medium-high heat. Have a splatter guard ready and turn on the vent hood (or open the windows and turn on a fan). When the oil shimmers, add the tomatillos and chile and cook, turning as needed, until the jalapeño is charred all over and the tomatillos are charred on the tops and bottoms (they can slide around too much to char the sides).

Remove the stem from the jalapeño and transfer it and the tomatillos to a blender or food processor. Puree until smooth. Stir in the salt, taste, and add more as needed.

Makes about 1¾ cups

2 tablespoons vegetable oil

1 pound tomatillos, husked, rinsed, and dried

1 large jalapeño chile

1 teaspoon kosher salt, plus more to taste

HERB-MARINATED TOFU FETA

This has the creaminess, tang, and saltiness of good feta, making it just the right finishing touch for so many bean dishes, including—of course—tacos. It gets better the longer it marinates. Note: Use firm, not extra-firm tofu, for the creamiest result.

Wrap the tofu in paper towels and microwave on high for 1 minute. Unwrap, rewrap with fresh paper towels, and repeat. Unwrap, let cool, and cut into ½-inch cubes.

While the tofu is cooling, in a medium bowl whisk together the lemon juice, vinegar, olive oil, miso, nutritional yeast, salt, and pepper.

Transfer the tofu to a tall jar and pour the marinade over it. Stuff in the lemon peel, rosemary, thyme, and oregano, cover, and refrigerate for at least 2 hours before using, turning the jar upside down and back a couple of times (to make sure the tofu gets coated).

Store in an airtight container in the refrigerator for up to 2 weeks.

Makes about 3 cups

1 (14-ounce) package water-packed firm tofu (preferably sprouted), drained

¼ cup fresh lemon juice

¼ cup apple cider vinegar

¼ cup extra-virgin olive oil, plus more for storing

2 tablespoons mild white miso

2 tablespoons nutritional yeast

1 teaspoon kosher salt

½ teaspoon freshly ground black pepper

4 strips of lemon peel

1 rosemary sprig

2 sprigs of fresh thyme

2 sprigs of fresh oregano

THE BEAN PANTRY

The right ingredients make all the difference, starting with the beans themselves and including herbs, spices, and more.

A Bean Glossary

Beans number in the thousands, especially when you count all the heirloom varieties available in seed catalogs. This list is by no means exhaustive, but here are some of the beans you're most likely to encounter.

ADZUKI (aka aduki, azuki). Little red beans native to Asia, where they are traditional in making sweets. Related to mung beans, they have a smooth texture and sweet, nutty flavor.

ANASAZI (aka cave, New Mexico appaloosa). This stunning maroon-speckled heirloom bean (which loses its coloring when you cook them, as most beans do) is native to the Southwest and is connected to ancient cave-dwelling native tribes. Meaty and a little sweet, it's good in baked bean dishes and southwestern stews. Bonus: It causes less gas than other beans.

AYOCOTE. Large, thick-skinned, firm-fleshed bean originally from Oaxaca that I've seen only in markets in Mexico—and from California's Rancho Gordo, whose Xoxoc Project supports small indigenous farmers in Mexico. Varieties: ayocote negro, ayocote blanco, ayocote morado.

BLACK-EYED PEA. One of the African cowpeas that came to America during the slave trade and are popular in the American South and in West Africa. Not really a pea, it's named for its trademark circular spot on one side. It's distinctive in flavor, a little starchy, relatively quick-cooking, and the main ingredient in hoppin' John, a traditional New Year's dish; in the Nigerian stew ewa riro; and more.

BLACK TURTLE (aka black, frijole negro, Mexican black, Spanish black, midnight black). Native to the Americas and beloved in Mexico, Brazil, Cuba, the American Southwest, and elsewhere. It's the main ingredient in traditional Cuban beans and rice (moros y Christianos), the Brazilian stew feijoada, and countless Mexican dishes. Earthy and meaty, they turn everything they touch an inky purplish black—especially if you cook them without soaking, which robs them of some color and flavor. (If you ever see black coco beans, snap them up: they're much bigger and even meatier than the turtles.)

BORLOTTI. See *cranberry*.

CANARY (aka mayacoba, Peruano, canario, Peruvian, Mexican yellow). Originally from Peru, where it is a staple in such dishes as tacu tacu, a pan-fried cake of leftover beans and rice, this mild, buttery yellow bean is also used in some regions of Mexico for frijoles refritos.

CANNELLINI (aka white kidney, haricot blanc). A versatile, large, kidney-shaped bean used throughout Italy. Its creamy-but-firm texture makes it a no-brainer in salads, where its thin skin helps it soak up flavor, but like most beans it is beautiful in soups and when pureed, too.

CHICKPEA (aka garbanzo, gram). An ancient bean and perhaps the most versatile one in the pantry as a roasted snack and for its ability to hold its shape in salads and to become creamy and fluffy as purees, including what has to be the most popular dip in the world: hummus. It's used widely in Italian, Spanish, Portuguese, Middle Eastern, Indian, Mexican, and American cooking, a crucial ingredient in countless traditional and modern soups, salads, and vegan "chicken" dishes. Try chickpea flour (besan in Indian markets) to make the pancakes/crepes called farinata in Italy, socca in France, and pudla in India. And try aquafaba, the liquid from a can or pot of chickpeas that can mimic egg whites (see page 18). The dried beans are famously slow to cook, so buy from a reputable source with high turnover so the beans are not too old. Unless you know they're pretty fresh, soak them overnight—and try them in a pressure cooker. Varieties: black chickpea, black gram, ceci siciliani, cicerchie, desi, kabuli (the most common in America), channa dal (Indian split chickpeas).

COCO (aka French navy). Ivory-colored and smaller and rounder than the navy bean, this creamy, tender, quick-cooking bean is lovely in salads. The giant white coco is in a different class of beans—the runners—and is akin to the giant lima or Greek gigante.

CORONA. A huge white Italian bean similar to the Greek gigante, it is super-creamy if you cook it long enough and can star in whatever dish you put it in.

CRANBERRY (aka borlotti, cacahuate, Roman, Tuscan, coco rose). Plump, rich, and meaty, it's popular in Italy, where it's known as borlotti and used in pasta fagiole, minestrone, and more. In Mexico, it's known as cacahuate, or "peanut," and in America as the cranberry bean. Its luxurious broth might be the most delicious of all the beans, IMO.

CROWDER PEA. A member of the cowpea family, like the black-eyed pea, this one gets its name for the way it crowds up inside the pod. It's rich and hearty, and it makes a dark, wonderful pot liquor.

FAVA (aka faba, broad bean, horse bean). One of the oldest beans in Europe, where it is especially beloved in Middle Eastern cooking. It's a little fussy to prepare from the fresh pods, because each bean is wrapped in a second skin, although plenty of cultures don't bother peeling. Dried varieties: large brown (which needs to be peeled), split/skinned (quick-cooking and good for making into soups and dips because they fall apart), and mini brown (my favorite; traditional in Middle Eastern ful).

FLAGEOLET (aka chevrier, flageolet de chevrier). This small, pale green bean, sometimes called the caviar of beans, is actually an immature kidney bean. Delicate, creamy, and thin-skinned, it's beloved in France, where it's traditional in stews, soups, and salads.

GIGANTE (aka gigande, giant lima, giant butter, elephant, elephante, yigante, hija). A dramatically large bean in the runner family, adored in the Mediterranean, particularly in Greece. Super-creamy and meaty, it shines when allowed to star without too many distractions.

GREAT NORTHERN. A white bean a little larger than the navy, it's very popular and versatile, with a subtle, slightly nutty flavor and starchy texture.

JACOB'S CATTLE (aka Appaloosa, trout). A gorgeous, plump speckled bean beloved in the American Northeast and used in New England baked beans; also traditional as Appaloosa in southwestern-style baked beans. Full of flavor, it holds its shape well.

LADY CREAM PEA. Another cowpea, it is completely white and creates a clear pot liquor. Sweet and, as the name would indicate, creamy.

LENTIL. The oldest cultivated bean, it plays a huge role in Indian cooking but also in many dishes of Europe and the Middle East. There are four main distinct types (plus regional varieties):

> **Common brown/green:** your all-purpose, rustic lentil, when you want something that gets tender enough to be mashed but can still hold its shape if you'd like.

> **Red/orange (aka split, Egyptian, massor dal):** it cooks quickly and collapses to a golden, easily digested mush, making it perfect for dals.

> **French green (du Puy):** A small lentil that stays firm, making it traditional in cold marinated salads. Brown varieties that are similar in Italy and Spain are Castelluccio/Umbrian and pardina, respectively.

> **Black:** Named "Beluga" by one company because it looks like caviar, meaning you can soak it in a brine to evoke just that thing—or use it anywhere you'd use the du Puy.

LIMA (aka butter, haba, Madagascar, fagioli di Spagna, potato lima). Named for its Lima, Peru, birthplace, this big, flat bean tastes a little sweet and has a creamy texture. Varieties: large white (buttery, a little mealy), baby white (creamier, a little fruity), Christmas/chestnut (large, with chestnut flavor and gorgeous markings that, unlike most beans, survive cooking).

LUPINI (aka lupin, tremoco). You're most likely to find this bean sold in jars, already cooked and pickled, which is a good thing: raw, it contains a toxin that requires exhaustive treatment. The pickled ones are fun snacks and the main ingredient in an Ecuadorian bean ceviche called cevichochos.

MUNG (aka moong, green gram). A small, sweet green Asian bean common in Indian cooking, especially in its split yellow form (moong dal), that cooks quickly and turns very soft. The starch is used to make noodles.

NAVY (aka haricot, Boston, pearl, white pea, alubias chicas). It takes its name from the fact that it was a staple for sailors on ships. It's soft, a little starchy, and very versatile.

PIGEON PEA (aka congo pea, gandule, googoo, yellow lentil). This ancient bean native to Africa got its name because it was fed to pigeons. Earthy and soft, it is popular in the Caribbean (rice and pigeon peas), Africa (the stews of Ethiopia), and India (dals made from the split version).

PINK (aka habichuelas rosada). This is a very creamy, oval bean that is revered in Puerto Rico. Variety: pinquito, small, thin-skinned cross between pink and white bean native to the central coast of California, where it is a traditional side to barbecued meats.

PINTO. By some accounts, this mottled pinkish bean is the most popular in the United States and parts of Mexico, where it stars in frijoles refritos, borrachos (drunken beans), and all manner of tacos, burritos, soups, salads, and more. That's due to its creamy, mild flavor and versatility. Look for Rio Zape.

RED KIDNEY (red, chili, rajma). Named for its shape, this deep crimson bean is popular in India, Latin America, the Caribbean, and the United States, particularly in Louisiana, where it is de rigeur for New Orleans red beans and rice. It is beautiful, stays firm but creamy when cooked, and tastes mildly sweet. Throw as much spice at this bean as you'd like: it can take it!

SOYBEAN. Ubiquitous the world over, this Asian bean is popular not as a dried bean but made into products such as soy sauce, miso, tofu, tempeh, and more. Fresh edamame gained trendiness as a 1980s snack before, or alongside, miso soup in sushi bars.

SPLIT PEA (yellow or green). This Middle Eastern native is popular in Morocco and Tunisia (for tagine) and India (for dal). Like red lentils, it completely collapses when cooked.

TARBAIS. If you want to get *really* serious about your French cassoulet, this large white bean is the one you want; it is named for the city of Tarbes in the French Pyrenees and is preferred in the region. Mild, with a smooth texture, it holds its shape well.

TEPARY (aka terpari, yori mui, pavi). Small and dense, it has long been grown by Native Americans in Arizona because it can thrive in the desert. Good in soups and in southwestern dishes.

Herbs

AVOCADO LEAF. Mexican cooks, particularly in Oaxaca, add this to pots of black beans to give an earthy flavor.

BASIL. The Italian stalwart, added at the end of many a pasta dish.

BAY LEAF. A requirement, IMHO, when cooking beans from scratch.

BLUE FENUGREEK. The traditional herb in Georgian cooking, including lobio (beans).

CILANTRO. Just the thing to add a fresh green bite at the end of many Mexican and Indian dishes. For the haters out there, substitute parsley or mint.

DILL. For Greek beans, it's a must.

EPAZOTE. The Mexican herb thought to help with digestion.

MINT. One of my favorite ways to offset spiciness.

OREGANO, DRIED. Another great addition to a pot of dried beans.

PARSLEY. An Italian and Middle Eastern favorite. As with cilantro, mint, dill, and basil, add it at the end of cooking.

ROSEMARY. The strong herb adds a piney note to Mediterranean dishes.

Spices

ALEPPO PEPPER. Spice plus fruitiness makes this a wonderful addition to Middle Eastern dishes. Substitute a smaller amount of crushed red pepper flakes for it.

ANCHO CHILE POWDER. Rather than using supermarket chili powder, which includes other ingredients, I like pure ground ancho chile.

ASAFOETIDA (aka hing or heeng). An Indian addition that smells more pungent than it tastes and purportedly helps with bean digestion.

BERBERE. The Ethiopian spice blend adds fiery complexity.

CARDAMOM. One of my favorite spices for its intoxicating aroma, it adds an almost mysterious quality to everything it touches. Be careful: a little goes a long way.

CAYENNE PEPPER. For a zing of back-of-the-throat heat, this is the thing.

CHIPOTLE CHILE, GROUND. One of my favorite ways to add smoke and spice in one fell swoop.

CINNAMON. This warming spice goes surprisingly well with beans, especially pinto and black beans.

CORIANDER. The dried seeds of the cilantro plant, it is an Indian standard.

CUMIN. It's hard to imagine beans without cumin—especially, but not exclusively, in Mexican and Indian cuisine.

GARAM MASALA. This wonderfully versatile Indian spice mix varies by maker (and cook) but will add layers of warmth to your cooking.

KASHMIRI CHILE. When I want heat in an Indian dish, this is what I reach for.

MADRAS CURRY POWDER. There's no such thing as curry spice, as it's a highly variable mix, but this is my favorite variety.

SALT. My favorite, all-purpose, everyday salt is Redmond Real Salt's kosher sea salt. It's got the big grains I love in kosher salt, making it easy to pick up with my fingers, and the taste is so clean.

SPANISH SMOKED PAPRIKA (PIMENTON). What would I do without it? I use it to add depth and, obviously, smoke to so much of my cooking, but with beans, there's nothing like it.

SUMAC. The tart spice so essential to Middle Eastern cooking—but it's great for adding a lemony punch to anything, really.

TURMERIC. This Ayurvedic superfood brings color and an almost musty earthiness to dishes.

ZA'ATAR. There are as many blends as there are families in the Middle East, but I love them all.

Other Ingredients and Product Information

BLACK GARLIC. These fermented cloves are sweet and almost licorice-y.

CANNED TOMATOES. I am a longtime fan of Muir Glen canned tomatoes, especially the fire-roasted ones for their concentrated, slightly smoky flavor.

CHOCOLATE. It used to be difficult to find excellent dairy-free chocolate. No more. Theo makes beautiful vegan dark-chocolate bars.

COCONUT MILK AND COCONUT CREAM. These are essential for adding creaminess to plant-based dishes, and Native Forest brand is my favorite.

KOMBU. The dried seaweed that brings minerals and digestive enzymes to a pot of beans.

LIQUID AMINOS. Bragg's brand has been a vegetarian staple since the hippie era, and it's as good as ever at adding a touch of umami (plus nutrition) to dishes with less sodium than soy sauce. I also like coconut aminos by Coconut Secret for its touch of sweetness.

MASA HARINA. For making tortillas, sopes, and soup dumplings, I prefer Bob's Red Mill brand over the more widely available Maseca.

MISO. In many varieties, it adds wonderful umami.

PRESERVED LEMON. Salty, tart, bright, with a little depth from fermentation. I love using it instead of lemon in hummus. Good store-bought versions abound, but it's also easy to make your own.

SALSA. When I'm not making my own, I purchase Frontera salsa, made by the team behind Chicago chef Rick Bayless.

TAHINI. My favorite brand is Wicked Sesame, imported from Israel. It tastes good—and, almost as important, it comes in a very convenient squeeze bottle. I also like Soom, made in Philadelphia, and two other Israeli brands: Al Arz and Karawan.

VEGAN BUTTER. For a neutral flavor, I use Earth Balance. When I want something more interesting (such as when I'm serving it on its own with bread), I go for Miyoko's European-Style Cultured Vegan Butter, which has an amazing tang and is, quite simply, the best plant-based butter I've ever tasted.

VEGAN FETA. When I don't have time to make Herb-Marinated Tofu Feta (page 217), I buy Violife's vegan feta, made from coconut oil. Once you get used to the color—which reminds me of overly whitened, Hollywood teeth!—you'll love it.

VEGAN RICOTTA, CREAM CHEESE, AND RAVIOLI. I like Kite Hill brand for all three, and Miyoko's for its cream cheese.

SOURCES

Beans

Baer's Best

A twenty-five-year-old farm that grows heirloom and specialty beans, particularly those of interest to the Northeast, such as Marfax, Vermont Cranberry, and Boston Roman.

baersbest.com

Bob's Red Mill

Known for its variety of grains (especially gluten-free ones), this Pacific Northwest company also carries a good selection of beans.

bobsredmill.com

Camellia

Louisiana purveyor of very high-quality beans, including the red beans beloved in New Orleans and such southern favorites as crowder peas, lady cream peas, and field peas.

camelliabrand.com

Goya

The behemoth of Latino foods is probably your best bet for dried beans in most mainstream supermarkets.

goya.com

Gustiamo

Importer of stellar beans from Italy, including the rare cicerchie (wild chickpeas) and tiny lentils.

gustiamo.com

Kalustyan's

This New York purveyor started out selling Indian goods but long ago expanded to include beans and many other foods from around the world, specializing in India and the Middle East. Look here for mini fava beans, best for slow cooking with their skins on for traditional ful.

foodsofnations.com

La Tienda

Importer of top Spanish foods, including fabada beans from Asturias, premium chickpeas, and more.

latienda.com

Masienda

This company partners with traditional farmers in Mexico to grow corn for masa, and sells masa harina, tortillas, and black beans.

masienda.com

Native Seeds/SEARCH

This nonprofit specializes in the traditional crops of northern Mexico and the U.S. Southwest, including beans from Rancho Gordo and other purveyors.

nativeseeds.org

Patel Brothers

This Indian chain of stores sells a host of products, including a huge selection of dals and other beans and spices.

patelbros.com

Rancho Gordo

The premier source of beautiful beans in heirloom varieties that are always less than two years old and often less than a year.

ranchogordo.com

Timeless Natural Food

A grower of organic heirloom lentils and other beans in Montana.

timelessfood.com

Zürsun Idaho Heirloom Beans

Works with three hundred small farms in Idaho's Snake River Canyon region.

zursunbeans.com

Spices

Bazaar Spices

A deep list of spices and mixes from around the world.

bazaarspices.com

Gryffon Ridge

A Maine-based organic spice merchant.

gryffonridge.com

La Boîte

A New York master of spices, beloved by chefs.

laboiteny.com

Penzeys

A Wisconsin-based purveyor of spices and mixes with stores nationwide.

penzeys.com

PRESSURE COOKING TIMETABLE

DRIED BEAN & LEGUME TYPE	DRY, COOKING TIME (IN MINUTES)	SOAKED, COOKING TIME (IN MINUTES)
Adzuki beans	20–25	10–15
Anasazi beans	20–25	10–15
Black beans	20–25	10–15
Black-eyed peas	20–25	10–15
Cannellini beans	35–40	20–25
Chickpeas (garbanzo beans)	35–40	20–25
Gandules (pigeon peas)	20–25	15–20
Great Northern beans	25–30	20–25
Kidney beans, red	25–30	20–25
Kidney beans, white	35–40	20–25
Lentils, French green	15–20	N/A
Lentils, green, mini (brown)	15–20	N/A
Lentils, red, split	15–18	N/A
Lentils, yellow, split (moong dal)	15–18	N/A
Lima beans	20–25	10–15
Navy beans	25–30	20–25
Peas	15–20	10–15
Pinto beans	25–30	20–25
Scarlet runner beans	20–25	10–15
Soybeans	25–30	20–25

STOVETOP COOKING TIMETABLE

DRIED BEAN & LEGUME TYPE	COOKING TIME
Black beans	1–1½ hours
Black-eyed peas (not soaked)	1–1½ hours
Chickpeas (garbanzo beans)	1–1½ hours
Crowder peas	40 minutes
Field peas	2 hours
Great Northern beans	1–1½ hours
Kidney beans, red	1–1½ hours
Lady Cream peas	30 minutes
Lentils (not soaked)	30–45 minutes
Lima beans, baby	1 hour
Lima beans, large	45 minutes–1 hour
Navy beans	1–1½ hours
Pink beans	1–1½ hours
Pinto beans	1–1½ hours
Split peas, green/yellow (not soaked)	30–45 minutes

BIBLIOGRAPHY

Albala, Ken. *Beans: A History.* New York: Bloomsbury, 2007.

Bakunina, I. Y., Nedashkovskaya, O. I., Kim, S. B., et al. "Diversity of glycosidase activities in the bacteria of the phylum Bacteroidetes isolated from marine algae." *Microbiology* 81 (2012): 688. https://doi.org/10.1134/S0026261712060033

Carlisle, Liz. *Lentil Underground: Renegade Farmers and the Future of Food in America.* New York: Gotham Books, 2015.

Chandler, Jenny. *The Better Bean Cookbook.* New York: Sterling Epicure, 2014.

Dragonwagon, Crescent. *Bean by Bean: A Cookbook.* New York: Workman Publishing, 2011.

Food and Agriculture Organization of the United Nations. *Pulses: Nutritious Seeds for a Sustainable Future.* fao.org/pulses-2016.

Green, Aliza. *Beans: More than 200 Delicious, Wholesome Recipes from Around the World.* Philadelphia: Running Press, 2004.

Jood, S., Mehta, U., Singh, R., Bhat, C. "Effect of processing on flatus-producing factors in legumes." *Journal of Agriculture and Food Chemistry* 33, no. 2 (1985): 268–271.

Khattab, R. Y. and Arntfield, S. D. "Nutritional quality of legume seeds as affected by some physical treatments." *LWT: Food Science and Technology* 42, no. 6 (July 2009): 1113–1118.

Winham, Donna M. and Hutchins, Andrea M. "Perceptions of flatulence from bean consumption among adults in 3 feeding studies." *Nutrition Journal* 10 (2011): 128. https://nutritionj.biomedcentral.com/track/pdf/10.1186/1475-2891-10-128

ACKNOWLEDGMENTS

One bean doesn't make a meal, and one person doesn't make a book. This project has been on my mind for almost five years, and it took plenty of help for me to pull it together.

Many thanks to:

Kristen Hartke, for her expert recipe testing, invaluable insight, and good-natured outlook.

The visuals dream team of light-whispering photographer Aubrie Pick, genius food stylist Lillian Kang, and assistants Bessma Khalaf and Veronica Laramie for one of the best professional weeks of my life, as they brought my vision to gorgeous life, creating the most beautiful images of beans I've ever seen, while finding time to draw tiny portraits of me on favas, gigantes, and giant limas.

The stellar Ten Speed Press pros: editor extraordinaire Kelly Snowden, art director Betsy Stromberg, designer Lisa Bieser, production editor Kim Keller, copy editor Dolores York, proofreader Kathy Brock, and production manager Serena Sigona. You make me look better than I deserve, and I hope to return the favor someday.

My agent, the incomparable David Black, for looking out for my interests, for letting me geek out about beans in multiple conversations, and for always—always—taking my call.

My sister Rebekah, who first taught me to cook a pot of beans (kombu and all) and whose instinctive wisdom in the kitchen I will always honor.

My brother-in-law Peter, who put up with me on a yearlong stint at the Maine homestead and indulged me in bean-variety disagreements.

Sheri Codiana, whose project management released me from the shackles of my own procrastination and terror and freed me to focus on what I like best about this sort of project: cooking and writing, not organizing.

Tess Masters and Kitty Greenwald, who gave me the best advice I could hope for, just when I needed it most.

Kat Kinsman, for the mental-health check-ins she accomplishes with such compassion and strength. You are a gift.

Friends who listened to me vent about my anxieties and obsessions: Jamie Bennett, Carol Blymire, Maddy Beckwith, Bill Addison, Devra First, Edouard Fontenot, Christopher Bellonci, Allan Kesten, Tanya Voss, Swati Sharma, Nancy Hopkins, Sally Swift, Lauren Rosenfeld, Kathy Gunst, Penny de los Santos, Laura Gutzwiller, Rachel Alabiso, Von Diaz, and more.

My colleagues at *The Washington Post* (Liz Seymour, Mitch Rubin, Matt Brooks, Bonnie S. Benwick, Maura Judkis, Becky Krystal, Tim Carman, Tom Sietsema, and others), for understanding what it means to try to fit a book project on top of a more-than-full-time job.

My siblings, Teri and Michael, for energizing me with your own passion for food.

My mother, Dolores Jones, for tasking me to do the grocery shopping for the family when I was eight—I loved every minute—and for just being you.

All the chefs, restaurateurs, home cooks, and fellow writers who offered your time, your recipes, and your advice—or in some cases just your unknowing inspiration—to help drive me to make my own bean-centered creations in the kitchen: Michael Solomonov, Rich Landau, Kate Jacoby, Maria Speck, Eduardo Garcia, Ran Nussbacher, Pati Jinich, Ozoz Sokoh, Tunde Wey, José Andrés, Priya Ammu, Dan Buettner, Aglaia Kremezi, Ron Pickarski, Sandra Gutierrez, Ana Sortun, Naomi Duguid, Lina Wallentinson, Cathy Barrow, Mike Friedman, Brad Deboy, David Lebovitz, Ashok Bajaj, Vikram Sunderam, Michael Costa, Amy Chaplin, Ani Kandelaki, Gerald Addison, Rose Previte, Katy Beskow, Gena Hamshaw, Dina Daniel, Elmer Ramos, Oyin Akinkugbe, Udai Soni, Neha Soni, Sara Franklin, the late Edna Lewis, Annisa Helou, Emily and Alon Shaya, John Delpha, Brian van Etten, Valerie Erwin, Kara and Tami Elder, Deb Perelman, Lisa Fain, Roberto Martin, Brooks Headley, Lenny Russo, Christopher Kimball, Nick Stefanelli, Michelle Fuerst, Judy Witts Francini, Shirley Caesar, Polina Chesnakova, Tal Ronnen, Imani Muhhamad, the late Julia Child, Isa Chandra Moskowitz, Fran Costigan, Dennis Friedman, Dana Schultz, Robert Simonson, Samin Nosrat, Padma Lakshmi, Yotam Ottolenghi, Nik Sharma, Osayi Endolyn, Nick Wiseman, Ronen Tenne, Christian Irabien, Alton Brown, Paige Lombardi, Gabriel Frasca, Amanda Lydon, J. Kenji López-Alt, Dorie Greenspan, Ann Mah, and more.

Ken Albala and Crescent Dragonwagon, for paving the way with stellar previous books on this subject that I relied on for reality checks, perspective, and, in some cases, quotes.

Steve Sando, for being the bean evangelist. Period.

Finally, and most important of all, my husband, Carl, for eating more beans in a year than he could ever have imagined, and doing it with a minimum of complaints—and plenty of musical-fruit jokes.

INDEX

FOR CARL

Library of Congress Cataloging-in-Publication Data
  Names: Yonan, Joe, author. | Pick, Aubrie, photographer.
  Title: Cool beans : the ultimate guide to cooking with the world's most
    versatile plant-based protein, with 125 recipes protein / by Joe Yonan;
    photography by Aubrie Pick.
  Description: First edition. | California : Ten Speed Press, [2020] |
    Summary: "A modern and fresh look at the diverse world of beans
    and pulses, including 125 recipes for globally inspired vegetarian
    mains, snacks, soups, and even desserts"— Provided by publisher.
  Identifiers: LCCN 2019021681 | ISBN 9780399581489 (hardcover) |
    ISBN 9780399581496 (ebook)
  Subjects: LCSH: Cooking (Beans)
  Classification: LCC TX803.B4 Y66 2020 | DDC 641.6/565—dc23
  LC record available at https://lccn.loc.gov/2019021681

Hardcover ISBN: 978-0-399-58148-9
eBook ISBN: 978-0-399-58149-6

Printed in China

Design by Lisa Schneller Bieser
Food styling by Lillian Kang
Prop styling by Glenn Jenkins

10 9 8 7 6 5 4 3 2 1

First Edition